D0944616

West Side Story as Cinema

CULTUREAMERICA

Erika Doss
Philip J. Deloria
Series Editors

Karal Ann Marling
Editor Emerita

West Side Story as Cinema

The Making and Impact of an American Masterpiece

Ernesto R. Acevedo-Muñoz

JUL 0 2 2014

PROPERTY OF
SENECA COLLEGE
LIBRARIES
@ YORK CAMPUS

 University Press of Kansas

Published by the University

Press of Kansas (Lawrence,

Kansas 66045), which was

organized by the Kansas

Board of Regents and is

operated and funded by

Emporia State University,

Fort Hays State University,

Kansas State University,

Pittsburg State University, the

University of Kansas, and

Wichita State University

© 2013 by the University Press of Kansas
All rights reserved.

West Side Story by Leonard Bernstein and Stephen Sondheim
©Copyright 1956, 1957, 1958, 1959 by Amberson Holdings
LLC and Stephen Sondheim. Copyright renewed.
Leonard Bernstein Music Publishing Company LLC,
publisher. Boosey & Hawkes, agent for rental.
International copyright secured.
Reprinted by permission of Boosey & Hawkes, Inc.

WEST SIDE STORY ©1961 METRO-GOLDWYN-MAYER
STUDIOS, INC. ALL RIGHTS RESERVED.
Courtesy of MGM Media Licensing.

Library of Congress Cataloging-in-Publication Data
Acevedo-Muñoz, Ernesto R., 1968–
    West Side Story as cinema : the making and impact of an
American masterpiece / Ernesto R. Acevedo-Muñoz.
        pages cm.—(CultureAmerica)
    Includes bibliographical references and index.
    ISBN 978-0-7006-1921-4 (hardback)
    1. West Side Story (Motion picture) 2. Musical films—
United States—History and criticism. I. Title.
    PN1997.W456A93 2013
    791.43′72—dc23
                                            2013018936

British Library Cataloguing-in-Publication Data is available.

Printed in the United States of America
10 9 8 7 6 5 4 3 2 1

The paper used in this publication is recycled and contains
30 percent postconsumer waste. It is acid free and meets
the minimum requirements of the American National
Standard for Permanence of Paper for Printed Library
Materials Z39.48–1992.

A mis padres Rolando Acevedo-Lorenzo y Luz María Muñoz-Ríos por su inspiradora historia de amor.

To my brother Carlos R. for the complicit motivation and his inquisitive spirit.

In loving memory of my uncle Antonio Muñoz-Ríos (1933–2013), who gave me a home when I first went to New York to study cinema, and my cousin Haydée Muñoz-Bermúdez (1958–2011), who first took me to see a Broadway musical play.

CONTENTS

ACKNOWLEDGMENTS

I would first like to thank Michael J. Briggs, editor in chief; Kelly Chrisman Jacques, production editor; and the rest of the staff at the University Press of Kansas for giving my book a home and for mentoring and championing this humble volume. Thomas Hischak read the manuscript and was most helpful in pointing out inconsistencies and imperfections, as well as being very generous and encouraging about the book's prospects. His recommendations significantly improved the quality of the final product.

My luck in finding the University Press of Kansas was in great part due to the diligence and intelligence of my compadre Steven Wingate, who showed me the UPK catalog in the fall of 2009. Steven and his lovely family—Jennifer, Lucas, and Landon—have given me a sense of friendship and kinship that I treasure deeply.

I wish to thank the good people at the University of Southern California's Cinematic Arts Library, Special Collections, particularly Ned Comstock for his kindness and patience in dealing with my requests and for pointing me in directions I had not thought of. The staff of the Margaret Herrick Library at the Douglas Fairbanks Center for Motion Picture Study at the Academy of Motion Picture Arts and Sciences was tremendously helpful and courteous during my research time there. Through the generosity of research archivist Barbara Hall, I was given access to Special Collections materials as well as the Core Collection, clippings, and photographs, which significantly facilitated my mapping of this history.

At MGM Licensing, Jeremy Lott and Megan Bradford guided me through the process to obtain permission to use publicity and production stills. John White at Boosey & Hawkes Inc. facilitated the attainment of consent to transcribe song lyrics.

At the University of Colorado at Boulder, the staff of the Film Studies Program—Donald Yannacito, Rhonda McCuan, and Jacob Barreras—were extremely good sports who minded the store diligently and cheerily for the better part of three summers while I conducted research in Los Angeles and New York and was writing in Boulder. The

College of Arts and Sciences generously awarded me the Eugene M. Kayden Research Grant to help cover research and publication costs. Also, my friends and colleagues Victor Jendras, Teresita Lozano, and Anna Vrieling gladly gave me technical advice and support when I called on them. My research assistants Elizabeth T. Hanna and Dana L. Kopenhefer were extremely effective in helping me organize my research and track down library sources that were essential for background work. I am thankful to the students in my courses on the Hollywood musical from 2005 to 2011. They started this process with their curiosity, and in many ways, this book is for them too.

In my childhood, I was too restless to pay attention when my parents took me to music lessons, so unfortunately, I never learned to play an instrument or to read sheet music. That is a mistake I now regret. Luckily for me, my student, assistant, and dear friend Larissa Jean Rhodes is a talented musician and music intellectual. She was instrumental (if you will pardon the pun) in helping me understand the complexities of *West Side Story*'s notoriously tricky musical score. As a result, her fingerprints can be found all over this work, and I will never be able to express my gratitude properly. I can only say thank you.

Finally, I am very grateful to Christina Isabelle Smith for her time, the urgency of her encouragement, and the intelligence of her criticism. She too helped make this a better book by giving me so much to think about. All errors and omissions are entirely my responsibility.

West Side Story as Cinema

Introduction
"My Heart's Devotion": Finding *West Side Story*

On 26 September 1957 the stage version of *West Side Story* premiered in New York's Winter Garden Theatre after previews in Washington, D.C., and Philadelphia that summer. The show was conceived, choreographed, and directed by Jerome Robbins from a libretto by Arthur Laurents, inspired by Shakespeare's *Romeo and Juliet*. Leonard Bernstein composed the difficult, eclectic, yet catchy musical score, and Stephen Sondheim and Bernstein co-wrote the memorable if uneven lyrics.[1]

According to many accounts, possibly apocryphal, Montgomery Clift had approached Robbins in 1949 in search of direction, or inspiration, to play Romeo with a fresh perspective. Intrigued by the idea of a new, contemporary look at *Romeo and Juliet*, Robbins scribbled down a short treatment, setting the story in modern-day New York City, and took it to Bernstein.[2] Playwright Arthur Laurents was brought in to build a structure around Robbins's idea: a story about the doomed romance between a Jewish girl and a Catholic boy from the East Side of New York, set during the Passover season. But Bernstein judged it to be too close to *Abie's Irish Rose*, a popular 1920s play with the same plot. The idea lingered in Robbins's mind for several years, until a chance meeting between Bernstein and Laurents at the pool of the Beverly Hills Hotel resurrected the project in 1955. According to Laurents, a *Los Angeles Times* headline about gang activity and juvenile delinquency in the city led them to consider moving the setting to New York's West Side and using the perceived rise in

Puerto Rican gang violence there as the story's catalyst. They contacted Robbins immediately, who happened to be in Los Angeles choreographing the film version of The King and I, and West Side Story was conceived.[3]

Robbins, Bernstein, and Laurents then shopped around for lyricists. Bernstein was concerned that, given the amount and difficulty of the music he was composing, he might be overwhelmed if he had to write the lyrics as well. They approached the husband-and-wife team of Adolph Green and Betty Comden, whom Bernstein and Robbins knew from their previous collaboration on the 1944 Broadway production and the 1949 film version of On the Town, but the lyricists were busy with other projects and opted out. Laurents then suggested Stephen Sondheim, a young, fairly unknown songwriter from New York who was looking for his big break as a composer. Though initially concerned about his ignorance of Puerto Rican migration and gang warfare—Sondheim had "never been that poor, and never known a Puerto Rican"—he agreed to collaborate after consulting with his mentor Oscar Hammerstein II.[4]

With the principal creative team in place and the setting moved to the familiar streets of the West Side of New York, Bernstein wrote the music and Sondheim wrote the lyrics based on Laurents's scenes and dialogue. Meanwhile, the search for a producer proved problematic. Many potential producers and investors were turned off by the story's dark tone, its decrepit setting, and the death of two principal characters at the end of the first act. The show's first financial mentor, theater producer Cheryl Crawford, was on board, but as late as April 1957, the property was still struggling to find investors. A "backer's audition" was held on the West Side that month, but the wealthy audience was not impressed. As the show continued to develop, even Crawford started to lose faith. She wanted more sociological content explaining the resentment between the gangs and the Puerto Rican poverty angle. She wanted to know how Puerto Ricans and African Americans had replaced Jews as the city's poor population. Crawford gave the team an ultimatum about their creative differences, and they let her walk out.[5]

Nearly convinced that the show would never happen, Robbins contacted Roger Stevens, another early mentor of the project.

Stevens recommended the producing duo of Roger Griffith and Harold Prince, whose recent Broadway hits included *The Pajama Game* and *Damn Yankees*; Bernstein and Robbins also knew the two from their 1953 production of *Wonderful Town*. Prince and Griffith, who were in Boston previewing *New Girl in Town*, agreed to come to New York and listen to the score. They did so in May 1957, immediately agreed to take on the production, and reportedly raised the $350,000 budget within a week. *West Side Story*—then using the working title *Gangway!*—was finally on its way to the stage.[6]

A Show "Unlike Any Ever Seen"

The last pieces of the complex puzzle of the theater production of *West Side Story* fell into place with the addition of scenic designer Oliver Smith, costumer Irene Sharaff, and lighting director Jean Rosenthal. All had vast theatrical experience and were known as innovators—something the unorthodox *West Side Story* could benefit from. Smith's credits included the original 1956 Broadway production of *My Fair Lady*, Rosenthal had worked for Orson Welles's Mercury Theatre, and Sharaff was a veteran costume designer who had already won the Tony and the Oscar for *The King and I*, among many other accolades. Sharaff was the only member of the design team who would later work on the movie version of *West Side Story*.

Once the script, music, and dances were set, there was little variation in the concept, although some tryouts and rehearsals for friends and colleagues (including Richard Rodgers of Rodgers and Hammerstein fame) resulted in a few minor changes. In an article published in the *New York Herald Tribune* on 4 August 1957, Laurents noted that, from the beginning, *West Side Story* needed to be new yet recognizable and faithful to its Shakespearean origins. "Our hope," he wrote, "was to make the stage more theatrical, more lyrical, more magically exciting" and to aim for a "lyrically and theatrically sharpened illusion of reality."[7]

Even with a hasty schedule (the show went on to tryouts in the summer of 1957), a complicated musical score, a tragic tone, and unprecedented demands on the actors, singers, and dancers (mostly unknowns who were chosen after grueling auditions and went through six weeks of intense, exhausting rehearsals), *West Side Story* previewed in Washington, D.C., on 19 August 1957 to a reported seventeen curtain calls. Vice President Richard Nixon was in attendance.[8] The show's run in the nation's capital was soon sold out, and Robbins, Bernstein, and Sondheim were honored with keys to the city for their contributions to the fight against juvenile delinquency. From Washington, the show went briefly to Philadelphia for more tryouts, where the reception was positive and the box office quite promising.[9]

Finally, on 26 September 1957, the show that would later be promoted as "unlike any ever seen before" opened in New York's Winter Garden Theatre.[10] Initial reviews were mixed, and the stunned audience sat "open mouthed, and gasping" when the curtain dropped.[11] Many critics seemed unsure what to make of the show, but it looked like Laurents's predictions in the *Herald Tribune* were not far off. Positive reviews came from some of the most influential reviewers in New York. The day after the opening, they wrote that the show was "splendid and super-modern"; "eye popping, ear soothing, and conscience-busting"; "a somber tragedy"; "superlative"; and even "the most exciting thing" since *My Fair Lady*. Others described its material as "savage, restless, electrifying," and "horrifying," while praising the "workmanship" as "admirable." Critics called it "as exciting (and sordid) as a subway mugging with music" and "a chiller, a thriller, as up-to-the-minute as tomorrow's headlines." Most, it seemed, agreed with the notion that *West Side Story* was "a bold new kind of musical theatre" and a "departure" from the usual styles and themes of musicals.[12] Even *New York Times* drama critic Brooks Atkinson (dubbed "the most important reviewer of his time") set aside his reservations about Bernstein and wrote that "everything in *West Side Story*" was "of a piece," giving a "total impression of wildness, ecstasy and anger." Atkinson called the show "an achievement of the first order."[13]

While *West Side Story* may not have been an entirely "new kind of musical theatre," music historian Elizabeth Wells has argued that its greatest contribution was to create an intersection among "American musical theatre . . . popular culture and classical art music." According to Wells, Sondheim himself described *West Side Story* as "sui generis"—literally, "its own kind"; thus, it had little influence on subsequent musical theater.[14]

Whether *West Side Story* did or did not change the course of American musical theater, its longevity and nearly unprecedented international success certainly made it a force to be reckoned with and a landmark in theater history. Significantly, Wells and other historians point to the commercial and critical success of the 1961 film version, directed by Robert Wise and choreographed by Jerome Robbins, as being partly responsible not only for the show's staying power and popularity but also for bringing the concept of musical theater to audiences around the world who had little access to or even awareness of the Broadway musical.[15] In short, music and theater historians consider the movie version of *West Side Story* an important turning point in American entertainment history.[16]

"Puerto Rican *Birth of a Nation*"

I was a young boy in Puerto Rico in the 1970s when my father brought home the sound-track album from the movie version of *West Side Story*. My brother and I played it over and over, and by the time we finally saw the movie on a pan-and-scan Betamax videotape sometime in the early 1980s, we were both sold on it. I was in awe of and enamored with *West Side Story* before I understood much about movies in general or the musical genre in particular (I had never seen a Broadway musical, either). First, I was intrigued by the words "Puerto Rico . . . my heart's devotion" on the album, for I had rarely heard the name of my homeland mentioned in any movie. Later, I was overwhelmed and giddily proud to see "Puerto Ricans" represented onscreen, however inaccurate or stylized the portrayal. Other than the New York–based comedy *Popi* (Arthur Hiller, 1969) starring Alan Arkin, which my family had seen on television, I did not know of any Puerto Rican characters in American cinema. Throughout my childhood and into my college years, *West Side Story* was one of my family's "go to" choices whenever we had an at-home movie night. We showed it to all our friends and neighbors who did not own videocassette players, which were quite rare at the time. Even as a child, the names Robert Wise and Jerome Robbins were familiar to me. I was not quite sure what a movie director did, but my father was a high school drama teacher, so I understood to a certain extent. Natalie Wood and Rita Moreno, who played the "Puerto Rican" girls (Moreno actually was Puerto Rican), were my first movie crushes.

Cultural critic and Columbia University professor Frances Negrón-Muntaner once wrote that *West Side Story* is the "Puerto Rican *Birth of a Nation*: a blatant, seminal, valorized, aestheticized eruption into the (American) national 'consciousness.'"[17] It was thus inevitable for Puerto Ricans on the island and on the mainland to be confronted with *West Side Story* as a product of Hollywood popular culture. It was the first look at any form of "Puerto Ricanness" that many of our friends and peers came across. As a Puerto Rican native and an American film historian, an interest in *West Side Story* was doubly inevitable for me. In short, *West Side Story* is the reason why I study films.

In the early 1990s, when I was applying to graduate schools, I noted that "one day, I'd like to do something with *West Side Story*." I did not know what that might be, and my studies took me in other directions. Eventually, as I attained a better understanding of the formal and visual complexities of *West Side Story* as cinema, I started to incorporate the movie into my Introduction to Film Studies classes. I found it to be a good teaching tool to explain to my students, mostly freshmen, the possibilities of cinematic mise-en-scène. As one critic wrote of the movie in 1961, viewing *West Side Story* was like watching a film for the first time. So I used it to teach my students, most of whom were born in the home video era, how to really pay attention to a film. Later, *West Side Story* became the centerpiece of my very popular course titled The Hollywood Musical. The movie helped my students focus on strictly visual qualities and a holistic design that made sense; at the same time, the film enhanced and revised many of the narrative and structural conventions of the classical musical genre.

Soon, my students at the University of Colorado in Boulder started to ask questions about *West Side Story* that I found difficult to answer. Why does it feel so modern? Why can't María and Tony just live happily ever after, like the couples in other musicals? What is the meaning of all the chain-link fences? How did the filmmakers do that dissolve? Why is the lighting so peculiar? These questions, and the desire to satisfy my students' curiosity, led me to do further research on *West Side Story*. To my surprise, there had been little scholarly work on the film. The few books available were based mostly on secondhand accounts, marketing materials, "making of" publicity, and advertising copy. The few articles I found were mostly sociological or cultural criticisms of the treatment of the Puerto Rican characters. There was precious little information about how the movie was conceived, what the technical difficulties were, why a codirector left before the production was "wrapped," what really happened with the ghost singers, and many other genuine questions.

Thus, my search for answers led to several years of research and analysis that culminated in the current volume. After intense research conducted during the summer and winter breaks between 2007 and 2011, I carefully pieced together many different elements that did not always seem to be related. Although a portion of the story of West Side Story has been told in memoirs, interviews, and secondary accounts, I consulted original sources that I believed would complete the picture, including the Robert Wise and Ernest Lehman Collections at the University of Southern California and the Linwood Dunn and Boris Leven files at the Academy of Motion Picture Arts and Sciences. I also read contemporary newspaper accounts, trade journal updates and gossip, "buzz" features in magazines, oral histories, and published memoirs. The result is probably an imperfect chronicle and a somewhat biased assessment of the film's contribution and impact, but it is more complete than any other history or analysis of West Side Story published so far. It contains the answers to many of the questions that guided my research, and it even answers some questions that nobody asked or imagined.

The book is meant to appeal to a crossover readership. On the one hand, its historical information will be of use to general readers who are interested in West Side Story as a landmark in American filmmaking and to those who are curious about how deals are closed and movies are made. On the other hand, its formal analysis and assessment of the film's controversial topics, especially the Puerto Rican issue, will interest a scholarly audience, perhaps those concerned with film genres or cultural studies.

Chapter 1 chronicles the early visual and formal concepts of the film and the gathering of a creative and artistic team to consolidate those ideas. Chapter 2 presents many details about the production—scripting, casting, filming—and the creative differences and financial difficulties that led to the dismantling of the directorial duo of Robert Wise and Jerome Robbins. Chapter 3 is a sequence-by-sequence and number-by-number analysis of the film's content and narrative, emphasizing the technical achievements and the visual and aural logic of the finished product. Chapter 4 is a "post-history" of West Side Story, including its distribution and reception, legacy, precedent-setting practices, longevity, and currency in contemporary media. Chapter 5 is a theoretical and historical exploration of Puerto Rican identity in the film, which is not as transparent or as abject as some critics have argued. With evidence from the movie itself—details of the mise-en-scène, narrative subtleties, and some of the lyrics—I argue that although the "identity" of Puerto Ricans in West Side Story is certainly problematic, it is also much more complex and possibly better articulated than that of their assorted "American" rivals. Although the original creative team for the theatrical production of West Side Story insisted that the show was not about Puerto Ricans, that it was "a poetic fantasy, not a sociological document,"[18] it remains a much-debated text in Latino and cultural studies.

Perhaps my own familiarity with West Side Story has led me to write of the characters as if they are people I know and to reveal plot information that might be, for the uninitiated, shocking or disappointing. I thus confess that I have written this book for those who are at least acquainted with the plot: a rivalry between gangs, a doomed love story, a few gruesome deaths. If you are not familiar with West Side Story, I would advise you to put down this book and watch the film first. Knowing who the characters are and how the story unfolds will lead to a better understanding of my arguments and examples. I hope you enjoy the movie, and I am grateful that you have chosen to give this book your precious attention.

1 "Not a Photographed Stage Play": Creating *West Side Story*

The process of adapting the stage version of *West Side Story* into a suitable motion picture began in 1959 when United Artists acquired the rights to the play for nearly $400,000 and brought it to the Mirisch Corporation to produce.[1] The Mirisch brothers—Walter, Harold, and Marvin—had established solid reputations as maverick producers after arriving in Hollywood in 1943. They began their filmmaking careers producing jungle adventures and exploitation fare—shot in eight days on budgets of $80,000 to $100,000—for Monogram Pictures and its "B plus" wing, Allied Artists, in the late 1940s. By 1951, Walter Mirisch was head of production at Monogram. Eventually, their ambition, business savvy, and innovative, cost-saving filmmaking techniques allowed the brothers to branch out, acquiring more serious properties and attracting A-list talent. In 1952 Walter and Harold Mirisch raised $250,000 to independently coproduce, with British partners, *Moulin Rouge* for United Artists. It was directed by John Huston and starred José Ferrer, who had won an Oscar for *Cyrano de Bergerac* (1950). *Moulin Rouge* was a commercial and critical success, garnering seven Oscar nominations in 1953, including one for Ferrer and two for Huston, and winning two Academy Awards for color art direction and costume design. With that precedent and some successful independent experiments produced by their Moulin Productions, including Huston's 1956 *Moby Dick*, the Mirisch brothers built important relationships with directors such as Huston, John Sturges, Billy Wilder, and William Wyler, who had all become disillusioned with the major studios. Primarily, these directors sought greater creative control and a larger share of the profits.[2]

By taking risks, operating independently, and working largely outside the declining studio system, the Mirisch brothers produced a number of important films distributed by United Artists, including Wilder's *Some Like It Hot* (1959) and *The Apartment* (1960), Sturges's *The Magnificent Seven* (1960), and Wyler's *The Children's Hour* (1961). In the autumn of 1959 the *Los Angeles Times* had reported that the Mirisch Corporation was developing a "big musical" for United Artists and announced the partnership among versatile director Robert Wise, Seven Arts Productions, and the Mirisch Corporation to produce *West Side Story*, which was already "slated to be one of the highest-budgeted productions ever made under the Mirisch banner." Wise, who had started out making B pictures at RKO in the early 1940s, had eventually made A-list status and tried his hand at a variety of genres—war, horror, science fiction, film noir, and all sorts of melodrama—at RKO, Warner Bros., 20th Century–Fox, and United Artists. But Wise had never directed a musical, and like Huston, Sturges, Wyler, and Wilder, he was looking to escape the constraints of the studio system and had recently partnered with the Mirisch Corporation. He also had a reputation for being fast and reliable and had enjoyed recent success as an independent, directing *Odds against Tomorrow* for Harry Belafonte in 1959. As Walter Mirisch put it, Wise had "experience with gritty subject matter." After seeing *West Side Story* on stage in 1958 and finding it "stunning," Walter Mirisch had determined to produce it for United Artists. Early on, he considered bringing in Jerome Robbins as artistic director, and he offered Wise the possibility of codirecting with Robbins, who had precious little motion picture experience.[3]

On 27 November 1959 the trade paper *Daily Variety* announced that Robert Wise was en route to New York City to scout exterior locations for the film. Wise was accompanied by screenwriter Ernest Lehman, who had written *Executive Suite* for him at MGM in 1954.[4] Wise wanted to explore the possibility of adding more realism to the movie by filming some of it in real New York City locations—a rare but certainly not unique practice for a musical.[5] As part of his preparation, Wise watched short-subject movies such as *Gang War* (1928), which also involves a love affair in the middle of a gang turf conflict. "It's a very interesting little film," Wise wrote in a letter, "and I think [it] adds appreciably to our store of knowledge about juvenile gang warfare."[6] Wise told an interviewer in June 1979 that, "right off the bat, I was the one that insisted that [they] open the picture actually in New York."[7]

During their New York research trip, Lehman composed a lengthy memo to himself in which he recorded some helpful trivia and information that could be used to enhance their project's authenticity. For example, he noted that "a '1013' is a radio signal meaning there's a cop in trouble," and "anybody on the street after 1 o'clock is either a cop or a robber." He observed that the corner of 106th Street and Third Avenue in East Harlem was the "dividing line between PR and white gang." Lehman also gathered from the police the names of some real street gangs in the area, including the "Viceroys, Dragons, Bishops, Chaplains, Red Wings, Crusaders, The Golden Guineas, The Daggers, [and] The Baldies." Significantly, Lehman noticed that rooftops were among the few places "where a kid [could] be alone," and they were good spots for addicts to shoot up. Evidently, this made an impression, since the movie has several scenes set on the tenement rooftop—notably, the "America" number and María's meeting with Chino after the rumble—although this location was absent from the stage play.[8]

Lehman and Wise also met with New York City Youth Board Workers, gathered information about settings and statistics about juvenile delinquency, compiled a list of valuable gang lingo, noted the street nicknames of gang members, and cited police reports on tensions between Puerto Rican and Italian residents of the neighborhood. As I explore further in chapter 5, since the mid-1950s, there had been widespread suspicion among many sociologists, law enforcement officers, social workers, and especially the popular press that hikes in juvenile delinquency rates were commonly associated with "immigrant" or minority groups in cities such as Los Angeles and New York. In the latter, that typically meant Puerto Ricans, who were considered "the largest and increasingly most problematic of New York's minority populations," and they were often accused of instigating violence against unsuspecting white victims.[9]

The research trip thus provided a sense of legitimacy and realism, and Wise, Lehman, and the Mirisch brothers agreed early on that the "Prologue" sequence (eventually extended to nearly double its length in the play) would be filmed on location in New York City. For Lehman and Wise, it was evident that both the New York setting and the Puerto Rican background would be essential to making *West Side Story* as authentic and realistic as possible.

Shortly after the New York excursion, Lehman began writing a rough outline of the screenplay. Early in the writing process, Lehman also decided to make important changes to the lyrics of "America." The original theater version of the song was considered controversial, with its lampooning, derogatory lyrics about Puerto Rico and the island's inhabitants, such as "Puerto Rico, you ugly Island." The song offered a cartoonish portrait of a nation of violence, poverty, disease, underdevelopment, and overpopulation, and Lehman found the lyrics improbable and untenable, a farcical misrepresentation of the realities of immigration. Many years later, Lehman recalled in an interview his reaction to the lyrics of "America" and his decision to shift the focus from the infelicity of life in Puerto Rico to the paradox of immigration: "I looked at it and I said to myself . . . they're singing about Puerto Ricans in Puerto Rico. This is ridiculous. This is a show about Puerto Ricans coming to America and what they go through."[10] Arguably, Lehman's research in New York City's Puerto Rican neighborhoods and his meetings with social workers, neighborhood leaders, and local police helped him redirect his emphasis to Puerto Ricans in New York.[11]

At this early stage of preproduction, Jerome Robbins, credited with the concept, choreography, and direction of *West Side Story*'s theatrical version, had not yet finalized his deal to codirect the feature film. An article in the 27 November 1959 issue of *Variety* named Robert Wise as the sole producer and director of the movie. It was a month later, on the day after Christmas, when the *Hollywood Reporter* broke the news that Robbins had signed on as "co-director," adding that this would be "his first motion picture." The *Reporter* also mentioned that Ernest Lehman would be the screenwriter for the project.[12]

Thus, the trip to New York City in the fall of 1959 was essential in shaping Wise's ideas about the design of the movie, what it would look like, and how to make it different from the theatrical version. Perhaps more important, it cemented the concept of the film as something with a distinct visual style.

"Problems of Style"

In his memoir, producer Walter Mirisch recalls that Jerome Robbins expressed "grave doubts" about filming dance sequences on real-life locations, fearing that the dancers would look "ridiculous." But Wise and Mirisch did not want the film "to look like a photographed stage play."[13] In preparation for a pitch to the Mirisch brothers and executives at United Artists, Wise drafted a memo in which he expressed his dissatisfaction with the realistic treatment of song-and-dance numbers in contemporary musicals and concluded—paradoxically, I might add—that they had "a very unreal feeling" and were often "embarrassing" onscreen. Wise was especially concerned because *West Side Story*, he correctly argued, was "a musical drama, not a musical comedy," and thus could not be expected to follow the conventions of its generic relatives.[14]

The pitch to the Mirisch brothers and United Artists executives outlined three possible stylistic approaches to *West Side Story*. The first approach was a mixture of realistic settings and locations, with dialogue and dramatic scenes treated like "documentary photography," along with discernibly theatrical mise-en-scènes for the music and dance sequences. The second proposal was to make all locations and sets "completely realistic" and to combine these with a "strong theatrical" style in the musical numbers. In this approach, the theatrical elements and effects would be transitioned in inconspicuously, minimizing the shock between realistic settings and theatrical (or fantastic) effects. Wise envisioned that this would create a visual style that was "larger than life, . . . a not-quite-real-world."[15] The third option was a more conventional approach in which all sets would be realistically constructed and dressed in the sound stage, with no location shooting; however, camera and lighting effects would be foregrounded as a sort of curtain between the dramatic and musical segments.

It is evident that Wise preferred the second approach—the "not-quite-real-world" depiction—from the start. He had already decided to incorporate location shooting, and he argued that the movie had to have a "distinctive cinematic style," combining realistic and fantastic or "stylized" effects and mise-en-scènes. "The screen is a very real medium, and doesn't take kindly to stylization," Wise told an interviewer in 1995. His concern was "how to take all the stylized aspects of [West Side Story] and deal with them effectively in the reality of the screen."[16] For these purposes, Wise needed a select team of cinematographers, special and optical effects experts (for these two roles, he hired Daniel L. Fapp and Linwood G. Dunn, respectively), and production and set designers (notably, Boris Leven). Wise was aiming to achieve an "imaginative but controlled color concept," a specifically visual rendition of the themes of the play, as he saw them, that emphasized contrasts: difference and violence in the background of a doomed love story. For this, he needed "pointedly theatrical treatment in lighting," along with "soft romantic textures" and "dynamic angles" that would presumably underscore the recurring mood swings of the source material.[17]

Early correspondence from production designer Boris Leven indicates the design team's commitment to creating a vastly cinematic version of the play. After praising the onstage achievements of the play's production and lighting designers, Leven emphasized the need to liberate West Side Story from the perceived constraints of the theatrical space. "We have no proscenium, there is no audience and our stage is limitless in size," wrote Leven. "We are working in a different medium employing a different technique. . . . Let us create a style applicable to our medium." Among other ideas, Leven insisted that although the settings should be realistic, the design team would add "stylization . . . for dramatic emphasis, for accents." Moreover, Leven explained (perhaps superfluously), settings, like characters, must have meaning, and it was important to "be in control" of the style of the picture.[18] Echoing Wise's own words, or perhaps the other way around, Leven called for an "imaginative approach to the subject" and ended on a dramatic note, declaring, "the star of this show is the style, the treatment, the design, the photography. . . . We are reaching for new effects, a new approach."[19] Paradoxically, in a handwritten letter to a curious fan dated November 1982, Leven argues that he insisted on retaining a degree of realism in set design, while Wise and Robbins wanted to go "way out: non-representative backgrounds, stylized beyond recognition." "In the end, I won out," Leven claims, "the rest is history." Surely, there was less tension than Leven implies in this personal letter, in which he also characterizes his relationship with Wise, with whom he made six films between 1960 and 1971. Leven recalls it as being "the most ideal relationship. . . . He trusted me with the look of the film and I treasured the artistic freedom given to me."[20] Ultimately, the compromise worked out, resulting in realistic but not conventional sets, combined with fantastic, imaginative lighting and photographic effects.

By May 1960 Leven had been given a list of sets for the movie. These included, in order, the bridal shop, María's apartment, the rooftop, the back alley, Doc's Candy Store, Anita's bathroom (which never made it into the film), and "under the highway." An interoffice memo dated 23 May also urged Leven to visit the "New York Streets" sets at MGM and Universal Studios to get ideas and assess their suitability.[21] Although the New York City locations for the "Prologue" had been chosen by April 1960, a number of other sets, including the one for the rumble (referred to as "under the highway") were going to be built or substituted when production went back to Los Angeles in late summer, after the New York City location shoot was completed. Attached to the list of sets to be built by the design department was an inventory of the twenty-two New York City locations scouted earlier by Wise, Lehman, Leven, and other members of the preproduction team. These included assorted streets and alleyways, parking lots, parks, a public swimming pool, and several storefronts, some of which were actually featured in the film: "Commercial alleyway and fence— between West 59th & West 60th," "Street—68th West of Amsterdam —CONDEMNED AREA," "Street—71st West of Amsterdam—DEAD END SECTION OF BROWNSTONES," "Handball court and fences—126th and Amsterdam," and "Playground and street—West 47th—between 9th and 10th Avenue," among many others.[22] Wise and the location scouts had found two whole blocks of old tenement buildings between West Sixtieth and West Sixty-Sixth Streets that were scheduled to be demolished to make space for construction of the Lincoln Center complex. Wise and the Mirisch brothers eventually secured permission to use some of the buildings and surrounding areas, which, aided by a bit of set dressing from the art department, became the turf at the center of the street war between the Jets and the Sharks.[23] Significantly, the distinct style sought by Wise and his team came to symbolize one of the characteristic qualities of *West Side Story*: the odd, sometimes uneasy combination of realism and fantasy—or "stylization and theatricality," as the filmmakers often referred to it—that gave the movie its "not-quite-real-world" quality.

As early as February 1960, while Lehman worked on the screenplay, Wise was studying photographic processes, in search of some particular types of effects. He consulted photographic manuals and magazines such as *LA Times Week* magazine, *Look*, and *Life* and was particularly interested in urban scenes of New York City. Among the photographs he collected were ones depicting bright red urban sunsets, red brick buildings, brightly colored windows, bridges, brunette women in red and yellow dresses with bright red lipstick, a Hispanic-looking young man, neon signs in Times Square, highways and streets, graffiti, the New York City ports, details of chain-link fences, the Manhattan skyline, cranes, buildings under construction, scaffolding, and traffic signs. Many of these visual images became part of the film's production design and cinematography. Among Wise's research papers and notes is an article titled "The Changing Faces of New York," with lots of color illustrations, that he clearly studied in his search for stylistic inspiration.[24] He also wrote to the Ziff Davis Publishing Company and requested a copy of its *Color Annual* so that he could "show his cameramen and art director," he explained, "the photographic effects and colors" he wanted.[25] Another document, unsigned but presumably written by Wise himself, contains philosophical notes, questions, and musings on color cinematography. Under the heading "What Makes a Good Picture?" the author of the typewritten document calls attention to the need for realism, pointing out that color photography, though very expressive, should be "a reasonable facsimile" of reality. The writer criticizes the film version of *South Pacific* for having "nothing to do with reality" and concludes, "color should suit the mood of the picture."[26]

Perhaps in pursuit of that "reasonable facsimile" of reality, Wise engaged the services of costume designer Irene Sharaff. Her prolific career in Hollywood and on Broadway had earned her several Oscars and Tony Awards and multiple nominations, including a 1957 Tony nomination for *West Side Story*. She was the only key member of the original theatrical creative team, other than Jerome Robbins, who was retained for the film version. Sharaff began her career in the theater in the late 1920s, worked in classic ballet, and received her first solo design credit for a Broadway musical in 1936. Her first Hollywood musical was Vincente Minnelli's *Meet Me in St. Louis* (1944). Her subsequent work included such design-heavy productions as the stage and film versions of *The King and I* (1951 and 1956, respectively) and Minnelli's *An American in Paris* (1951). Sharaff may not have seemed an obvious choice for a show with a contemporary urban setting in which the costumes were, to a certain extent, ordinary.

In preparation for the stage version of *West Side Story*, Sharaff researched gang styles and dress codes and observed the youths in their own environment on 110th Street, discovering patterns of teen apparel that she used in her designs. Sharaff chose windbreakers and hooded sweatshirts, T-shirts and blue jeans, and sharp color contrasts to distinguish the two gangs. Her designs for the play, largely re-created for the movie, gave the Jets "muted, indigo blues, ochre and musty yellows" and the Sharks "sharp purple, pink-violet, blood red and black." Likewise, the Jets' girls wore "pastels and homogenous" colors, while the Sharks' girls dressed in "brilliant colors."[27] Sharaff had her team dye the boys' T-shirts in various gang-related colors, and she employed a special blended fiber that allowed the dancers to jump around without splitting their blue jeans.[28] This special fabric was especially important in the movie, where multiple takes might cause additional wear and tear on the costumes. She created various new designs for the film, of course, but they were based on the same patterns, colors, and fabrics she had developed for the stage version.

Early concepts for the movie costumes included distinctive "uniforms" for the gangs: for the Jets, white sneakers, tight jeans, and "hoodies" with the word "JETS" on the back; for the Sharks, black street shoes, tight-fitting pin-striped slacks, long-sleeved zipped-up baseball jerseys, and baseball caps (paradoxically, reminiscent of the 1950s New York Yankees). Sharaff and Wise later abandoned this "uniform" idea in favor of more vivid, color-coordinated costumes, similar to the model used in the stage version. This choice became essential to the movie, especially as María's and Tony's costume colors tend to become more harmonious, and even shift, over the course of the movie (see chapter 3). Wise's pursuit of an "imaginative but controlled color concept" encompassed treating costumes, settings, locations, and production design as part of a singular cinematic vision in which color cinematography and special effects would play a major—if not *the* major—expressive role.

A Not Quite Real World

Evidently, Wise spent a significant amount of time in the first half of 1960 researching the photographic and scenic peculiarities he needed for the "imaginative" look of *West Side Story*. For principal set photography, Wise eventually hired Daniel L. Fapp, a noted craftsman who had recently worked in both color and black and white with directors George Cukor and Billy Wilder in *Let's Make Love* (1960) and *One, Two, Three* (1961), respectively. Tellingly, my research yielded relatively few materials on Fapp and his vital contribution to *West Side Story*, probably because his main concern was recreating a fundamentally "realistic" look on the sets and on location. By contrast, it seemed that Wise and the Mirisch brothers spent more time thinking about and discussing special effects. Wise examined various photographic formats and corresponded with colleagues (among them George Stevens, who was already researching cinematography for *The Greatest Story Ever Told*), but he also considered many options for laboratory processes, special photography, and optical effects. As early as October 1959, the filmmakers explored the possibility of making the movie in Cinerama, but the Cinerama company declined because *West Side Story* might be "a controversial picture."[29] The TODD-AO company, known for its high-definition sound systems, was trying out its new high-definition wide-screen formats at the time and offered its services to Wise and Mirisch. It did not get that contract, but TODD-AO was hired to provide sound recording and reproduction.

Meanwhile, a television broadcast of the "Rumble Ballet" scene from the play had been verbally authorized by Jerome Robbins and was scheduled to air on 31 January 1960. Upon learning of the broadcast, Wise and his lawyers stopped it. Their rationale was photographic. In a letter dated 7 January 1960 Wise wrote to the New York City law firm of Stillman & Stillman, representing Robbins, and argued that "showing this number on a small screen cannot convey to the public what we hope to convey in making the motion picture in a large screen process."[30] Wise objected to the limitations of the television format—he was thinking of "big" and wide for the film. Since the rights had been acquired by Mirisch and United Artists, the television broadcast never happened.

The movie was ultimately shot using the Super Panavision 70 format—actually, 65mm film printed on 70mm stock to make room for the optical sound track—although most release prints would be reduced to 35mm and masked for theatrical projection. Super Panavision 70 was a wide-screen format with an aspect ratio of 2.20:1, which had been especially well exploited in Otto Preminger's *Exodus* (1960). It had been invented to compete with TODD-AO's format and Ultra Panavision, but with a narrower aspect ratio. The format could accommodate the New York City locations gracefully and allowed space for mobility and choreography, while potentially reducing camera movement. Deciding on a cinematographic format and color photography was not as complex as Wise's search for the special effects that would provide the "not quite real" quality he had pitched to the Mirisch brothers and United Artists.

Special effects pioneer Linwood G. Dunn and his company, Film Effects of Hollywood, were hired to handle the complicated trick cinematography. Dunn's company, founded in 1946,. was the first independent optical effects company serving the Hollywood film industry. Before going independent, Dunn had risen through the ranks of the camera department at RKO Studios in the 1930s and 1940s and was particularly well known for his special effects photography, most notably in Merian C. Cooper and Ernest B. Schoedsack's *King Kong* (1933) and Orson Welles's *Citizen Kane* (1940)—for which Robert Wise was the film editor. Surely, Wise and Dunn knew each other from their postproduction years at RKO, especially since editing and special effects were closely related. Dunn was contracted for specific work on *West Side Story* over a twenty-two-week period, initially to run from 1 September 1960 to 1 February 1961. By 11 April 1960, Dunn and his team had already drafted a list of "possible methods" to achieve some of the optical printing effects; among the failed suggestions were split screens, changes from color to black and white and vice versa, and even "animated cartoon effects." More important, Dunn's company recommended the use of photographic manipulation "in every song"; these effects would come in fast or slow, "depending on the mood" of each number.[31] Many of these suggestions never got off the ground, but by 16 May 1960, Dunn had already completed four weeks of "experimental" effects and submitted film tests to Wise and his team at the Mirisch offices. Specifically citing Wise's desire for "unusual techniques" for a number of sequences and musical numbers, Dunn assured the producers of *West Side Story* that "nothing [was] really impossible in the realm of special effects."[32] Dunn's company also offered a verse-by-verse outline of the special effects that would accompany the "Tonight" duet between María and Tony. Here is a sample of what Dunn proposed:

> "*Tonight, tonight the world is wild and bright.*" New clusters of star-like forms are born, which appear and die out . . . increasing in size and number. (During the above, the set is dimmed down.)

> "*Going mad, shooting sparks into space.*" With sudden bursts, appear larger clusters of star-like forms, similar to skyrockets at maximum brightness and with almost blinding intensity.[33]

Few, if any, of these ideas actually made it into the finished film. But they provide evidence of a coordinated effort at a rather early phase—some three months before the beginning of principal photography, and only four months after Wise's trip to New York City—to produce visual concepts and effects that were new, imaginative, and even experimental.

By 30 June 1960, Dunn's company estimated the cost of its services to Mirisch/United Artists at $106,560, including the purchase and retrofitting of two 65mm optical printers for certain special effects shots.[34] Some haggling and requests for budget revisions ensued in a series of letters between Dunn and Marvin Mirisch, resulting in fewer special effects and composites in the film. In a letter to Mirisch dated 25 August, Dunn in fact mentions specific budget revisions "due to the lesser amount of effects desired."[35] Arguably, these negotiations explain why so many of Dunn's original ideas were left out of the movie. Evidently, financial considerations affected the final result, although the style and overall effect Wise envisioned were maintained to the extent possible.

In keeping with their determination to emphasize the visual qualities of their adaptation, Wise and the Mirisch brothers retained the services of noted graphic designer Saul Bass. Bass had made his reputation designing title sequences and movie posters for Otto Preminger (Carmen Jones [1954], The Man with the Golden Arm [1955]), Alfred Hitchcock (Vertigo [1958], North by Northwest [1959], Psycho [1960]), and Stanley Kubrick (Spartacus [1960]), among many others. Although Bass is listed in the screen credits as "visual consultant" for West Side Story, a memo from the Mirisch Company describes his work as "technical work design" and sets his fee at $25,000.[36] Bass's work began with the creation of various storyboards and designs for the "Prologue" sequence. He also designed the movie's distinctive, dynamic, animated title card, with its shifting color dissolves and its mysterious abstract line design (somewhat reminiscent of his Psycho concept); the film's title is dramatically revealed as the screen dissolves to the Lower Manhattan skyline. Bass was also responsible for the end credit sequence, where the credits are either handwritten or optically imposed on building walls, doors, storefront windows, and traffic signs.[37]

Bass rehearsed a number of different concepts for what he called "the time before" prologue. Color drawings show men in color-coordinated costumes fighting in dramatic poses; orange and black geometric patterns wipe through the entire screen, pushing dancing figures in silhouette off the screen. Several frames show slanted, broken fences with arrows indicating the actors moving through the frame, always left to right. In others, store signs and assorted words ("BODEGA," "SE HABLA ESPAÑOL," "TAQUERIA") or indiscernible fragments of words occupy the entire screen; there are dark walls with the gangs' names in graffiti, traffic signs depicted in close-ups and long shots, chain-link fences, and even a rooftop, apparently in the dawn light.[38] These designs emphasize visual motifs: dramatic, even unnatural colors; letters and signs; choreography; camera angles; and "stylized" or theatrical uses of locations. It is also evident that these early designs, presented in storyboard form, are based on a more "artificial" scheme than that presented in the finished movie; they are part of the initial design based on early versions of the shooting script, dated June 1960, when Lehman and Wise meant to create a much more unrealistic look for the "Prologue." Nevertheless, many of these visual motifs were adopted and implemented in the movie, such as the chain-link fences, rooftops, street signs, and graffiti. Not coincidentally, Wise had discovered many of these motifs himself, as his early research folders from the winter of 1959–1960 demonstrate. Although Bass's stylized designs were not formally adopted for the "Prologue" sequence, it is evident that his influence permeated both Lehman's screenplay and Wise's approach to mise-en-scène. In the forty-eight Bass storyboard frames I have seen, there is a discernible pattern of dark and bright colors alternating in rapid succession. For instance, six consecutive, mostly dark backgrounds are followed by four bright ones, then two dark, one bright, two dark, two bright, and so on. Since a good portion of the action in *West Side Story* takes place at night (María and Tony have barely known each other for twenty-four hours), it is logical that light and dark contrasts accompany Bass's design pitch. The shifting "moods" of the action (also brought up by both Boris Leven and Linwood Dunn) is clearly visible in the Bass storyboards.

"Second Thoughts"

While the design and technical team of Daniel Fapp, Boris Leven, Irene Sharaff, Linwood Dunn, and Saul Bass drafted concepts and developed the film's look through trial and error, under Robert Wise's close supervision, Ernest Lehman continued to work on the screenplay, often with feedback from Wise and Jerome Robbins. By April 1960, Lehman and Wise had created a list of characters and their traits. For example, Action was described as "angry, aggressive, always itching for a fight." Many of the secondary characters, including the Jets, the Sharks, and the girls, were similarly described with a few general terms. Interestingly, there was also a space for "María's parents," left blank and awaiting further input. Clearly, this would have been an important departure from the play and would have added a number of complications, but Lehman evidently did not pursue it.[39]

A long memo from Robbins to Lehman describes the "Rumble scene" in cinematographic "treatment" form, going into specific detail as to the actions, movements, and moods of the characters; exact lines of dialogue; and complete stage directions. At the end of the note Robbins writes, "O.K. Ernie, that's it, as well as I can remember it. NOW LEAVE IT ALONE! (polite laugh)."[40] Though it is difficult to determine the amount and type of Robbins's involvement in the screenwriting phase of West Side Story, there is evidence of some amiable friction between him and Lehman. Lehman's personal papers, memos, and letters depict a man of great humor; even as he was handing them over to a university archive, he added numerous handwritten notes, many on index cards, contextualizing and editorializing about the writings themselves. Lehman writes that he started "officially on West Side Story in November 1959, after finishing some on-location rewrites for From the Terrace." In a lovely, careful cursive, he explains his method of breaking down scenes, sometimes even shots, into brief descriptions on five-by-eight index cards:

> After the usual notes, outlines, conferences, etc., I made up this set of cards and tacked them up on a cork board on the wall facing my typewriter. This was my "step outline" to be followed while writing the screenplay. In almost every picture, I used this card system. I didn't always follow what was on the cards. In some pictures I never looked at the cards once I had tacked them up. But their presence was always reassuring, and sometimes even helpful.[41]

Some of Lehman's earlier notes involve simple, descriptive breakdowns of plot elements: "Scene 1. Two forces fighting each other established in prologue in first scene. . . . Scene 4. Gym—All forces join and fuse at the dance hall."[42]

An early approach to the "Prologue" (probably suggested by Robbins) was deemed "too documentary in flavor," according to Lehman, which led to the "stylized" yet still realistic fashion adopted later.[43] Lehman's first two index cards in the "Step Outline" describe the opening of the film. After the main titles and credits, the first card reads: "Over stylized 'views' of NY's WEST SIDE. Music—Overture."

Card number 2 continues: "PROLOGUE (Music). Exteriors, *Day* + *Night*, . . . semi-balletic—growing hostilities, Jets + Sharks, ending in free-for-all."[44] Though Lehman called for an "overstylized" atmosphere and Robbins lobbied for more realism, the finished product was a compromise in which the real locations served as the setting and background for "semi-balletic" dance choreography, in lieu of fighting.

Lehman and Robbins also discussed what the Jets' "turf" would be like: "Spheres of influence. Establish at what level they function, the world they move in and influence. The worlds they deride and the worlds they hide from." Lehman credited Robbins with creating that tension and conveying the narrative information: "it was done, in dance, by Mr. Robbins," he writes. Lehman also gave Robbins credit for moving the "Officer Krupke" number to a "different place"—whether he meant in space or time, Lehman does not specify. Lehman himself proposed moving the number to an earlier time in the story. In the stage version of *West Side Story*, the comical "Officer Krupke" number, with its "fast, vaudeville style," comes midway in the second act, after the rumble and the deaths of Riff and Bernardo, and it takes place in an unspecified alley between buildings.[45] It thus arguably disrupts the somber tone of the rest of the play. Lehman, thinking in terms of the film's narrative structure, proposed moving the song to the street in front of Doc's Candy Store and having it take place before the "War Council" scene. With a screenwriter's logic, under the heading "SECOND THOUGHTS ON THE ABOVE SEQUENCE," Lehman argued:

> It would be better to have Krupke come along before the PRs do—and then have the boys do "GEE, OFFICER KRUPKE" while the mood is still light. The number ends, and THEN the Sharks arrive. The war council takes place—SCHRANK comes along—the PRs disperse, and Tony is left alone with Doc. In this way, the mood is not destroyed by the number, with the need to revive the mood again for the proper ending.[46]

Clearly, Lehman's suggestion made a noticeable difference in the mood of the film compared with that of the play and was arguably an improvement.

The same logic applies to the rearrangement of two other musical numbers: "I Feel Pretty" and "Cool." In the movie, "I Feel Pretty" is moved ahead to immediately follow the "Tonight" duet; it comes right before Tony and María's mock wedding, which leads to the song "One Hand, One Heart." In fact, the song seems uncannily plausible at this point in the narrative, as it describes María's gleeful, bubbly mood while she excitedly anticipates Tony's visit, agreed upon in the previous number. In the play, the fizzy and funny "I Feel Pretty" comes at the beginning of the second act—after the rumble and the deaths of Riff and Bernardo. The first act ends on a noticeably solemn, depressing note: two principal characters lie dead in the middle of the stage; Tony runs away heartbroken, screaming María's name; and a "distant clock" starts to boom before the curtain falls.[47]

In a theater setting, with the convenience of an intermission, opening act 2 with "I Feel Pretty" is, in fact, a relief.[48] In the same way, the "Officer Krupke" number places narrative distance between Riff's and Bernardo's deaths—at the end of the first act—and Tony's death—near the end of the second act. In other words, in the play structure, although these songs are potentially jarring, their original placement can be justified. In the movie, though, the songs "Cool" and "Officer Krupke" effectively swap positions, sustaining the dark tone the film acquires after the rumble. In an undated note (probably from the summer of 1960), under the heading "Continuity of music and numbers in script," Wise had already shifted these three numbers, as proposed by Lehman, for purposes of mood continuity.[49]

Even more friction arose between Lehman and Robbins around the treatment of the "Tonight" quintet, which serves as the dramatic setup for the rumble sequence. Lehman wanted to start the film's second act, when all the principal characters are preparing for the night's events, with the "Tonight" quintet. (At this time, the movie was still imagined as having an intermission.) With this shift, the mock wedding and the cautiously optimistic "One Hand, One Heart"—with its promising lyrics "Now it begins, now it starts"— would end act 1. Lehman was unsure that the quintet itself would work in the revised order of scenes. In the stage version, the two gangs, plus María, Tony, and Anita, sing in unison but not together.

They occupy different areas of the stage, and spotlights bring each one in turn to the public's attention, leading to an en masse conclusion. In the book of the play, Arthur Laurents describes scene 8 in these terms: "6:00 to 9:00 PM. The Neighborhood. Spotlights pick out Riff and the Jets, Bernardo and the Sharks, Anita, Maria and Tony against small sets representing different places in the neighborhood. All are waiting expectantly for the coming of night, but for very different reasons."[50] This breakdown of the action is arguably the live theater version of what is called "montage" in classical cinema. Lehman envisioned opening up the sequence similarly, putting all the parties in separate settings, matching some of the sets Boris Leven had been instructed to design in the 23 May memo. The Jets and the Sharks would be seen preparing and strutting toward the rumble in opposite screen directions. María would be sitting by the bedroom window, dreamily looking forward to her next rendezvous with Tony. Anita would be getting ready in her bathroom, anticipating a sexual encounter with Bernardo. Tony, at Doc's Candy Store, would be thinking of María and planning to stop the rumble.

Card number 31 in Lehman's "Step Outline" describes the scene as "quick flashes" of the principals singing their lines. Lehman adds a dramatic montage of consecutive close-up and medium shots of Tony, Schrank ("in car, cruising"), Riff and the Jets, Bernardo and the Sharks, Anita ("in bath"), and María at the end of the number, as "all [are] caught in close shots during the holding of the final word of [the] song—*Tonight*." Following his common practice, Lehman added "CUT TO:" at the bottom of the card, and the action continues on card 32, where he describes the rumble sequence per se. But the bottom of card 31 reads "CUT TO: Jerry, leaving"—the last two words in a different handwriting. Lehman's notes explain that this handwriting belonged to Jerome Robbins. Another card describing a shot from the rumble reads: "EXT. STREET NIGHT. Jets on the move—singing: 'We're gonna rock it tonight / We're gonna jazz it up and have us a ball.'" To this particular card, Robbins added the editorial quip, "CUT TO: Jerry—worried." According to Lehman, Robbins probably wrote those comments, expressing his worry and threatening to leave (presumably the movie theater, or maybe the production itself) while Lehman was away from his office.

Robbins's reservations about the treatment of the scene baffled Lehman. He wrote, "I don't know *why* Jerry felt like swearing at this cinematic treatment of a difficult musical number . . . because my suggested treatment of this particular section of the picture, which made him 'nervous . . . worrying . . . leaving,' turned out to be so exciting on the screen."[51] But Lehman himself had been unsure if the musical number would work, since it takes place over the course of three hours in different locales. He considered dropping the song altogether and rewriting the sequence in a different format, but his close-up montage solution makes sense in terms of cinematic form and structure. A montage is designed to compress a significant amount of narrative information into a single, self-contained unit.

Ultimately, Lehman prevailed, and the sequence indeed turned out to be quite "exciting." He used a "cinematic" treatment to solve the problem of continuity of action and mood, while indicating dynamic relations of time, space, and movement. As promised, Lehman's adaptation of *West Side Story* was faithful enough to the source material to convert the stage experience of the play into cinematic language without looking like filmed theater. Insistently pursuing a distinctive visual style and effectively employing the tools of the cinema, Robert Wise, Ernest Lehman, Boris Leven, Daniel Fapp, and Linwood Dunn were determined to make the adaptation of *West Side Story* "not a photographed stage play." Codirector Jerome Robbins, however, was not always confident that the material he had so successfully brought to the Broadway stage was destined to achieve comparable success as a motion picture.

"To Contribute in the Same Way"

On 26 December 1959 the *Hollywood Reporter* announced that Jerome Robbins—the principal creative force behind the stage success of *West Side Story*—had been signed by the Mirisch Company to "co-direct his first motion picture." The *Reporter* also informed its readers that Ernest Lehman was writing the screenplay; Saul Chaplin, formerly of the MGM Music Department, had been hired as associate producer; and Robert Wise, Robbins, and Chaplin were "conferring in New York."[52] Although Robbins had evidently come on board earlier, his contract was not finalized until the spring of

1960; meanwhile, Wise, Lehman, and the creative team were already in place and working full time on preproduction matters. A 4 March letter from Raymond Kurtzman, representing the Mirisch Company, to Sidney H. Levin, of the law firm Stillman & Stillman, requested the latter to prepare a contract for Jerome Robbins as codirector of *West Side Story*. This letter states that Robbins was to provide "exclusive services" for $175,000 compensation to be paid over three years. These services would begin 1 May 1960 and would continue for no less than twenty-eight weeks, "until completion of principal photography." Overtime compensation, if needed after the initial twenty-eight weeks, would be paid at the rate of $6,250 per week. Among other particulars, Robbins was required to be in Los Angeles when production moved there after the New York location shoot, with additional compensation of $500 per week "in lieu of living expenses." Robbins would be allowed to travel between Los Angeles and New York after the conclusion of the "exclusive" part of his contract, but the producers were obliged to reimburse him "for only five such trips." Robbins was also contracted on a nonexclusive basis for the postproduction or "cutting" of the picture; however, his participation in this phase was voluntary and would depend on his "desire to be involved" and, presumably, on the film's producers—namely, Robert Wise and the Mirisch brothers.

Item number five of the letter addressed the issue of screen credit: Robbins's credit would be in the same size and color as Wise "but in second position," reading "Directed by Robert Wise and Jerome Robbins." On this matter, Kurtzman anticipated "some problems with regards to guild regulations," but he promised to look into it before the contract was finalized. Item number six established that Robbins would receive screen credit for choreography on a separate card reading "Choreography by Jerome Robbins," but this would not appear on paid advertising, presumably to keep costs down. (As discussed in chapter 2, the choreography credit provoked a good deal of extra haggling and negotiation between the Mirisch Company and Robbins's legal representatives in New York.)

More important were Kurtzman's caveats on item number seven, covering creative control. Citing a previous telephone conversation with Levin, Kurtzman warned, "It is easy to see that this could be a big problem, both contractually and practically." Under the clause proffered by Kurtzman, creative control would be "shared jointly by Wise and Robbins," subject to United Artists' final approval under the distribution deal. In the event Wise and Robbins could not agree on any "artistic matter," arbitration, followed by a final decision, would fall to Harold Mirisch in his capacity as executive producer and partner in the Mirisch Company. The significance of this proviso cannot be understated. As executive producers of the film, Walter, Harold, and Marvin Mirisch were at least titular partners with Robert Wise, the sole credited "producer." The Mirisch brothers also had a standing collaboration with Wise and had entered into a multiple-picture deal with him. It could thus be argued that Wise had more clout with the Mirisches than Robbins ever would, and when it came to potential creative differences with Robbins, Wise could exert more pressure on his partners. In fact, Wise was able to prevail over Robbins on some on-set decisions, eventually leading to Robbins's exit midway through production (see chapter 2).

A final clause proposed by Kurtzman addressed the issue of succession in the event Wise became unavailable to direct the film either before or after the beginning of principal photography. In either case, the Mirisch Company would "consult with Robbins in good faith" concerning a replacement director but would retain the right to make the final decision. If Wise became unavailable *before* the commencement of production, and if Robbins did not approve of the substitute codirector, the Mirisch brothers gave him the option to resign. If, for any reason, Wise could not carry on *after* the beginning of production, Robbins remained contractually obliged to "continue to render his services," regardless of whether he approved of the replacement director. Evidently, the producers were appreciative of Robbins's position and respectful of his collaborative role, but they did not want Robbins to take over solo directing duties on the set if Wise were to resign, fall ill, or die during production.[53]

The fact that Robbins did not have much experience with filmmaking was apparently on the producers' minds. Robbins did have some prior screen credits, however: as choreographer in the 1942 Mexican film I *Danced with Don Porfirio* (Gilberto Martínez Solares); for providing the "idea" for the 1949 film version of On *the Town*, directed by Gene Kelly and Stanley Donen; for staging the dance and musical numbers in the 1956 movie version of *The King and I*, directed by Walter Lang; and for choreography and adaptation in the 1960 TV movie *Peter Pan*, directed by Vincent J. Donehue.[54] It is evident that Robbins was involved in different aspects of preproduction on *West Side Story*, including his notes to Lehman in the early writing stages and his correspondence with Wise beginning in April 1960. In one letter to Wise, Robbins states, "I have taken a fairly passive position on the film so far . . . because I have not been sure of where to go or in which direction we were headed, and even more so because I trust your taste so very much."[55]

As he was not yet contractually obligated, Robbins apparently yielded to Wise on whatever decisions, if any, were made. These included some early brainstorming about casting, presumably an area in which "taste" was a factor. Wise had begun preliminary cast interviews in New York and Los Angeles as early as 8 January 1960, when Rita Moreno first read for the part of Anita. But casting and screen tests did not begin in earnest until sometime later in the spring.[56] As per early decisions about casting, in a 25 May memo, Robbins suggested to Wise that there be "ten Sharks and ten Jets," as well as a third group in the "dance at the gym" sequence. Robbins recommended that this third group be dressed in a color scheme that made them clearly stand out from the Jets and the Sharks, who had to be equally and readily identifiable.[57] This was a particularly important directorial recommendation from Robbins, since the stage version of *West Side Story* included no such cast members.[58] In the play, the "dance at the gym" is strictly a "duel" between the Sharks and the Jets; the presence of this third group (identifiable in the movie standing in the background in their drab, olive green costumes designed by Irene Sharaff) was a new idea that showed Robbins was trying to think "cinematically," beyond the spatial constraints of the theatrical stage.

Robbins's participation in the preproduction phase increased in the months leading up to principal photography, and a 16 June memo broke down the "choreographed areas" of *West Side Story* from the "Prologue" to the "Taunting" of Anita. Ten "areas" were named on this list, corresponding to scenes or sequences from the play and the screenplay. Recognizable on the list were a majority of the musical numbers, yet notably missing were both versions of "Tonight" (the duet and the quintet), as well as Tony's "María" solo.[59] It is possible that these two numbers were omitted because there is less "dancing," in the theatrical sense of the word: the actors in these sequences are mostly standing or walking, making choreography unnecessary. As the codirectors developed their "division of labor" approach, this led to the drafting of an actual breakdown of sequences and an implied hierarchy of directorial duties. An undated document from Wise's papers, most likely compiled in June 1960, divided the film into twenty sequences, from the "Prologue" to the "Final Sequence," including every major setting and action to be filmed. Each sequence was given a descriptive title and a setting; when necessary, the accompanying song or musical number was listed. For instance, the list included the following: "Jet scene—Schrank and Krupke—*Jet Song*," "Balcony scene and *Tonight*," "Drugstore—*Taunting Scene*." Details about the featured characters were often included. Also listed next to each entry were the names of the codirectors, in primary and secondary order. Entry number 11 on the list, for example, reads "Bridal Shop—*I Feel Pretty*—mock wedding—*Robbins*—Wise." Entry number 12 says, "Quintet of *Tonight*—*Wise*—Robbins." The codirector with the underlined name would assume primary responsibility on the set. The segments were divided fairly equally, with Wise listed as principal director on eleven, and Robbins on nine. Robbins was generally responsible for the scenes considered heavy on dance, closely approximating the list of "choreographed" scenes drafted on 16 June. At the bottom of the document, a typed note from Wise adds an earnest stipulation: "I would count on having and considering all Robbins' ideas, thoughts and suggestions on the scenes that I handle and would expect to contribute in the same way to the sequences that Robbins has precedence on."[60]

It is clear from this document that the codirectors and producers of *West Side Story* meant to approach filming in an evenhanded manner, giving Wise and Robbins equal authority, at least nominally, when it came to creative decisions. It also suggests that Wise and Robbins were expected to play to their own strengths: Wise, who had no musical credits, would be responsible for the dramatic sequences, and Robbins would be in charge of the musical numbers and their lead-in scenes.

The codirector system worked out for *West Side Story* was not unusual in itself, although such arrangements have always been quite rare in Hollywood productions. Codirector credits, usually in the form of "Directed by . . . and . . . ," were seldom seen in Hollywood films, but in practice, codirectors were not unheard of in the musical genre. As far back as Busby Berkeley's early days at Warner Bros., credit for choreography and the "staging" of musical numbers was separate from credit for directing the dramatic segments, with the latter typically receiving the major credit.[61] Nevertheless, codirector collaborations, along with shared credit, had occasionally worked well, at least from a business standpoint. The partnership of Gene Kelly and Stanley Donen at MGM's Arthur Freed unit in the movies *On the Town* (1949), *Singin' in the Rain* (1952), and *It's Always Fair Weather* (1955) serves as the most visible and profitable example in the studio era, although even Kelly and Donen's professional relationship ended not so happily. At the outset of *West Side Story*, Wise had imagined some sort of creative arrangement with Robbins. But, according to Wise, Robbins wanted a more active role in the production, one that went beyond just choreography. Aware that Robbins was "a special talent" and that he had created the entire *West Side Story* "concept," Wise even suggested to Harold Mirisch that Robbins be allowed to direct the movie, since Wise could not "see any way for a co-directing situation to work out." But Mirisch thought the film was too big and too expensive for Robbins's limited motion picture experience. As one of the film's producers, Wise finally came to the conclusion that "the best thing for the film" was to work out the codirecting deal, eventually leading to the division of labor between Wise and Robbins in a prearranged breakdown of sequences.[62]

It was clear from the beginning that although his involvement had been proposed early on, Robbins's official duties began later and involved mostly the musical numbers in the film as initially scripted.

Lehman, Wise, and the Mirisch brothers all had concerns about the codirectorial scheme at one point or another. With a planned production schedule running from July to December 1960 and a release date of October 1961, *West Side Story* was ready to start filming in New York City in the summer of 1960, with its two directors in tow. Still missing was a leading actress to play the part of María.

2 "A Different Medium":
Making *West Side Story*

Both the budget and the production schedule of *West Side Story* had expanded significantly by the time of its October 1961 theatrical release. From an initial estimate of $5 million, the budget had grown to about $6.75 million, reportedly the highest figure for any musical film at the time.[1] In the 7 December 1960 edition of *Daily Variety*, Larry Tubelle's column, "The Feature Story," was dedicated to a gossip-style report of the apparently troubled production. Tubelle began with some musings on the decline of the musical genre in Hollywood filmmaking, wondering what had "killed" the musical and pointing to *The King and I* (1956) as the genre's last dignified stand. Tubelle also put in perspective some of the difficulties and peculiarities of *West Side Story* and predicted that it "could reverse the trend and reinstate the stature and prominence of this vanishing cinematic art form." Tubelle warned that the original property was considered "holy" in theatrical circles because of its unusual blend of music, drama, and dancing, and he reported "suspicion that all may not be well" at the Samuel Goldwyn Studios, where the movie was shooting. Tubelle cited "'family' turmoil, a mushrooming budget, production delays, uncooperative talent, questionable casting, and untimely illnesses." He also reported that the production budget had risen from $5 million to $6 million[2] and that the wrap on principal photography had been pushed from December 1960 to February 1961. He offered the first public news about the lyrics change in "America" and about the swap in song sequence between "Officer Krupke" and "Cool" to "fit the mood"; he announced that the "Prologue" had been expanded to eight minutes (from the original four and a half in the play) and that the movie's running time was expected to be two hours and fifteen or twenty minutes. Tubelle was also the first to report that a professional singer would dub Richard Beymer's singing voice and that the same might be true of Natalie Wood, whose singing was "still on the borderline." Furthermore, Tubelle announced that Jerome Robbins had exited the production earlier than planned, and he quoted Robert Wise, whom he had interviewed on the lot: "It was merely a matter of time, not of artistic differences or personal friction," Wise said of Robbins's early departure. "It took too much time to coordinate our thoughts," and the arrangement had become "unwieldy and time-consuming . . . it became unmanageable."[3]

However, a lot happened before Robbins's departure from the film. Through the spring and early summer of 1960, with the technical and design teams in place, the casting of West Side Story began in earnest.

"A Name Actress"

Jerome Robbins, Robert Wise, and Ernest Lehman had agreed that the principal cast would consist of ten Jets, ten Sharks, their "girls," five adults (this includes the addition of Madame Lucía, who does not appear in the play), plus the leading female characters of María and Anita. However, the "Work Script" belonging to script supervisor Stanley K. Scheuer, dated 17 June 1960 and containing revisions up to 26 October 1960, listed eleven Jets, with separate cast and crew lists dated 2 and 4 August, respectively.[4] Interviews, readings, and testing with potential cast members began as early as 8 January 1960, shuttling between New York and Los Angeles. It seemed that every young actor and dancer on either coast was on the list at some point. A memo from Lynn Stalmaster's casting office listed thirty-four possible Tonys, many with check marks, scratch-outs, highlights, and question marks next to their names; some additional names were penciled in. Early candidates on this list included Russ Tamblyn and Richard Beymer, who went on to win the parts of Riff and Tony, respectively, along with Richard Chamberlain, Warren Beatty, George Peppard, Burt Reynolds, Dean

Stockwell, Ricky Nelson, Anthony Perkins, Michael Landon, Troy Donahue, Alan Reed Jr., Robert Redford, and Robert Blake. The list of potential Marías contained twenty names, including Suzanne Pleshette, Diane Baker, Barbara Luna, Susan Kohner, Yvonne Craig, Roberta Shore, and Elinor Donahue.[5] According to Robert Wise's New York and Los Angeles casting files, from January through November 1960, as many as 486 actors and dancers were interviewed, tested, or considered for a number of parts in the movie. Among the notable names and dates were Rita Moreno (8 January), Jack Nicholson (9 February), George Segal (5 March), Keir Dullea (8 March), George Hamilton (25 March), Diane Baker (11 April), Joan Tewkesbury (30 April), Robert Redford (16 May), and Margaret O'Brien (23 May). Both Russ Tamblyn and Jill St. John were interviewed on 18 May. After Sheree North was interviewed on 7 April, the word "No" was written next to her name. Twenty-six-year-old George Segal was considered "maybe too old" to play Tony. Yvette Mimieux, who tried out on 26 April, was described as having "vacant eyes," yet she made a second early list of possible Marías that also included Jill St. John, Cathy Crosby, and Margaret O'Brien. Though she was in her fifties, Dolores Costello's name was also on the list, as Wise and his producing partners were considering "name" actresses to play María. As it turned out, the lead was not cast until later in the process.

As of 26 March 1960, a new list of "West Coast Tony Possibilities" again included Richard Beymer, Troy Donahue, and Robert Blake (none of whom read for the part), among a few others. By the same date, the actresses still under consideration for the part of Anita were Barbara Luna and Rita Moreno. Moreno's test from 26 March was judged to be an "excellent reading of Anita Test scenes," but there was some "question" about her dancing. Still, Moreno left the audition with a red pencil check mark next to her name. On the same date, Russ Tamblyn tested for the part of Tony and was deemed to have done "an excellent reading."

Through the winter and spring of 1960, Robert Wise had likewise been testing a number of performers under the category of "dancers." Some of them were eventually cast in small, supporting roles in the movie, including Tony Mordente, who had been in the original Broadway cast of *West Side Story* and was one of Jerome Robbins's assistants. Mordente tested in New York in February 1960 and ended up with a red pencil mark around his name, followed by the comment, "Played A-Rab here and a year in London. Has done two Sid Ceasar [sic] shows." Mordente eventually won the part of Action in the movie, a promotion from his less flashy stage role. Naturally, other performers from the original production were given the opportunity to try out: David Winters, who had played Baby John on stage, was cast as A-Rab in the movie; Jay Norman was promoted from the background figure Juano to the role of Pepe, Bernardo's lieutenant; and Carole D'Andrea reprised the role of Velma. D'Andrea was one of only three original Broadway cast members who repeated their roles in the film; the other two were William Bramley, who played Officer Krupke, and Tommy Abbot, as Gee-Tar. Carol Lawrence, the original stage María, tested for the lead role in New York on 7 March, along with newcomers Yvonne Othon and Suzie Kaye, both of whom, paradoxically, got their roles (as Consuelo and Rosalía, respectively). Also in March, Wise and Robbins held a number of on-location screen tests with some of the aspiring actors in New York City. The *New Yorker* ran the story in its 2 April issue, detailing Robbins's coaching of dancer Eddie Verso, who won the part of Juano. The reporter commented on the cold weather and the state of the location on West Sixty-Seventh Street between West End and Amsterdam but made only brief mention of Wise's presence there. The list of dancers interviewed and tested in Hollywood in late March 1960 included their phone numbers, height, weight, and hair color. Maria Jimenez and Joanne Miya got the dancing parts of Teresita and Francisca, respectively; Jimenez had been on the list of possible dancers since 27 January. Jose de Vega, who got the featured part of Chino, tested in Hollywood on 10 March; his note reads, "Read Chino—All right with work—Good Quality." Eventually, the New York casting tour brought in Eliot Feld as Baby John and the brother-and-sister team of Gus and Gina Trikonis on opposite sides of the gang conflict: he as the Shark Indio, and she as Riff's girlfriend Graziella. Susan Oakes (listed as Sue Oakes) appeared in the cast records in June 1960 attached to the role of Anybodys, described as "a tomboy." The final New York casting tests with Wise were held on Monday, 2 May 1960.

The Carlos Alvarado Agency, which had been representing Hispanic actors in Los Angeles since the 1940s, sent a number of actors and dancers to audition and test for bit and background parts in November 1960, well after the Los Angeles studio shoot had begun. None of them was featured in the movie. The last of the adult parts was also cast in November 1960. John Astin (his name misspelled in the schedule as "Aslin") was interviewed on 2 November for the part of Glad Hand, described in the screenplay as "a social worker." Penciled notes on the schedule describe Astin as "30, 6'1"—dark hair large nose, out here 2–3 months, original 3 Penny Opera, Broadway, much off Broadway, Phoenix, etc." Astin got the part; *West Side Story* was his first movie. Veteran character actor Ned Glass got the part of Doc. Simon Oakland, fresh off Hitchcock's *Psycho*, had worked with Wise previously in *I Want to Live!* (1958); he rounded out the adults in the movie, cast as Lieutenant Schrank.

Through the spring of 1960, major parts remained unfilled. Late in March, among the actresses still being considered for María were Anita Sands, who had appeared in the TV series *Surfside 6*, *77 Sunset Strip*, *Hawaiian Eye*, *Maverick*, and *Bonanza*, and Susan Kohner, who had earned a supporting actress Oscar nomination in 1960 for playing the mixed-up, mixed-race teen Sarah Jane in Douglas Sirk's remake of *Imitation of Life* (1959). Arguably, this particular short list, however unofficial, shows some attempt to find an actress who could play "ethnic" (or at least "tanned") parts, as indicated by the tropical and western settings of Sands's résumé and Kohner's real-life background (she was the daughter of Mexican actress Lupita Tovar). This list also reveals that the search for a somewhat recognizable "name" actress to play María was still going on; among others, former MGM child star Margaret O'Brien had been considered. Natalie Wood's name had not yet come up, however.[6]

Still other major roles remained uncast as spring rolled into summer. Filming in New York City was now scheduled to begin on 1 August, but by mid-June, there was still no final decision on the role of Bernardo. It is clear, though, that George Chakiris was the top candidate. In a production memo dated 10 June, Wise delivers a gentle, redundant ultimatum to Robbins: "We will have to make our decision on 'Bernardo' immediately, for if we need [George] Chakiris from the London company he should know immediately." Wise also discussed Carole D'Andrea in this memo, somewhat urgently exhorting his assistants to "see if she [is] available."[7] Evidently, a decision about Bernardo was made quickly, and Chakiris was summoned from the London company, where he had been playing Riff. Negotiations were still ongoing with Rita Moreno, who had read for the part of Anita in the spring. From 8 to 18 July, Moreno's agents and Ray Kurtzman of Mirisch's Legal Department had been negotiating the size of her onscreen credit. Because there was still no María, Kurtzman insisted (and Moreno's agents agreed) that her credit could be reduced to "the larger size allowable under Maria's contract." Kurtzman explained in a memo to Wise that this clause was necessary "in the event [they] had a name actress to play Maria."[8] Moreno had been acting in movies since 1950, including the featured part of Zelda in *Singin' in the Rain*, so her agents were demanding suitable screen credit for her flashy, key role in *West Side Story*. The parties agreed on the screen credit proviso, and the search for María continued. Moreno was the only native of Puerto Rico in the principal cast.

Meanwhile, by early July 1960, the cast was reportedly rehearsing and preparing for location shooting in New York City. On 3 July the *New York Times* ran an article about the two-month period of "intense rehearsal" that had already begun in Hollywood, focusing on Robbins's careful casting and precise instructions to his dancers. "Look," Robbins is quoted as telling the cast, "I want the movements sharp, like a pistol shot." In a candid aside with the reporter, Robbins admitted some of his concerns, including the fact that theater dancing, which he knew very well, was supposed to be broad and visible "to the last row of the balcony," whereas the movie camera was always sitting "front row center." Somehow, he had to make the choreography fit the cinematic medium. Furthermore, Robbins had to work with "dancing actors and acting dancers," because the "rough and tumble action" in *West Side Story* would be performed by the principals, not by stunt doubles. Robbins pointed directly to Russ Tamblyn, whose acrobatics in *Seven Brides for Seven Brothers* had caught his attention. As a demonstration, in the middle of rehearsal, Tamblyn practiced the back handstand from the "Officer Krupke" number, "much to Mr. Robbins' delight."[9]

While the majority of the dancers were already rehearsing with Robbins, fifteen actresses were still scheduled to test for the part of María in Hollywood. On 16 July seven of the fifteen aspirants ended the day with check marks next to their names, presumably making a new short list. On top of the list was singer and actress Carol Lawrence, nearly twenty-eight years old at the time. Lawrence had tested with the "Bridal Shop" and "Balcony" scenes. Also making the list were Lynn Loring, who would soon appear in a small role alongside Natalie Wood in Elia Kazan's *Splendor in the Grass*; Elizabeth Ashley, who would go on to win the 1961 Tony Award for *Take Her, She's Mine*; Ina Balin, who won a featured role that same year with John Wayne in *The Comancheros*; Susan Slavin, an aspiring actress who later married acting coach Larry Moss; Barbara Luna, ubiquitous in TV westerns and variety shows; and Diane Baker, who had debuted as Anne Frank's older sister in George Stevens's *The Diary of Anne Frank* (1959). Both Luna and Baker were holdovers from the list supplied by Lynn Stalmaster early in the process. Except for Carol Lawrence, most of the hopefuls were asked to perform the "Chino" scene—the dramatically charged exchange in which Chino announces to María that her boyfriend Tony has killed her brother Bernardo. Apparently, only one candidate, Angela Dorian (aka Victoria Vetri), was asked to sing ("I Feel Pretty").[10] Curiously, another survivor from Stalmaster's preliminary list was the Italian-born, classically trained coloratura Anna Maria Alberghetti. As a teenager, Alberghetti had appeared with Bing Crosby in Frank Capra's *Here Comes the Groom* (1951) and with Rosemary Clooney in *The Stars Are Singing* (Norman Taurog, 1953); more recently, at age twenty-four, she had played the featured role of Princess Charming in the modest box-office hit *Cinderfella* (Frank Tashlin, 1960), starring Jerry Lewis. As a young, beautiful, accomplished opera singer with movie experience, it is no surprise that Alberghetti was being considered for María, seemingly from the beginning. Paradoxically, she did not get the part, although she won a 1962 Tony Award for *Carnival!* and eventually played María onstage in a 1964 revival. Evidently, none of the women remaining on the short list was enough of a "movie star." Wise, Mirisch, and Robbins passed on both Carol Lawrence and Larry Kert (the original Tony), who had been in competition for the leads at one point. They had no movie experience and were judged too old to portray María and Tony onscreen, although both were back on Broadway that spring playing the parts.

The Mirisch Company was reportedly under pressure from United Artists not to risk a $5 million production by relying on a cast of mostly unknown actors. Reportedly, UA executives suggested Harry Belafonte and Elizabeth Taylor to headline the film. In late July the producers began to consider Natalie Wood, who had just turned twenty-two. Walter Mirisch had known Wood since she was a teenager, from his days as a producer of $125,000 B movies at Monogram Pictures; Wood had appeared in *The Rose Bowl Story* (William Beaudine, 1952), which Mirisch had produced. "She was the right age for Maria," recalled Mirisch, "and a good actress."[11] Though the producers were somewhat worried about her singing prowess and the potential challenge of re-creating a Puerto Rican accent, Natalie Wood was hired for an upfront salary of $250,000. Robert (Bobby) Tucker, a vocal coach, was retained to help Wood navigate the intricacies of Bernstein and Sondheim's music and lyrics.[12] Even so, music producer Saul Chaplin kept soprano Marni Nixon on hand for dubbing purposes, predicting that although Wood wanted to do her own singing, she might not be up to the vocal challenge.[13] Nixon was purportedly expected to "loop" in the high notes that Wood could not reach and perhaps "sweeten" some of Wood's voice takes.

Twenty-two-year-old Richard Beymer, an early candidate for the lead, was finally cast as Tony. Beymer had been playing small roles in movies and TV series since he was eleven years old, and at age fifteen, he had been directed by Wise in the Warner Bros. remake of *So Big* (1953) with Jane Wyman and Sterling Hayden. Beymer was hired with the understanding that another performer—in his case, jazz singer and arranger Jim Bryant—would dub his songs.[14] Tucker Smith, who had landed the role of Ice, a part adapted from the stage roles of Diesel and Action, would dub the voice of Riff, played by Tamblyn, in the "Jet Song." It is unclear why Chaplin decided to do this, since Tamblyn was an accomplished singer; he had been in various musical films, including Stanley Donen's *Seven Brides for Seven Brothers* (1954), and had a recording contract with MGM.[15] Most likely, Chaplin was seeking a particular type of harmony that, for whatever reason, he thought Smith would deliver better. The dubbing of actors' singing voices—a common practice since the invention of the musical genre—ended up being a contentious affair during the production of *West Side Story*. This was especially true of the Natalie Wood–Marni Nixon pairing.

"In Bad Taste": Censorship Difficulties

As required by the Motion Picture Association of America (MPAA), Robert Wise submitted two copies of the shooting script of *West Side Story* for the censorship board to review on 24 June 1960. At this point, Lehman and Sondheim were still revising the lyrics for the song "America," so Wise explained that these would be forwarded "the moment" they were ready. Wise politely asked that the board move quickly, for music prescoring sessions were already under way at the recording studio.[16] Geoffrey M. Shurlock, vice president of the MPAA and director of the Production Code Administration (PCA), responded on 28 June that the news was generally good. The board had ruled that the story of the film was "acceptable," but it asked for one specific change: the lyrics to "Anita's song"—actually, her solo section of the "Tonight" quintet—were deemed to be "unacceptably sex-suggestive," as they included the word "hot" to describe Bernardo.[17]

Lyrics revisions for "several musical numbers" were submitted to the PCA on 28 June and 28 July 1960. These latest submissions included the new "America" lyrics, which the board readily cleared. However, there were still no final revisions for Anita's solo in the "Tonight" quintet, and new objections arose concerning words in the "Officer Krupke" number. Mistakenly referring to it as "the Jet song," Shurlock personally "urged" the writers to "eliminate the reference to social disease." He observed that many spectators might consider this reference "offensive," which could make the movie "vulnerable" to charges of "bad taste."[18] Even after the film was in production and music recording sessions were in full gear, Wise and Lehman continued to forward revised song lyrics and lines of dialogue to Shurlock and to Eugene Dougherty and Albert Van Schmus, the top censors at the MPAA. On 12 October the revision of Anita's "hot" line was presented to the censors—changed from "what/hot" to "dear/here"—and news of the board's approval reached the set two days later. Technically, the *West Side Story* shooting script was approved for production in late June, even though changes continued to be demanded and incorporated during the first two months of principal photography. However, every letter from the MPAA and the PCA dated between June and October 1960 ended with the warning that "final judgment" would be issued only when the finished film, or a good approximation thereof, was fully reviewed by the censors. Surprisingly, the "social disease" reference in the "Officer Krupke" song survived intact, though not without controversy.

"Pick up the Pace"

While writing the screenplay, Ernest Lehman (who had also scripted the movie version of *The King and I* for Walter Lang) broke down the action and the book of the play into 112 scenes and 126 pages. The initial preproduction schedule, set up in March 1960, proposed that principal photography begin in New York on 18 July, although it warned, "This date will have to be flexible." A 6 June memo from Wise's assistant director, Robert E. Relyea, to Mirisch production manager Allen K. Wood estimated twelve shooting days and four nights in New York City, with thirty-one cast and crew present and a "test budget" of $175,000.[19] By the next day, shooting in New York City had been rescheduled; it was now set to begin on 1 August—delayed by exactly two weeks. The ambitious production breakdown listed forty-four scenes, most estimated to take between a quarter day and a full day, to be filmed in New York from 1 to 18 August. Two Sundays, 7 and 14 August, were listed as days off. First on the scene breakdown were exterior shots of the city; this was second-unit work, with two days set aside for "stylized shots of N.Y." The schedule for 3 August included two scenes—one of the Jets "moving and dancing" through a parking lot, and one of Sharks being "chased off" by Jets. Pencil marks on these and two other scenes in the New York locations indicated they would be based on Saul Bass's storyboards. Thirty-two of the scenes named on this production list involved the "Prologue" sequence, up to and including the "free for all" fight and the "Jet Song," scheduled to take four days at the end of the daytime shoot. The nighttime shoot included more "stylized shots of New York" for the "Prologue," which never made it into the movie; part of Tony's walk during the "María" number; "Anita's P.O.V. shot" of Tony in an alley after leaving María's bedroom; and assorted Jets and Sharks hide-and-seek action occurring after the rumble.[20]

The "Prologue" production schedule, however, was soon simplified and altered from Lehman's original screenplay. The "Prologue" now took place entirely during the daytime—in fact, all the action seemingly occurred in a single day; it was also compacted and produced with no costume changes.[21] In the interest of simplicity, and to make up for production delays, all eleven scenes scheduled for nighttime filming in New York were eventually moved either to the alley sets on the back lot of the Samuel Goldwyn Studios or to locations in downtown Los Angeles that Boris Leven and his team had scouted; others were just scrapped altogether.[22]

Meanwhile, before filming began in New York, many of the songs were being recorded in Los Angeles in June and July under the guidance of associate producer Saul Chaplin. According to the recording schedule, "Cool" and the "Taunting" of Anita would be recorded on 21 June, the "Jet Song" on 27 June, and "Officer Krupke" on 1 July.[23] Because the "Jet Song" was scheduled to be filmed in New York on 10 to 13 August, it had to be recorded early so that it could be played back on location in New York for the actors to lip-synch. Sid Ramin and Irwin Kostal had begun new orchestrations of the musical score in July, and Leonard Bernstein was composing new music for the "Prologue"; orchestrations and recordings went on until May 1961.

On 4 August Wise asked Irene Sharaff for an update on the costumes for the "America" number. Production was already behind schedule, which was leading to budget concerns. By then, Bob Relyea and Al Wood had received instructions to cut out one of the two budgeted hairdressers in New York and to "drop [the] 11th Shark and 12th Jet," also in response to budget concerns.[24]

According to both Robert Wise and Walter Mirisch, the first scenes to be filmed were for the opening sequence of city sights:

beginning with extreme high-angle and vertical aerial shots of Lower Manhattan; moving west with helicopter views of the Empire State Building, rooftops, streets, parking lots, and city landmarks; leading to the introduction of the Jets and the "Prologue." This was second-unit work—establishing shots that required neither actors nor Jerome Robbins; however, it had been budgeted and allotted a two-day schedule. Wise wanted to introduce New York City in a way that had not been done before—something other than "that same shot across the river, the bridge, and the skyline" seen in so many movies. Drawing from the similar but more modest approach he had used in *Odds against Tomorrow*, Wise decided to film "the canyons of New York, straight down." He wisely reasoned that this "almost abstract" view of the world's most famous skyline would allow the audience to transition more easily into the state of mind demanded by the film's blend of realism and stylization.[25]

The late casting of George Chakiris in mid-June, the last-minute casting of Natalie Wood, plus the grueling rehearsal schedule established by Robbins had added to the delay, and the cameras did not start rolling until 10 August on West Sixty-Eighth Street and the surrounding neighborhood.[26] Photographs from the location shoot show the razed buildings where space was being made for Lincoln Center, a multitude of onlookers, crew members with electrical and camera equipment, and even the Jets stretching before rehearsing a scene. Several photographs show Robbins and Wise in various directorial positions, including setting up shots, and, significantly, talking separately to dancers and crew (a division of labor that was blamed for delaying production from the start). The stylized gang war that had taken over the neighborhood created some excitement, too. *Time* magazine ran a short feature on the location shooting in its 22 August issue, quoting onlookers, commenting on the oddity of the dilapidated location, and featuring an impromptu on-set interview with extras coordinator Sally Perle. Already behind schedule and over budget, it is unlikely that either Wise or Robbins would have indulged the reporter's questions, in contrast to Robbins's lively chat in the spring with the *New Yorker* reporter.

The New York location shoot extended until mid-September, doubling its budget and its initial sixteen-day schedule. By all accounts, disagreements between Robbins and Wise and Robbins's insistence on long on-set rehearsals, multiple camera setups, and numerous takes were responsible for the delay. Wise, accustomed to storyboarding, had agreed to two or sometimes three camera setups for the dancing sequences to ensure coverage and to give the editor, Thomas Stanford, a good choice of shots in postproduction.[27] But Walter Mirisch recalls that the shooting went slowly because Wise and Robbins "would have long discussions about shots before [they] made them," and before every take there was always a lot of "talk, more indecision, more choices."[28]

After further delays caused by weather problems in New York, the production was already a great deal over budget and behind schedule when it moved to Los Angeles in September. Because of the delays, a number of planned New York scenes were not yet "in the can," but it was decided that they could be shot either on location in Los Angeles or on the MGM and Universal Studios' back-lot sets. Back at the Samuel Goldwyn Studios, Boris Leven and his team had prepared fifteen sets in stages 3, 4, and 5. These included almost all the interiors (with the exception of the tenement hall and stairway where María chases Chino after hearing about Bernardo's death), as well as Anita's bathroom, which was eventually replaced by a dark, nondescript bedroom set. It also listed a variety of exteriors and semiexteriors such as rooftops, an alley and fire escape, a street and playground, the garage for the "Cool" number, "under the highway," and Schrank and Krupke's police car, which was to be processed with back projection. Eight days of shooting had been set aside for the "Somewhere Ballet" sequence that Lehman planned to adapt from the play. Stage space for it, however, had not yet been determined. Eventually, this idea, which involved the entire cast and complicated "dreams and visions of pleasure and warmth," was dropped for creative, budgetary, and especially scheduling reasons, in favor of the simpler, more intimate "Somewhere" duet with María and Tony (see chapter 3 for additional details).[29] At this time, with the "Somewhere Ballet" still on the schedule, approximately ten weeks of sound-stage work would be needed.[30]

Upon arrival in Los Angeles, however, Wise and Robbins received a warning memo from Harold Mirisch: "Now that the New York shooting is completed and you're back in the safety of the studio, *you must pick up the pace of the shooting* so the picture doesn't get impossibly behind schedule and over budget." Mirisch cautioned that they must cut down on the number of takes and consider the cost of 65mm film stock, which he called "fantastically expensive." Calling attention to the fact that they were already "far over" budget on this item, Mirisch advised the directors: "Please do not start filming a set-up . . . until it is *really* ready so you'll have a chance to 'get it' in the first couple of takes."[31] Mirisch, executing his producer prerogative, would be keeping a watchful eye over the two directors.

"Jerry, Leaving"

On 15 September 1960, just three days after the "pick up the pace" memo, Harold Mirisch again saw the need to scold his two directors. Shooting had immediately fallen behind schedule, and Mirisch cited the shooting log for Tuesday, 13 September, which lists rehearsals and multiple takes of only two shots: "From 9:00 AM to 9:52 AM—rehearse Anita's song; 10:35 AM to 11:06 AM—shot 171—14 takes; 1:28 PM to 2:10 PM—shot 172—14 takes; 3:55–4:52 PM—rehearse."[32]

For any producer, an eight-hour day of filming that yielded twenty-eight takes of only two *shots* (not scenes) was nothing short of alarming. It was particularly distressing for a movie that was already significantly behind schedule and over budget. Increasingly, the blame fell on Robbins's rehearsal demands and requests for multiple takes. Rita Moreno told *TV Guide* in 2001 that Robbins was "the most demanding person I ever worked with. . . . 'Difficult' is really a kind word."[33] And Russ Tamblyn reported to *People Magazine* in 2002 that they "would rehearse and rehearse and Jerome Robbins would always want more. . . . Bob Wise would say, 'Geez Jerry, it looked good to me.'"[34] The Mirisch brothers, as executive producers, were directly accountable to the financiers and were already under pressure from United Artists to speed things up on the set.

At some point in early October, Wise and Robbins were summoned to the front office for an urgent conference with Harold and Walter Mirisch, but it did little good. The "Cool" number (one of the most complicated in the movie, as I argue in chapter 3) was scheduled to be shot on 3–6 October, followed by the "Bridal Shop" number, on the same sound stage, on 7–14 October, but the report from the set was not encouraging. In an anxiously worded memo to Wise and Robbins dated 5 October, Harold Mirisch wrote: "In spite of our last conversation, it appears from the work accomplished yesterday that the 'Cool' number will not be finished on Thursday. [I] want you to know that whether it is finished or not, as far as I'm concerned we will do no further work on it, and I will expect that the 'Bridal Shop Number' be started on Friday."[35] As progress failed to be made, Mirisch's memos took the form of an ultimatum: "Under no circumstances," he wrote around Columbus Day, "can I allow the shooting of [the Bridal Shop] number to continue past Friday."[36] Walter Mirisch did "everything [he] could think of" to speed things up, including, presumably, authorizing his brother's ultimatum.[37]

Yet, by Thursday, 13 October—the forty-fifth day of filming—only 33¼ pages of script had been marked off as being in the can, amounting to forty minutes and four seconds of "printable" footage for editing purposes.[38] On any average picture, normal progress (measured in eighths of a page) is considered two to four pages per day. Even by the most conservative measure, the movie was already at least twenty-four days behind schedule. By way of comparison, only ten years earlier, Singin' in the Rain—with a similar codirecting arrangement and division of labor between Gene Kelly and Stanley Donen and a considerable amount of complicated musical material—started production on 18 June 1951 and completed seventeen scenes in the first week of filming. Nine scenes of the "Good Morning" number were shot on one day alone, and by 25 June, Singin' in the Rain was already two and a half days ahead of schedule.[39]

On top of the delays, the budget was showing signs of escalating fast. As early as 5 October, production manager Al Wood estimated that the exterior sets for the Candy Store, an alley, a rooftop, the park, and the "Cool" garage were already $94,000 over budget. Wood urged the Samuel Goldwyn staff to control costs.[40] Twenty-three women's costumes, including two that were never fitted, plus accessories, shoes, and sweaters for the "Gym" and "America" numbers cost $68,205. The men's costumes and shoes for the same two sequences (plus shoe lifts for George Chakiris) were estimated at $25,891 but had also exceeded the budget.[41] With the schedule and the budget threatening to jeopardize the entire production, the Mirisch brothers had shifted their strategy and were trying to get the musical numbers filmed first, perhaps already foreseeing Robbins's early departure. Ultimately, Walter and Harold Mirisch determined that the "two-director plan" was untenable. Since all the musical numbers had already been "intensely rehearsed" by Robbins and his assistants, Walter and Harold Mirisch, with Robert Wise in impartial agreement, decided that Jerome Robbins had to go.[42] Wise would continue on his own, with the dancing assistants overseeing the execution of Robbins's choreography.

Based on my estimate from Scheuer's "Work Script," Robbins probably left sometime in the fourth week of October, while the "Dance at the Gym" sequence was being filmed on stage 4. Walter Mirisch recalls that he and his brother Harold had gone to see Robbins at his house "over a weekend," with the intention of firing him. The "weekend" to which Mirisch refers was most likely 22 or 23 October, which means that Robbins was out by the fifty-second or fifty-third day of shooting (out of an eventual total of 124 days).[43] According to Walter Mirisch: "[Harold and I] told him what our problems were and what we intended to do. He was, of course, hurt, furious, and insulted. It was a terrible scene. But we stuck to our decision. We acknowledged that his contributions to the play were immense, and his contribution to the picture was equally great." When an indignant Robbins asked to have his name removed from the credits, Mirisch asked him to wait and see how the movie turned out before "decid[ing] whether or not it [was] so far afield from what [he] would have wanted it to be." Robbins agreed, but the matter of the screen credit would remain unresolved for many months.[44]

Robbins also agreed, as his contract allowed, to look at first and "fine" cuts of the film when Wise had them ready and to give his opinion to Wise and film editor Thomas Stanford. Wise always acknowledged, as did Walter Mirisch, that Robbins's departure was a hard blow for all involved, but especially for Robbins himself. In various interviews after the fact, Wise, always the gentleman, often stated that Robbins's departure had come after 60 percent of the film was already in the can, which was evidently not the case.[45]

Paradoxically, Robbins's own humorous handwritten note at the bottom of card 31 of Ernest Lehman's "step outline"— "CUT TO: Jerry, leaving"—turned out to be truer than anyone could have imagined.

"Push along to Completion"

The shooting log in Scheuer's "Work Script" shows a significant pickup of the pace after Robbins left, with nearly seven and a half pages of script completed by Friday, 28 October. However, the "Dance at the Gym" fell behind again without Robbins—his absence required a period of adjustment on the set. But even at this late date, casting was still not complete. Recall that the role of Glad Hand went to John Astin in early November, and background actors and dancers were still being interviewed in Los Angeles on 25 November. Furthermore, letters between Leonard Hirschman of the William Morris Agency and Ray Kurtzman of Mirisch indicate that Natalie Wood had been absent from the set on 19, 20, 28, and 31 October due to illness. Mirisch was threatening a lawsuit against Wood because of her irregular presence at work, coinciding approximately with Robbins's final days on the set.[46]

Over the course of the autumn, Wise (accustomed to working at a fairly fast clip since his days at RKO, when he was unexpectedly asked to substitute for Orson Welles on The Magnificent Ambersons) did a significant amount of catching up. For the week of 7 November, for instance, the log shows an average of one to two pages of progress per day, even though the company was off that Friday for the Veterans Day holiday. One by one, the seventeen musical numbers, including the "Taunting" and, surprisingly, "My Country 'Tis of Thee," appear scratched off in the "Work Script."[47] Yet progress varied through November and December, with Scheuer logging three minutes of printable footage on 14 November but only twenty-five seconds on the fifteenth (days 66 and 67 of filming).

Both Scheuer's "Work Script" and Wise's personal copy of the screenplay show numerous handwritten marginal notes involving descriptions of the action, setups, lines of dialogue, and even technical and editing instructions. These were almost always written in pencil and then written or rewritten on the spot by Lehman or Scheuer. These two copies of the screenplay are quite a contrast to the clean versions published in book or facsimile form with various DVD and Blu-Ray releases, but even the "clean" publishable copies show significant changes as late as 29 December 1960. What emerges from studying the two original documents is a rather "live" chronicle of the film's production. The most evident impromptu change made to the "Prologue" sequence, for instance, was the elimination of several "exterior night" scenes. It is also clear that some actors' scenes, proposed by Lehman to help characterize the individual Sharks and Jets, were dropped in favor of a more expeditious treatment of the introductory material.[48]

Wise's original screenplay, for example, describes the "jumping" of Baby John, referred to as "FINAL 'MOVEMENT' OF PROLOGUE," in these words: "EXT. ~~PLAYGROUND~~—LATE AFTERNOON—(FINAL MOVEMENT OF PROLOGUE) Baby John comes running into the deserted area, starts to play by himself like the child that he really is. Suddenly Bernardo appears, then another Shark, and another, and more. They surround him." The screenplay also contains a handwritten annotation over this description: "Painting Out Sharks."[49] Clearly, this scene was simplified in the movie, where we see Baby John not "painting out" the word "SHARKS" but adding the word "STINK" to the Sharks graffiti on a brick wall. The scene was also moved from the playground to an alley, most likely a set at the Los Angeles studios. As originally conceived, the scene demanded a more complicated real location and various extra camera setups.

Another function of these on-set screenplays was to keep track of special instructions for film editor Thomas Stanford and the special effects team led by Linwood Dunn. For instance, in the published screenplay, the scene in which the action dissolves from the bridal shop to the dance at the gym is described as follows: "[María] begins to whirl in the dress as we—EFFECT DISSOLVE TO: INT. GYM—THE DANCE—NIGHT—(MASTER SCENE)." But Wise's screenplay has a handwritten pencil annotation: "Study for Bass angle to cut," with an arrow pointing to the word "dissolve."[50] Always aware of the conveniences of storyboarding, Wise and his assistants ensured quality control in continuity and kept up with the demands of process photography and special effects, integral to the movie's design.[51]

There were ultimately more than a dozen special optical and

photographic effects shots in the movie, crafted by Linwood Dunn's company Film Effects of Hollywood. These include the transition from the abstract line and color patterns that dissolve into the Lower Manhattan skyline in the title sequence; María's twirling effect that marks the transition between the first bridal shop sequence and the dance at the gym, mentioned earlier; the diffusive "oil" effect at the gym when María and Tony first see each other; the shifting focus, soft iris, and purple and yellow lights that magically frame the "Tonight" duet; the conspicuous sun-ray effect in the bridal shop during María and Tony's mock wedding; bright red sunlight effects on the rooftop set; the chain-link transitions that serve as bookends to the "Tonight" quintet; as well as several other sunlight effects suggesting dawn during that same number. Beginning in September 1960 and continuing through August 1961, correspondence among Linwood Dunn, Robert Wise, Boris Leven, and the Mirisch Studio indicates a number of problems and delays involving many if not most of these effects. As late as 29 June 1961, Wise was urging the optical effects team and the Technicolor technicians to "push along to completion" eleven of these shots. By 18 August 1961, less than two months before the road-show release, Wise and Dunn were still in communication about finishing touches and corrections on seven special effects and transition shots, including the opening and end credits, which had run into printing problems at Technicolor Studios.[52] These problems led to budget revisions, with the special effects costs expanding from the original estimate of $106,560 to a revised $155,000 and a final sum of $162,559 when all the work was finally completed; this figure included Saul Bass's fee of $25,000.[53]

Early, optimistic schedules predicted a wrap of principal photography in December 1960 and then early January 1961, but these projections turned out to be flawed, especially after the slow start in New York the previous summer. Assistant director Relyea and production manager Wood estimated the finishing dates for four of the five principal actors as follows: "Natalie Wood December 14, 1960; Richard Beymer December 30, 1960; Rita Moreno January 3, 1961; George Chakiris December 15, 1960."[54] But 10 January 1961—the 100th day of production—achieved only one-quarter page of progress, totaling barely 90 pages of script and 104 minutes of printable footage. In an elegant cursive, Scheuer kept a daily record of each eighth of a page and each second of footage as an appendix to his "Work Script." By Tuesday, 24 January, the 110th day of shooting, Scheuer had recorded 115 minutes of footage and 102¼ pages of script. With a steadily increasing pace, shooting had progressed to 110½ pages by the end of the month. The studio shoot finally wrapped on Valentine's Day 1961, with a little over 125 pages completed, plus "one open," on the 124th day—almost two full months behind schedule.[55] Postproduction, involving editing, recording, and special effects, would continue almost up to the road-show release date of 18 October 1961.

"An Excellent Natural Voice"

Other complications involved the dubbing and recording of singing voices and the new music that Leonard Bernstein was composing. The "ghost singers"—Marni Nixon, Betty Wand, and Jim Bryant—had begun their work back in late September 1960, but Natalie Wood's insistence that she do her own singing was causing problems (Nixon was rarely even allowed in the music studio while Wood's vocal tracks were being recorded). Reporter Neil Rau chronicled his visit to stage 2 of the Samuel Goldwyn Studios "to watch Natalie Wood do her first big musical number." In a somewhat flippant tone, Rau commented on the "heap of people concentrating on seeing that little Natalie shines for the camera," and he seemed especially interested in the amount of work it took to shoot the scene: a few takes of "I Feel Pretty." Rau referred to Wood as "diminutive" in the middle of a small army of technicians, vocal coaches, assistant choreographers, assistant directors, and "dozens of well wishers," plus Wise and Robbins. Rau's article was clearly designed as a publicity report—what is now called "buzz"—but its frivolous tone about Wood's efforts to sing and dance came across nonetheless. Naturally, there was no mention of the ghost singers.[56]

Though dubbing itself was fairly common, the normal practice was for the "ghosts" to prerecord all the voice tracks, which were then played back in the studio or on location for the actors to lip-synch. But according to Marni Nixon's memoir, all of María's songs were prerecorded by Wood herself, and these takes (with one exception) were used as playback on the set. Nixon later had to substitute all of Wood's recordings with her own, while matching María's lip movements onscreen. Recall that Nixon (who was paid $300 a day but had no contract) was initially supposed to just "sweeten" and, presumably with the help of mixing technology, help Wood's voice reach the high notes that her natural alto could not accomplish. But the substitution of María's entire score meant that after Wood was finished with *West Side Story* and had moved on to rehearsals for her next project, *Gypsy* (where she actually did her own singing), Nixon had to go back into the studio and record her voice over Wood's on-screen images. This proved difficult because María's songs had "a high, angular range," and Nixon had to be careful to approximate Wood's gestures and movements with her own vocalization. Nixon also ended up "looping" two lines of dialogue in the last scene of the film—including the final "*Te adoro Anton*"—when Wood's takes were judged unusable.[57] Jim Bryant, who recorded Tony's songs, had little trouble imitating Richard Beymer's timbre, which was all that was required of him.

Also involved in the recording process was Betty Wand, who had done "ghost" singing in a number of films for Shirley Temple, Sophia Loren, Esther Williams, and Leslie Caron in Vincente Minnelli's *Gigi* (1958). Wand was what Nixon called a "stand-by" singer; she was attached to no particular part and was used when, for any number of technical or strategic reasons, an additional voice was needed. However, because of the difficult register duel in the joint numbers "A Boy Like That" and "I Have a Love," Saul Chaplin decided that Betty Wand would provide Rita Moreno's singing voice in those two songs, recorded on 15 December 1960. Moreno did her own singing in "America" and most of the "Tonight" quintet, but when both Wand and Moreno were unavailable to record some of Anita's lines, including the final sustained note on the word "Tonight," Nixon provided the vocals. Singing for both Anita and María in the quintet, Nixon quipped, "I'm actually singing a duet with myself!"[58]

All of Nixon's good humor, however, cannot negate the occasional injustices done to *West Side Story*'s ghost singers. As was customary (with rare exceptions), their names did not appear in any of the publicity, credits, or album releases. But the fact that many of the songs had been dubbed was not a secret, as Larry Tubelle had reported in December 1960. Also, during September and October 1961, when press previews were in progress in anticipation of the road-show engagements, Sidney Skolsky of Hollywood Citizen News and Barney Geazer of Limelight reported, respectively, that it was Marni Nixon's "singing" and "chirping" in the movie sound track. Even Robert Wise readily admitted as much (though he failed to credit Nixon). In a letter to a curious Minneapolis fan who had seen the movie in previews in September 1961, Wise wrote:

> Miss Wood's vocalizing is not her own. Natalie had had no voice training but, to our surprise, she had an excellent natural voice. She took singing lessons and worked very hard and, for a while, it looked as if she might be able to do her own singing. But in the end Bernstein's music turned out to be too demanding and we had to use another voice. However, I'm sure the singing lessons and all the work Natalie put in contributed greatly to her performance during the songs.[59]

Furthermore, because she had no contract, Nixon almost lost out on a share of the royalties for the movie sound-track album (released by Columbia Records), which went multiplatinum, selling three million copies by 1986. Nixon gratefully acknowledged that Leonard Bernstein generously granted her one-quarter of 1 percent, "not a negligible amount," out of his own royalties. Nixon claimed that the royalties eventually awarded to West Side Story's ghost singers constituted a historic first, leading to industry changes in onscreen credit and profit-sharing practices.[60]

While Marni Nixon left the negotiating largely to her managers, Betty Wand took the legal route. Dissatisfied with her lack of royalties and credit, and impressed by the movie's box-office success and critical acclaim, Wand filed suit on 8 February 1963 in Los Angeles County Superior Court against Mirisch Pictures Corporation and Columbia Records. Wand sought to block further showings of the movie and sales of the album, citing "a conspiracy . . . defeating and defrauding her."[61] The Los Angeles Times reported that Wand sought damages of $60,000 and had requested accounting reports on the film's profits and album sales.[62] After Wand gave testimony about the then-mysterious practice of ghost singing and dubbing before Superior Court Judge Charles A. Loring, she won a quick, undisclosed settlement from the respondents. Contemporary reports in the trade journals and other publications generally noted that Rita Moreno had won an Oscar—at the 9 April 1962 Academy Awards ceremony—although the "singing was not hers."[63]

"End Credits"

Before *West Side Story* could be released and gather its accolades, there was still the matter of departed codirector Jerome Robbins's participation and screen credit. Robbins's contract, amended on 10 October 1960, shortly before his departure, allowed him to see and comment on the film during postproduction, although his editing input was limited to "the scenes that he [had] actually choreographed and directed," leaving him out of decisions concerning the "dramatic segments" and, presumably, the remaining musical numbers.[64] Another exchange between the lawyers for both parties stated that Robbins would have no say with regard to the new music Bernstein was composing for the "Prologue."[65] By 21 March 1961, Robert Wise and Robbins's agent had agreed that Robbins would look at the film and work on the editing on two consecutive weekends, 1–2 and 8–9 April 1961. It was apparent that sore feelings persisted between the former directing partners, as Wise's response reads like an ultimatum: "I'll be ready for Jerry to see WEST SIDE STORY on Saturday April 1. He'll have to complete his work on the areas in which he's involved by Sunday, April 9." Wise added that the special effects shots on "Maria" and "Tonight" would not be ready for Robbins to see—these were still in progress at Film Effects—and oddly, he asked that Robbins not bring "a lot of people" to the screening with him. Wise explained that Robbins would be seeing "a cutting version and we're simply not running it widely until we have everything in and the dubbing completed."[66]

With such conditions agreed on, Wise showed Robbins an early, unfinished cut of the film in Los Angeles on 1 and 2 April. On Monday, 3 April, Wise reported to Harold Mirisch that Robbins had suggested "only a couple of minor changes" in the "Prologue" and "America" numbers and had given his reactions to "the balance of the picture." Wise admitted that "many of his points have merit," and he informed Mirisch that he had agreed to try to incorporate some of Robbins's changes, clarifying that "others with which [he] did not agree [would] be disregarded." Wise also informed Mirisch that Robbins would not be returning the following weekend, as previously planned, because his work "in the sequences he [was] involved in" was considered complete.[67]

On 12 April 1961, back in New York rehearsing the ballet *Moves*, Robbins wrote a long memo to Wise in which he explained in detail his concerns about the cut of the film he had seen ten days earlier. Over more than three pages and in several point-by-point entries, Robbins explained, among other things, his concern over the "Dance Hall" sequence. Specifically, Robbins thought the dance did not convey strongly enough the fierce rivalry between the gangs and their struggle for territory—here, symbolized by the dance floor itself. "One doesn't get the impression that this is a highly pitched and desperate gang fight for supremacy," wrote Robbins, adding, "this is terribly important to remedy." Robbins recommended shots that could be added or reedited to meet this admittedly important story requirement. He judged the first meeting between Tony and María on the dance floor "disappointing" and called it "prosaic, untouching and insensitive," whereas onstage it had been a "fantastically magical" moment. Robbins even suggested the addition of "opticals" or close-ups to improve it, willing to sacrifice his own dance creations to enhance the emotional effect: "I don't care about the *choreography* or the *steps* themselves. But I feel forcibly insistent that the story and the emotion be saved. I don't care what you do with the steps, even if you lose them, as long as the *action* and the happenings of the story are clearly told."

Robbins also expressed dissatisfaction with the reordering of the "Balcony" scene, which had been moved from immediately following Tony's "Maria" solo (in the play) to after the rooftop "America" number (in the movie). Robbins "strongly advised" that it be moved back to its original place, to build on the romantic mood of "Maria," opining that the new order made the romance seem "badly conventional." He also felt that Wise's "reshuffling" of the "Balcony" and "America" numbers made the picture seem "longer" and the conflict "not as *inevitable*." In contrast, Robbins agreed that swapping the "Officer Krupke" and "Cool" numbers worked for the better. In the "Rumble" sequence, Robbins complained that there was not enough dramatic buildup and that, surprisingly, the dancing got in the way of the action. On the positive side, Robbins was "overjoyed" with how the movie had turned out, and he found some of the particular effects and sequences "brilliant" and achieved "marvelously." In an almost apologetic tone, near the end of the letter, Robbins referred to the film as "your" picture and reassured Wise that his criticism was intended only to "help improve it."[68]

Judging by the finished product, it is evident that Wise incorporated some of Robbins's suggestions. The "Dance Hall" sequence includes a number of long shots that physically dramatize the distance between the Sharks and the Jets, as well as a particular visual effect that isolates María and Tony from their environments when they first see each other, smoothing the transition into the "fantastically magical" part of the sequence. Since Wise was using two or three camera setups for the musical and dance numbers, it is safe to assume that he would have had enough coverage (from close-ups to long shots) to reedit for the desired effect, as Robbins had argued. However, it is evident from the released film that Wise refused to change the order of the musical numbers ("America" and the "Tonight" duet, specifically), as Robbins had "strongly advised." In another letter dated 1 May, Robbins reiterated his insistence that what he had seen in the early cut of the "Dance Hall" sequence was simply not working to convey the emerging tension between the gangs. But by this time, Wise had moved on. Whatever the reasons for their creative differences, Wise felt comfortable ignoring Robbins's opinion whenever he did not agree with it.

While Wise was considering Robbins's input on the editing, a new source of friction arose that would lead to more hard feelings and offended parties. To meet marketing and publicity copy deadlines, Saul Bass had to get the credit sequence—devised by Wise as "end credits," except for the opening title card—into design and production by spring 1961.[69] Wise had reported to Harold Mirisch that the credits would read, "Directed by Robert Wise and Jerome Robbins," with an additional title card, as was customary for movies based on theater, giving Robbins credit for conceiving, choreographing, and directing the stage version. But Robbins's agents had asked for yet another card stating, "Choreography and Musical Numbers Staged by Jerome Robbins." On 7 April and again on 24 April, Wise objected in writing to this characterization of the division of labor and asked Mirisch to "immediately settle" the question of the credit wording.[70] The original agreement among Robbins, Wise, and the Mirisch Corporation, dating back to March 1960, described Robbins's credit as two separate cards reading "Directed by Robert Wise and Jerome Robbins" and "Choreography by Jerome Robbins."[71] Wise greeted Robbins's demand for additional credit with justifiable indignation. In an urgent memo to Mirisch Company lawyer Raymond Kurtzman, Wise wrote: "There is absolutely no justification in Robbins' demand . . . for the special card giving him credit for staging *all* the musical numbers in the picture." He continued, "I feel I am going way past halfway in according co-director credit to a man who *was not involved in the filming of 65 to 70% of the picture.*" This claim from May 1961 contradicts Wise's later, more conciliatory estimates that Robbins had left after 60 percent of the movie was in the can. But it is consistent with Robbins's exit in late October 1960, after only 52 or 53 slow days of shooting out of a total of 124 days. In the memo, Wise put Robbins's contribution in perspective and reminded the Mirisch brothers where things stood:

> It's true that Jerry rehearsed most of the numbers and was involved in staging five of them for the screen. But he simply was not around for the filming of the balance of the numbers and songs—or the balance of the picture. As co-director he will be getting credit for a great amount of material that he did not rehearse or help in staging. This should be strong compensation for whatever loss he feels about the [other] credit.[72]

While negotiations continued, Wise appealed to Robbins directly, explaining why the credit he sought was unjustified. Wise clarified that, as worded, the new credit could be interpreted "in motion picture terminology" as meaning that Robbins had directed the actual filming of all fourteen musical or dance numbers, and this implication, Wise stated, was "just not right." He invited Robbins to suggest some credit that would clearly convey that he had "conceived the choreography and developed" the numbers without implying that he had been explicitly involved in directing all the sequences.[73] On the evening of Wednesday, 31 May, immediately after receiving Wise's "ultimatum," Robbins telephoned Wise to express his "self-righteous hurt," arguing that he had been taken advantage of in the credits argument and had not known that the problem was so serious. Wise argued that he had brought the issue up "several weeks before"—on 7 April, to be exact—and blamed the misunderstanding on a "lack of communication" between Robbins and his lawyers and agents.[74] Finally, the matter was settled on 2 June when Wise informed Kurtzman that Robbins had agreed by telephone to a "Choreographed by" credit, as long as it was "put up above the cast in order of appearance on the screen."[75]

With this agreement in place, Wise continued to "push to completion" the complicated special effects and the dubbing and re-recording of the musical score and the new music composed by Bernstein. Meanwhile, *West Side Story* began its preview screenings less than two months after the credits dispute was settled. The earliest preview on record occurred 25 July 1961 in New York City. Jerome Robbins did not attend, as he was reportedly out of the country. The print that was screened in previews was not yet final, however; there was still optical work to be done in the gym sequence, final special effects to be added, and "color balancing of the entire picture."[76] Technicolor laboratory complications were not resolved until late August. In fact, as late as 15 September 1961, Robbins had not yet seen the fine cut that was making the preview rounds.

A few months later, record-breaking box-office receipts, nearly unanimous positive reviews, and eleven Oscar nominations had turned *West Side Story* into a veritable phenomenon. At that point, Wise and Robbins made their tenuous peace and, in increasingly conciliatory tones, acknowledged that in spite of the difficulties, they could all be proud of their accomplishments. In a letter written in March 1962, Robbins apologized to Wise for a misquotation by an interviewer from the *New York World-Telegram* that, coincidentally, gave Robbins more credit for the film's success than he now believed he deserved. Robbins concluded by acknowledging their differences, but he sent his earnest well wishes to Wise on his next film, *Two for the Seesaw,* and to "all of us on the Oscars." The letter was uncharacteristically formal, addressed to "Mr. Robert Wise" as opposed to the more customary "Dear Bob," and it was sent to Wise in care of the Mirisch Company, 1041 North Formosa Avenue, Los Angeles, CA. The signature at the bottom of the page was quite telling. Robbins had scratched out the typewritten, businesslike "Jerry Robbins" and scribbled over it, in his own handwriting, just "Jerry."[77]

Saul Bass created several storyboard versions of the "Prologue" for *West Side Story*. Many of the designs became visual motifs in the movie. (From the collections of the Margaret Herrick Library, Academy of Motion Picture Arts and Sciences.)

WEST SIDE STORY: PARTIAL STORYBOARD PROLOGUE "THE TIME BEFORE" (CONTINUED)

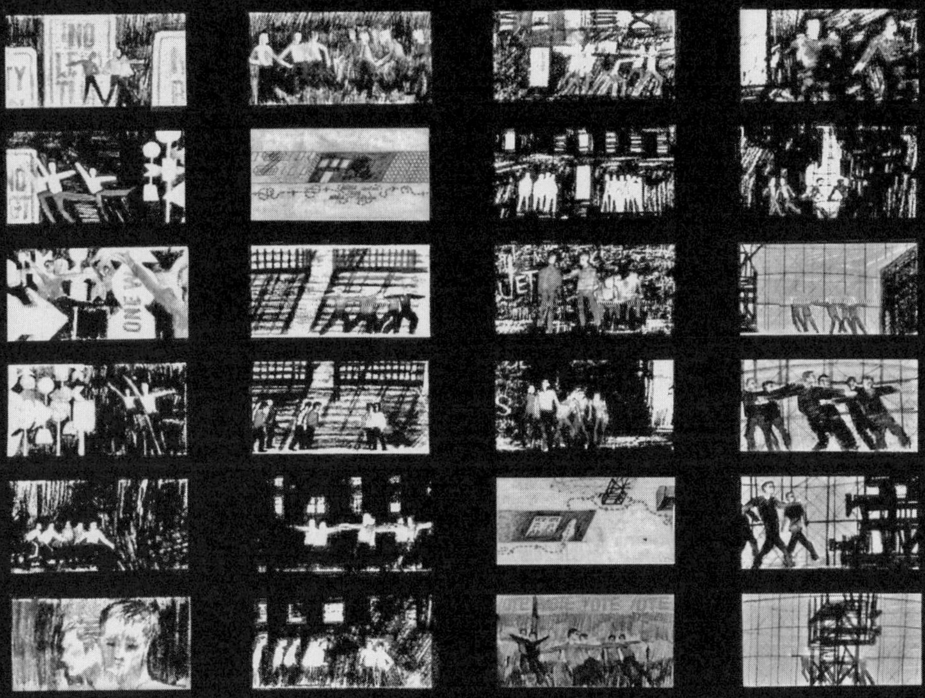

In her early costume designs, Irene Sharaff had the Jets wearing identical, branded uniforms. These were eventually dropped in favor of gang-specific color themes. (From the collections of the Margaret Herrick Library, Academy of Motion Picture Arts and Sciences.)

Always more stylish than the Jets, the Sharks' early costumes made them look, paradoxically, like the New York Yankees. Irene Sharaff's signature is clearly visible in the bottom right. (From the collections of the Margaret Herrick Library, Academy of Motion Picture Arts and Sciences.)

The Jets on location in New York City, stretching before a rehearsal in August 1960. (From the collections of the Margaret Herrick Library, Academy of Motion Picture Arts and Sciences. WEST SIDE STORY ©1961 Metro-Goldwyn-Mayer Studios Inc. All rights reserved.)

The Jets strut their stuff on location in New York City in August 1960. Notice the rubble of the recently demolished buildings, making room for Lincoln Center. (From the collections of the Margaret Herrick Library, Academy of Motion Picture Arts and Sciences. WEST SIDE STORY ©1961 Metro-Goldwyn-Mayer Studios Inc. All rights reserved.)

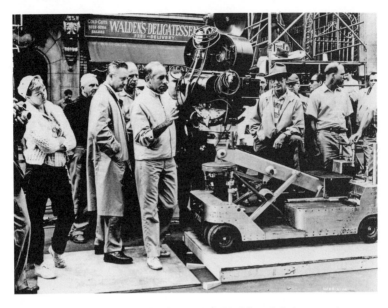

Jerome Robbins (center) and Robert Wise (third from left, in a trench coat) rehearsing a take and scouting locations in New York in the spring of 1960. (From the collections of the Margaret Herrick Library, Academy of Motion Picture Arts and Sciences. WEST SIDE STORY ©1961 Metro-Goldwyn-Mayer Studios Inc. All rights reserved.)

Jerome Robbins (left) and Robert Wise (right) setting up a shot for the "Prologue." Robbins speaks to dancers George Chakiris, Eddie Verso, and Jay Norman (hidden behind Robbins), while Wise considers a camera setup. (From the collections of the Margaret Herrick Library, Academy of Motion Picture Arts and Sciences. WEST SIDE STORY ©1961 Metro-Goldwyn-Mayer Studios Inc. All rights reserved.)

The "taunting" of Bernardo under the ominous "KEEP OFF" sign, with the Puerto Rican "fruits and vegetables" storefront in the background. The Jets' old neighborhood is evolving culturally. (From the collections of the Margaret Herrick Library, Academy of Motion Picture Arts and Sciences. WEST SIDE STORY ©1961 Metro-Goldwyn-Mayer Studios Inc. All rights reserved.)

Robert Wise looks rather silly showing Natalie Wood how to pose in the bridal shop set. (From the collections of the Margaret Herrick Library, Academy of Motion Picture Arts and Sciences. WEST SIDE STORY ©1961 Metro-Goldwyn-Mayer Studios Inc. All rights reserved.)

A publicity still from the rumble set. This shot was "killed by the MPAA" and banned from theater lobby displays because it was deemed too violent for general audiences. Notice the grease pencil mark around Bernardo's knife. (From the collections of the Margaret Herrick Library, Academy of Motion Picture Arts and Sciences. WEST SIDE STORY ©1961 Metro-Goldwyn-Mayer Studios Inc. All rights reserved.)

"Bernardo was right." The "taunting" and attempted rape of Anita is the film's dramatic climax and, arguably, its most violent scene. (From the collections of the Margaret Herrick Library, Academy of Motion Picture Arts and Sciences. WEST SIDE STORY ©1961 Metro-Goldwyn-Mayer Studios Inc. All rights reserved.)

Natalie Wood practicing a song with vocal coach Bobby Tucker. During production, she was always under the impression that her voice would be used in the finished film. (From the collections of the Margaret Herrick Library, Academy of Motion Picture Arts and Sciences. WEST SIDE STORY ©1961 Metro-Goldwyn-Mayer Studios Inc. All rights reserved.)

Natalie Wood in the recording studio. Her vocal takes were never heard in the movie. (From the collections of the Margaret Herrick Library, Academy of Motion Picture Arts and Sciences. WEST SIDE STORY ©1961 Metro-Goldwyn-Mayer Studios Inc. All rights reserved.)

During the "taunting" of Bernardo in the "Prologue," the Jets dominate more than four-fifths of the screen space. (From the collections of the Margaret Herrick Library, Academy of Motion Picture Arts and Sciences. WEST SIDE STORY ©1961 Metro-Goldwyn-Mayer Studios Inc. All rights reserved.)

"Miss America can just resign." In "I Feel Pretty," María usurps the ultimate title of white female Americana. (From the collections of the Margaret Herrick Library, Academy of Motion Picture Arts and Sciences. WEST SIDE STORY ©1961 Metro-Goldwyn-Mayer Studios Inc. All rights reserved.)

María and Tony's mock wedding in the bridal shop shows them exchanging improvised vows and gang colors: Tony's jacket lining is purple; María's dress is yellow. (From the collections of the Margaret Herrick Library, Academy of Motion Picture Arts and Sciences. WEST SIDE STORY ©1961 Metro-Goldwyn-Mayer Studios Inc. All rights reserved.)

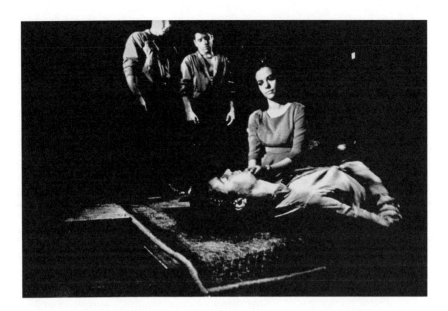

Dramatic red lighting underscores the tragedy in Tony's death scene. Actor Richard Beymer, however, rests comfortably on a padded surface. (From the collections of the Margaret Herrick Library. WEST SIDE STORY ©1961 Metro-Goldwyn-Mayer Studios Inc. All rights reserved.)

3 "You're the Only Thing I'll See": Watching *West Side Story*

West Side Story was ready to begin its road-show engagements in the early fall of 1961, with a scheduled premiere at the Rivoli Theatre in New York on 18 October. By that date, Robert Wise and the creative team had spent a significant amount of time preparing the film for what was generally expected to be a solid run. They had also overcome a number of creative, scheduling, and technical difficulties. *West Side Story* would eventually become the second-highest-grossing movie of the 1961–1962 season, behind Disney's animated *One Hundred and One Dalmatians*.[1] Because the movie was conceived and designed to be something of an "event" picture—a "road-show attraction," as they were called—Wise included specific instructions to theater owners and exhibitors on how they were to show the film. Wise's instructions to exhibitors were especially precise when it came to the opening title sequence: the abstract color and line patterns designed by Saul Bass, at a cost of $25,000, introduced musical, visual, and color motifs that ran throughout the movie. Wise specified the exact foot of film when the curtains were to be opened and the lights dimmed and the precise percentage of house lights allowed per segment so that the design could serve its purpose of creating a mood and establishing motifs. For example, Wise wrote: "The first whistle starts at 12½ feet. At this point the curtains should be opened slowly and the house lights lowered by 25%. Since the time required for opening the curtains varies from theater to theater it must be timed so that these operations are completed by the time the overture design fades in at 28 feet."[2]

The idea was to let the audience know when to be comfortably in their seats in order to see the design and listen to the overture music, as these were part of the entire movie experience. As I argue in this chapter, the integrity of the visual and aural design of *West Side Story* was extremely important not only to distinguish the film from its theatrical origins but also, as Linwood Dunn suggested, because "the style and design" were "the star of this show."

Fingers Snapping: The "Prologue" and the "Jet Song"

As announced in Wise's notes to exhibitors, *West Side Story* begins with the faint sound of the Jets' whistle call, the three ascending notes also heard in the "Prologue" score. This recognizable sound signature and rally call of the gang is heard first over an entirely dark screen that fades fast into Bass's color pattern and abstract design, seen over the new overture composed by Leonard Bernstein. Initially, there are only vertical lines of varying lengths over the changing color background: first orange, then red, a pinkish purple, a reddish orange, green, and blue. Over the course of this sequence, the music track visits sections of and transitions from the "Prologue," "Tonight," "Maria," the "Mambo," and more phrases from "Tonight," ending with the somewhat distorted tritone horns of the "Prologue," recognizable as the Jets' whistle.

The title card itself, after a brief fade to black, appears in a sharp blue screen with the words *West Side Story* at the bottom. Then the seemingly random black vertical lines of the abstract pattern suddenly transform into the New York City skyline, framed by the meeting of the Hudson and East Rivers. The dramatic revelation of the skyline is followed by images of the city, all from an extreme, fully vertical or zenith angle, imparting some familiarity to the scenes. This is the approach Wise decided on to introduce the city—something unusual that still allows the audience to recognize New York. Thus, we see a succession of shots: a bridge, a busy highway, ships on a pier, a waterfront parking lot, a park, the Chrysler Building, the Empire State Building, the United Nations, Columbia University, and other sights—some familiar, some unknown. Each shot lasts about three seconds, while the camera movement is consistently to screen left—or, rather appropriately, "west." We finally see various

images of the "projects"—the mass-constructed low-income housing where much of the city's poor and immigrant populations lived
in the 1940s and 1950s. Though it is not suggested that this is the
specific neighborhood where the Jets and the Sharks will battle, the
proximity of the projects is important to the social context of *West
Side Story*.

Over the introductory views, the sound track offers a series of city
sounds: traffic, car horns honking, general city bustle, all with the
underlying presence of the Jets' whistle. The whistle continues into
the introduction of the immediate setting of the film, as the camera
finally dissolves into closer views of the neighborhood scouted the
winter before by Lehman and Wise. At one point, the camera slowly
zooms in and dissolves into an asphalt playground, the location of
the film's first narrative action. The Jets are seen in a high-angle
long shot of the playground, on the upper left of the screen. The
shot then cuts to a closer long shot, before a quick zoom jerks in
closer onto the gang.

The origin of the finger-snapping sound that has accompanied
the introduction of the city is finally revealed in the next shot: a
close-up of Riff (Russ Tamblyn), in profile, leaning against a chain-
link fence. The chain-link fence motif is a repetitive and significant
symbol of "entrapment" in the movie, and it was one of the many
visual images that caught Wise's attention during his research in
New York. At this point, though, Riff is confident and "cool" in his
mustard yellow windbreaker, snapping his fingers in a rhythmic, relaxed beat. As the orchestra comes in louder, the first lines of the
"Prologue" music introduce the "spheres of influence"—that is, the
gang hierarchy that Lehman and Robbins had discussed earlier. The
camera pans slightly to the right to reveal Ice (Tucker Smith), who
is Riff's number two, and then the third in command, Action (Tony
Mordente, Robbins's dancing assistant). All have joined in the finger snapping when the next shot opens up to show numbers four
and five, Baby John (Eliot Feld) and A-Rab (David Winters). Rather
than uniforms (Irene Sharaff's early idea for costume design), they
wear general gang colors: yellow, light blue, gray, and cream, with
A-Rab in red. The next shot includes other assorted Jets, including

Tiger (David Bean) and Mouthpiece (Harvey Hohnecker), all snapping their fingers in unison.

The Jets' relaxed command of the playground is briefly disrupted by a baseball bouncing off the chain-link fence, startling the Jets and presumably violating their space. It is notable that the first apparent disruption of the Jets' supremacy is associated with the fence, but at this early stage, the symbol has not yet acquired the function of a motif. A boy dressed in drab, olive green (the color worn later by "the others" at the dance) enters the frame and shyly reclaims the baseball. After a slightly threatening look, Riff nods to Action, who returns the ball. The finger snapping gets faster at this point. With one shake of his head, Riff gets the gang moving through the playground. A wider tracking shot follows them as they seem to claim this territory with their strut, but now they are quite visibly trapped by the chain-link fence in the foreground and a building's black brick wall in the background. Suspiciously, a graffiti signature on the wall reads "BOBBY"—Wise's nickname.[3] The same signature appears much later in the movie, in the rumble setting, out of place but identical in design. The Jets loop around a young girl drawing concentric circles with chalk on the hard asphalt. Standing in the center of the pattern, she seems "trapped" in the circle, and she eyes the Jets cautiously. The gang then encounters a couple of boys playing basketball. They immediately surrender the ball to the Jets who, after taking a couple of playful shots, return the basketball without incident. But their dominance of this space is evident. On a background wall we see the name "Lakers" (which also appears in the rumble set)—perhaps a previously dominant gang. But in even bigger letters the word "JETS" commands the top of the brick wall. When the Jets turn in unison toward the young basketball players in their first choreographed movement, the gesture seems to be a warning. It is clear that other gangs have claimed this turf (the Jets later mention the Emeralds and the Hawks) but for now, it is firmly under the Jets' control.

The following shot establishes this particular motif and narrative information. The Jets take their first balletic steps in the next shot, in one of the New York street locations. Always moving left, each one takes a few steps—first Action, then Tiger, then Ice—spreading their arms and legs in a flying motion (they are, after all, the "Jets"), crossing the street defiantly as if to say, "Oh, yes. This is our turf." The dance continues, getting larger and faster, moving from the sidewalk into the middle of the street, dancing into the camera. A high-angle shot follows, coming down onto the seven Jets introduced thus far as they dance in the street over a white word painted on the pavement: "JETS." In the final movement of this dance, they confront Bernardo (George Chakiris) for the first time; he is dressed in a bright red shirt, black jeans, and black "Chuck Taylors" (with one exception, the Jets' sneakers are white). The seven Jets, with Riff in front, dominate three-quarters of the screen space; Bernardo is squeezed into the left quarter of the 2.20:1 frame. The Jets sardonically laugh Bernardo off while surrounding him, sizing him up, and then walking away. Significantly, this scene gives the audience even more site-specific information about the New York City location. In the background of the shot of Bernardo with Tiger and Ice, the frieze of St. Matthew's Roman Catholic Church, formerly at 215 West Sixty-Seventh Street, is clearly visible (the church closed in 1959). Tiger and Ice chase Bernardo and tease him with kissing and whistling sounds, as if they were harassing a woman. He crosses the street, and they cut off his path at one point. Tiger makes a fist in front of Bernardo's face: a challenge has been issued.

An indignant Bernardo retreats to a brick wall painted fire-engine red—exactly matching his shirt color and, clearly, his emotions. He too makes a fist and strikes the wall: challenge accepted, it seems. Bernardo walks in front of the red wall in medium close-up and is quickly joined by his lieutenant, Pepe (Jay Norman). Pepe is in Sharks colors: a black T-shirt with purple lines, and maroon pants. These two are followed by Juano (Eddie Verso). The three Sharks begin to snap their fingers, marking their walk. But it is an angry, anxious snapping, distinct from the Jets' "confident" tone. They walk through an alley as their pace gets faster—more a run than a walk now—and then dance-step over the word "JETS" painted on the pavement, entering a large, empty square in front of some tenement buildings. A few families are sitting outside on the stoops, a familiar sight in the summer. The picture of Bernardo, Pepe, and Juano dancing on location, with legs lifted high in the air, has become one of the iconic images of *West Side Story*. It establishes the film's urban setting and its energy in an exemplary fashion and has appeared in numerous publicity and art materials.[4] With all its stylized poses, however, the image looks almost natural. Since dancing is such a pervasive metaphor for fighting in the film, it suggests the Sharks' genuine claim to the neighborhood.

Here, significantly, as the Sharks stake their first claim to a piece of this turf, the tables briefly turn. The three Sharks surprise A-Rab and Baby John attempting to steal an orange from the local bodega, which might belong to Bernardo and María's parents.[5] More important, the bodega scene shows evidence of the cultural transition taking place in the neighborhood—the sort of place Ernest Lehman had described as a "dividing line between PR and white gang" in his New York notes.[6] There is evidence that the neighborhood's ethnic and racial makeup is changing. The storefront is painted mauve and purple—Sharks' colors. Along with the dark green peppers, bright red tomatoes, and light green cabbage are distinctly Afro-Caribbean produce: green and red bananas, green plantains, and brown West African yams. A-Rab's and Baby John's bright blond hair contrasts sharply with the Sharks' black hair (most of the actors had dyed their hair for the film). Empowered in their own territory, the three Sharks recover the orange and let the two Jets go. At the end of the block, however, they run into the rest of the Jets, and the power roles are reversed again. This brief scene best illustrates the transitions occurring in the neighborhood. The brick walls of the buildings surrounding the gangs are alternately white and mustard yellow (Jets' colors) and mauve, dark blue, and purple (Sharks' colors). The Jets stand in front of a small cargo truck with the menacing words "KEEP OFF" painted on it, while another storefront behind the Sharks clearly shows the words "Se Habla Español." In fact, the store behind the Sharks is a travel agency and displays the sign "Si Parla Italiano." This is evidently a neighborhood in transition, where the Jets, described in the play as "an anthology of what is called American,"[7] seem to be more and more out of place.

But they are not defeated yet. The outnumbered Sharks flee from the storefront standoff, and the Jets resume their joyous, triumphant dance down the street. They soon encounter three other Sharks (now characterized by their black leather wristbands)—Toro (Nick Covacevich), Indio (Gus Trikonis), and Loco (Jaime Rogers)—playing cards in front of a dilapidated building. After a tense moment of recognition, the Jets scare them off with a unanimous cry of "Beat It!" Still reclaiming their neighborhood, the Jets continue their dance down the streets and sidewalks; other people get out of their way, either annoyed or in recognition of their dominance. But they soon stumble onto three more Sharks in an extreme high-angle, zenith shot: the Jets command three-quarters of the screen, and the Sharks are squeezed into the extreme left quarter. This is our first glimpse of Chino (José de Vega), wearing Shark purple and khaki. Again, the Sharks are easily scared away, and they continue to be outnumbered through most of the "Prologue."

The high-angle camera shows the Jets' triumphant jump, arms stretched up in the air. The shot then cuts to the opposite low angle as a basketball falls into their hands from above. Once again, a long shot of the playground is cut short when Bernardo's hand (recognizable by the bright red sleeve and the leather wristband) comes into the left-panning shot and grabs the basketball. All the Jets' eyes are fixed slightly offscreen toward Bernardo's face. By now, all eleven Jets are present on the basketball court, occupying two-thirds of the screen; the other third contains Bernardo, Pepe, Indio, Loco, and Juano. Riff demands the ball back with a double snap of his fingers—the Jets' power sign—and the simple word "C'mon." Bernardo surrenders the ball but drops it; it bounces lightly off the floor, forcing Riff to bend over to pick it up. This amounts to the Sharks' second live challenge to the Jets, but they are still outnumbered five to eleven, so they retreat after Riff's second "Beat it!"

These brief scenes constitute the turning point in the gang hostilities, eventually culminating in the free-for-all that brings this gang war to the attention of the authorities. But as the gangs disperse from the playground, Loco trips Action with his foot and offers a mockingly apologetic gesture. Pretending to be friendly, Action attacks Loco and pushes him onto the ground. Loco responds with a powerful projectile of spit, and Action turns back to him. Indio tries to pull Loco away—possibly aware of their continued disadvantage—but it is too late: Action kicks Loco's behind, and Indio jumps him. Their choreographed dance/fight begins as Action yells out for the Jets and the other Sharks to come back to the playground. The war has begun in earnest.

The challenges continue, with first the Jets and then the Sharks taking advantage of their skills and the dividing lines within the neighborhood. Each gang in fact has an equal number of "winning" scenes, alternating the dominant role. These scenes include the patterns designed by Saul Bass and elaborated by Boris Leven, incorporating elements of the locations—the street, the playground, the fences, the empty lots, the alleys—into the drama. The Jets and Sharks chase one another through fences, narrow alleys, piles of rubble, empty lots, and rows of unhinged doors. The doors, like the fences, are symbols of entrapment and lead nowhere—denying the promise of the song "Somewhere." Storefronts, scaffoldings, and signs of construction and destruction in the neighborhood all come into play. At one point, Chino entices the Jets to chase him into an alley, where the Sharks splash them with yellow paint from a scaffold. Fast swish pans make transitions between scenes, adding a sense of urgency, speed, and chaos to the gang war. This part of the "Prologue" makes the best use of the New York City locations. The gangs' antics are rather mild—sloshing paint, throwing rotten produce, defacing the other gang's graffiti—but they underscore the struggle for the literal and symbolic "space" of the neighborhood, as Lehman and Robbins discussed at length in the spring of 1960, and as Wise chose to emphasize in his use of locations.

Eventually, the chase leads back to the playground, where, aided by various Sharks, Bernardo injures Baby John. A high-angle shot shows the Sharks stretching their arms into the air—a movement identical to that of the Jets when they ruled this turf uncontested. An extreme high-angle shot of the playground shows the gangs gathering for the free-for-all, which is more chaotic and less stylistically choreographed than previous scenes. The fight is interrupted by a police whistle and the arrival of Lieutenant Schrank and Officer Krupke. In an effective use of the wide-screen composition, the next shot puts the gangs on extreme opposite sides, with the policemen in the middle. It is clear that the gangs have one thing in common:

their hatred of the authority represented by the cops. When Riff claims that Baby John's injuries may have been caused by the police, Krupke responds, "Impossible!" Bernardo retorts, "In America, nothing is impossible," and he asks that the message be translated into Spanish. All the Jets and Sharks laugh, complicit in their contempt for authority. Still, the Sharks exit after Schrank's sardonic request, "Take your . . . friends out of here Bernardo. . . . Please." Then Schrank makes an overture to the Jets, taking their side. He clearly has a problem with the Sharks, stating in disgust, "As if this neighborhood wasn't crummy enough." But the Jets are deaf to Schrank's offer. It is one thing to hate the Sharks; it is another thing to do the policeman's bidding. Schrank and Krupke leave, contemptuous and disappointed.

At some point during the free-for-all, the character of Anybodys (Susan Oakes) makes her appearance. Described in the casting notes as "a tomboy" but in the play as one of the Jets' "girls," Anybodys begs Riff to allow her to join the gang. For Riff, the request is out of the question, regardless of her fighting skills. Riff's rejection of Anybodys enforces the motif of homosocial arrangements in the classical musical. Typically, all-male and all-female groups abandon their homosocial structure for the eternal promise of heterosexual coupling, a major theme and the most consistent convention of the classical form. This convention—with its implication that all humans are destined to join with a person of the opposite sex and that the promise of marriage can dissipate all conflicts—is eventually subverted in *West Side Story*. The rejection of Anybodys thus sets the scene for the "Jet Song," a signature number that enforces the homosocial bonds of the gang. It also sets up a significant plot development: the upcoming challenge to the Sharks at the gym that same evening.

The "Jet Song" is partially set on the playground and the surrounding street, combining some studio sets with ample location shooting. As such, it incorporates another important convention of the classical musical—the "audio dissolve," which typically serves to transition from dramatic scenes or spoken dialogue and natural sounds into music and song. The song starts with a few introductory bassoon notes in the background over the Jets' spoken dialogue;

they talk about their history in the neighborhood with other gangs and about their now estranged former number two, Tony. The dialogue then transitions into the first lines of the song, "When you're a Jet you're a Jet all the way," completing the audio dissolve and making the transition fairly inconspicuous (as Wise had first pitched). As noted earlier, for purposes of consistency of pitch and continuity, Tucker Smith sings for both Riff and Ice in this number. But Russ Tamblyn shows off his acrobatic skills, executing a few trapeze-style moves on a pipe, reminiscent of the sort of physical dancing he had done in Stanley Donen's *Seven Brides for Seven Brothers* (1954). Even in the high glory of the "Jet Song," the chain-link fences conspicuously frame the gang. Regardless of their apparent freedom—commanding the seesaw, for instance (an incorporation of location props that also recalls *Seven Brides for Seven Brothers*)—the fences remind the viewer of the "trapped" motif. The final stanza makes the best use of the location, showing the fences, the street—where the Jets are temporarily freed—cars and pedestrians, and a stadium in the background. The Jets confidently strut toward the backtracking camera, ending with an extreme close-up, slightly out of focus, of Mouthpiece as he yells the final note: "Yeah!"

Recall that Lehman had initially imagined this "Prologue" sequence taking place over several months, as implied in the play. Although there are apparent temporal ellipses, there are no costume changes in the "Prologue," and all the action takes place in the daytime, with consistent climate and lighting conditions. Thus, it all seems to occur over the course of a single day—that is, the day of the dance at the gym. Condensing the "Prologue" into a single day enhances the sense of urgency and speed. It makes the escalation of violence seem somehow more "inevitable" and logical, consistent with what Jerome Robbins called "a highly pitched and desperate gang fight for supremacy."[8] Ultimately, the directors chose the single-day structure to hasten the slow production and then made it work for narrative expediency. The "Overture," "Prologue," and "Jet Song" take more than twenty-three minutes of screen time, nearly 15 percent of the running time of approximately two hours and thirty-two minutes. Although this might seem disproportionate—the presumed principals, María, Tony, and Anita, have yet to be introduced—Robbins, Lehman, and Wise had discussed at length the importance of setting up not only the urgency but also the power of the gangs' rivalry.

"All the Spirit": "Something's Coming" and "The Bridal Shop"

The high-pitched, high-energy, harsh ending of the "Jet Song" cuts directly into the introduction of Tony (Richard Beymer), Riff's former second in command and the story's presumed male lead. The transition—called a "quick dissolve" in the screenplay but actually a clean, quick cut—goes from Mouthpiece's mouth in extreme close-up to Tony in medium shot, leaning forward in the frame. Tony and Riff are in an alley behind Doc's store, near the steps leading down to the cellar. In contrast to the Jets' idle ways, Tony is working, carrying crates of Coca-Cola down the stairs into the cellar, the first indication that he is no longer a part of the gang. Already, Tony is surrounded by a subtle combination of both Jet and Shark colors. The wardrobe and the sets display an array of purples and reds, with soft pastels and grays in the garments hanging from a clothesline high in the background. This setting is different from the play, where Riff and Tony are in front of Doc's store—Tony up on a ladder painting a new sign. This change is important because it allows a look at the alley—which eventually takes on a new significance in the movie—and because it continues the motif of colors and textures as personality traits. Tony and Riff's loyalty pledge to each other is also different, changed from the slightly homoerotic "Womb to tomb, sperm to worm" to the tamer "Womb to tomb, birth to earth" to appease the MPAA censors. It still establishes the sense of intimacy between these two childhood best friends. Furthermore, it is revealed that Riff has been living with Tony's family, which is presumably more stable than his own—more evidence of Tony's removal from the gang context.

After a playful, slightly homoerotic wrestling match in which Tony easily overpowers Riff, Tony is ready to reveal his secret desires. Tony recounts that every night he wakes up "reaching out" for something. There is something out there waiting to bring him happiness, but he has yet to discover what it is. It is Riff who guesses that it might be "a dame," prefiguring the breakup of this particular homosocial link, which is essential for Tony's pairing with María. Tony agrees to go to the dance that evening as Riff's lieutenant, and Riff speculates that whatever Tony is looking for might be there, "twitchin' at the dance." This serves as the setup and introduction to Tony's "I want" song, "Something's Coming."[9] The background of the set conspicuously displays the clothes hanging on the line— soft pastels in silk, light cotton, and lace that denote a much gentler environment than the harsh asphalt, cement, bricks, rubble, and chain-link fences of the "Prologue" and "Jet Song." This setting aligns Tony with the softer, "feminine" environment of the bridal shop, where we first see María. It is also quite different from the spartan, dark, angular setting of the song's theater version. Tony's "personality dissolve"—a generic feature of musicals by which each member of the principal couple acquires the characteristics of the other—is already taking place in the setup for the song.[10] Notably, the entire song is covered in only six shots, mostly medium shots and close-ups; a smoother cutting style further distinguishes it from the harder, faster editing—including swish pans—of the two previous numbers. The editing also aligns Tony with María: his final close-up tilts up into the clothesline, toward the silky white and pastel fabrics, and then goes slightly out of focus before slowly dissolving into nearly identical fabrics and clothes inside the bridal shop (also in soft focus). This creates the illusion of being a continuation of the previous shot, which pans slowly from Tony's extended arm and hand into the fabrics.

At twenty-eight minutes and fifty seconds, the shot tilts down, in an apparent continuation of the preceding camera movement, to reveal María (Natalie Wood) in a shot described by Lehman as capturing "all the spirit and radiant beauty of the lovely young MARIA in one quick, breathtaking CLOSE-UP."[11] Significantly, María is dressed only in a white slip, a neutral color that only she wears in the movie. The light cotton undergarment is adorned with a small gold medal of the Virgin Mary on a baby-blue ribbon attached to the left strap with a safety pin. This type of charm was common in traditional Catholic society; typically, a mother gave it to her child to serve as a constant prayer to the Virgin Mary for protection. By contrast, the next shot introduces Anita, described in the play as having "loose hair and flashy clothes."[12] She is dressed in a purple sewing smock, and a bright purple satin fabric hangs in the background—Shark colors. As a "gang girl," Anita is quite distinct from the virginal, childish María, who is still untainted after "one month" in New York. But María refuses to wear the white dress Anita is altering for the dance, protesting, unconvincingly, that "white is for babies." María wants Anita to lower the neck of the dress by an inch, but Anita, enforcing her authority and acknowledging María's lack of experience, argues that it is too late. "Next year," she says.

Besides the visible distinctions between the two women, it is intimated that Anita is sexually active. María, annoyed by Anita's refusal to alter or dye the dress, threatens to reveal to her parents something about Anita and Bernardo "in the balcony at the movies." Whatever happened there, the threat affects Anita, who offers to "rip [the] dress to shreds." But when María tries the dress on, it takes only a moment for her real self to come out, as she marvels at the garment—and herself—in the mirror with a charmed, "Oh sí." Spreading the white dress in front of the mirror, María stands out against the Shark purple surrounding her reflection, but it is clear that she is eager for some kind of sexual thrill. While the white dress, the gold crucifix around her neck, and the Virgin Mary charm mark her as presexual and virginal, she longs for something else. In lieu of an "I want" song, María protests about working all day at the bridal shop and "sitting at home" every night. "One month have I been in this country," she protests. "Do I ever even touch excitement?" Her purported beau, Chino, does "nothing" for her, and she longs for something to happen at the dance. Like Tony, María seems to anticipate that "something's coming."

Enter Bernardo and Chino in black suits, purple shirts, and red ties. Afraid to come into "a shop for ladies," they seem consciously aware of this "feminine" space and subconsciously mindful of the homosocial arrangement, the gender segregation of the classical musical. But since Anita and Bernardo are already paired, Chino too aspires to the promise of heterosexual coupling. After all, Bernardo has brought María from Puerto Rico "to marry Chino." The ensuing repartee between María and Bernardo—that she is "a precious

Tony in the alley. The light, soft pastels and lighting eventually turn dark, ominous, expressionistic. ©1961 Metro-Goldwyn-Mayer Studios Inc. All rights reserved.

jewel" and he is "a silly watch dog"—is new to the movie but stresses
Bernardo's possessive, brotherly protection of María. The few lines
of dialogue added by Ernest Lehman make Bernardo's motivation
for accepting the Jets' challenge—and wanting to fight Tony specifically—somewhat more convincing and a bit more logical than
its portrayal in Laurents's book of the play. The movie clarifies that
the animosity is not just about turf but also about gender expecta-
tions: the desire to possess María is an insult to Bernardo. Finally,
along with her muted but emerging sexual curiosity, the bridal shop
sequence expresses María's initial desire to assimilate culturally. By
cheerily and somewhat naïvely welcoming "the real beginning of
[her] life as a young lady of America," María is upholding the tradition of the classical musical and conforming to the expected personality dissolve with Tony.

The classical musical creates a series of apparent conflicts that
threaten to thwart the principal heterosexual couple's destiny to be
together. These conflicts or differences can be cultural (Sandy and
Danny in *Grease*), social or economic (Professor Higgins and Eliza
Doolittle in *My Fair Lady*), professional (Don Lockwood and Kathy
Selden in *Singin' in the Rain*), moral (Jerry Travers and Dale Tremont
in *Top Hat*), or even species based (Prince Eric and Ariel in *The Little
Mermaid*). But they are almost always illusory rather than real conflicts. The personality dissolve serves to appease these conflicts and,
in general, to show that they are really just misunderstandings or
confusions that can be easily and comically resolved. While this
is true of any number of romantic films and a variety of genres in
the Hollywood tradition—both classical and contemporary—in
the musical, singing and dancing are the most visible tools for the
resolution of these conflicts.[13] Tony and María go through the process of the personality dissolve, first seen in certain similarities of
clothing and setting. But this also takes the form of various cultural
adjustments, the most significant, so far, being María's search for
"excitement" at the dance and her willingness to become "a young
lady of America." Sadly, the conflicts that separate María and Tony,
however trivialized in the narrative, are real. Singing and dancing
will not bring compromise, relief, or the dissolution of tensions.
For the moment, though—as Bernardo, Anita, Chino, and María get

ready for the dance—*West Side Story* has not yet broken these classical conventions.

"Fantastically Magical": The "Dance at the Gym" and the "Mambo"

With the words "a young lady of America" still ringing in the sound track, María begins to twirl in her white dress, like a toy ballerina in a music box. As she slowly moves away from the camera, the dress takes on an aura of colors, and María is seen briefly in triplicate, like a "persistence of vision" effect. This is the first of the many special effects shots and transitions designed by Linwood Dunn and his company Film Effects of Hollywood. María's image is shadowed in red, green, and blue—suspiciously, the photographic red-green-blue color model—before the shot tracks in and dissolves into an identical pattern, transforming into three soft-focus dancers in fiery red silhouette against a sharp black background. This is one of the shots that gave Dunn so much trouble at the lab (a remake was ordered on 29 June 1961), owing to its three complicated segments of figure, lighting, and color transformation.[14] The silhouettes finally turn into—and the shot cuts to—three of the Jets' women twirling like María on the dance floor, but concluding with discernibly "modern" dance moves. The next shot is a high angle of the entire dance floor, with the Jets and Sharks and their partners already in full motion.

There is a gauzy quality to Daniel Fapp's cinematography in the gym scene, invoking the "dreamy" quality of the setting—"a not quite real world"—while also anticipating the "fantastically magical" moment of María and Tony's meeting (which Jerome Robbins had argued for after seeing an early cut of the film).[15] The visibly artificial, stylized set helps emphasize the gangs' color coordination: even the girls' underpants match their dress colors—a clever run around possible censorship issues. Barely discernible because of their drab, olive green costumes are the background players that Robbins requested for this sequence; they are alongside but do not mix with the Jets and the Sharks. Even a few African American extras can be seen in the background, a detail completely absent from the stage version but that seems logical and historically more accurate in the 1950s "West Side" context. As usual, the two gangs are clearly distinguishable by their colors, especially the Sharks, in their purples and reds.

The first potential conflict is shown in medium long shot, with the gangs lined up on opposite sides of the wide screen: Sharks on the left and Jets on the right. As they start to approach each other menacingly, they are interrupted by Glad Hand (John Astin), the jolly, clueless social worker who is chaperoning the dance. Glad Hand introduces the "get-together" dance to sneers, wisecracks, and ad-libs from the kids. This is one of the scenes that concerned Robbins, and he asked Wise to reedit it to dramatize the sense of space and the "turf" motif. Although the introductory medium long shot does not clearly exploit the set, the following long shot does, putting each gang on opposite sides of the 2.20:1 Panavision 70 frame. Glad Hand and Officer Krupke occupy the uncomfortable middle. With a slight high angle, the spread of the two circles of dancers—"boys on the outside, girls on the inside"—further exposes the physical distance Robbins argued for. As the couples rearrange themselves in the "correct" order to avoid mixing the gang lines, the beginning of the "Mambo" scene complements the effect even more. The choice of a slightly shorter wide-angle lens reveals the floor, the ceiling, and a mezzanine in a longer shot, where the Jets and the Sharks are actually several feet farther away from each other. The camera then cuts to consecutive, formally opposite medium long shots of each gang shouting "Mambo!" to the other. When the Sharks take the floor first for their display—of talent, energy, anger, skill, and color—the Jets retreat to their corner, screen right. The action is repeated in the exact opposite screen orientation when the Jets reclaim the floor in counterattack. This is precisely the symbolic "turf war" Robbins had insisted on, with the dance floor representing the street, the neighborhood, the West Side, the city itself, and maybe even the country.

Bernardo and Anita, followed by Riff and his girl Graziella (Gina Trikonis), take consecutive turns on the floor. This is a duel, repeating the motif and pattern of the "Prologue," yet it takes the form of a dance competition, as opposed to the "stylized" fighting choreography of the extended opening sequence. At one point, the two competing couples and their respective gangs share the massive wide frame, "splitting" it exactly in half, with each gang safely on its own side: Sharks on the left, Jets on the right. Dunn had suggested at one point using an actual "split-screen" effect, presumably for this scene and possibly for the "Tonight" quintet.[16] But Wise and Fapp create the same impression, and convey the same message, with their effective use of wide-screen composition. It is like a montage within the frame that creates division, paradoxically, in a single space, yet it delivers the sense of distance—cultural and social—that Robbins thought was missing from the earlier cut of the sequence.

Out of this sharp division arises Tony and María's first meeting. Cheating in composition, again employing a slightly longer lens, Wise and Fapp still take advantage of the wide-screen frame, placing María on the left and Tony on the right, on extreme opposite sides of the screen (this is the original "magical" moment Robbins asked for). The shot gradually changes to include the opaque "oil" effect designed by Dunn to artificially mask the middle two quarters of the screen, blocking a clear view of the Jets and the Sharks and their dancing partners. Meanwhile, María and Tony—who had arrived moments before—are clearly visible and notice each other for the first time, all in a single wide frame. What had been done in the theater with lighting—dimming the middle, spotlighting the corners—is accomplished here with a simple photographic trick that not only enhances the "love at first sight" moment but also offers a "not quite real" representation of an otherwise realistic set. Opposite, alternating medium long shots of María and Tony repeat the effect by containing and isolating the characters from the gangs, which are still obscured by the opaque oil effect (this effect was still being processed as late as the end of June 1961). These shots are followed by alternate close-ups of María and Tony, replicating the same effect and literalizing the metaphoric assumption that the "world has gone away." From this point on, the lovers have eyes only for each other, as María and Tony later confirm in the "Tonight" duet: "I see you. . . . " "Oh, María, see only me."

The oil effect continues for the next few shots as María and Tony slowly walk toward each other, while the frenetic dancing in the background slows down. The lighting suddenly turns dark, theatrical—the only scene in the movie that deliberately looks like a stage.

The oil effect gradually disappears, and little flakes of light (red, green, and blue again), called "falling stars" in the special effects list, begin to descend, superimposed, as if it is snowing light. This new special effects shot—still in the "experimental" stage at the lab in July 1961 and remade in August to produce the "exact effect" Wise wanted—was arguably prompted by Robbins's request for a "magical" effect.[17] In any case, it is clear that a transformation—from real to magical, from anger to love—has taken place. Surprisingly, even in a visibly theatrical setting, it is a cinematographically convincing moment: we can "see" the teenagers' infatuation as the rest of the world "goes away" (just as María later sings in "Tonight"—"I saw you and the world went away"). The pace of the music and dancing onstage slows down to the "courtship" pas de deux number, and the illusion is now complete as the lighting, dancing, and feelings are transformed into a romantic (as opposed to a dueling) setting. With a few extra lines of dialogue added by Lehman—presumably to make an otherwise utterly unbelievable event more plausible—the scene slowly but steadily returns to "reality" at the moment of Tony and María's first kiss. The kiss seems to reawaken the reality of the imminent gang violence and the urban setting as the lights quickly come back on, the "falling stars" disappear, a drum bangs loudly four times, and the pace of the dancing returns to its "normal" angry, jazzy frenzy.

The ensuing argument between Bernardo and Tony also returns us to the dramatized division of space onscreen, with the Sharks and the Jets sharply splitting the screen in the usual orientation in a medium long shot. The argument is broken up by Glad Hand and Krupke, but the Jets and the Sharks have enough time to agree to a "war council" later that night at Doc's Candy Store. At this point, Chino gently, kindly takes María away with a soft, "Come, María," and Tony hears her name for the first time, setting up the upcoming solo song, "Maria."

"A Bit of Loving": "Maria" and "America"

After the brief exchange between the gangs, Tony, who is not a party to their arrangement, slowly walks out of the gym as the other unaffected parties continue to dance in the background.

Tony speaks, then sings the name of his object of desire, while disembodied voices in the background of the sound track repeat her name in the familiar tritone of the song "Maria." Tony is in medium close-up in the center of the screen. The shot is a composite, and as Tony begins to sing the first line—"The most beautiful sound I ever heard"—the couples in the background move in slow motion against Tony's natural speed. While Tony walks and sings the first lines, the background of the shot changes from the (slowed down) interior of the gym to a very stylized street outside, and Tony is suddenly flanked by buildings arranged in a symmetrical composition behind him. Lehman suggested that Tony be shown "lost in a dream" and that the transition in space be "imperceptible." What Lehman sought here was to "ignore the physical realities" of the setting to convey to the audience Tony's state of mind.[18]

The background then turns from the ocher and red of the gym to a purplish or fuchsia sky as he sings the word "María" for the first time. His movement and the shot size do not change, however, so the change of setting is "magical" as well, with no apparent temporal ellipsis in spite of the break in spatial continuity. Tony is surrounded by a red glow as he continues to occupy this magical space, removed from his real environment—and the reality of violence and urban decay around him. The scene then cuts to a long shot of Tony in the street setting (obviously a studio set), returning to the gauzy lighting effect of the gym's interior; it has turned realistic yet remains removed. Back in close-up, Tony's face goes slightly out of focus before the scene cuts to a high-angle shot in a fenced-in handball court (presumably, based on the one scouted in New York in the spring of 1960). This is the first time Tony is associated with the chain-link fence motif, seemingly predicting the coming tragedy in spite of his present joy. From the handball court, Tony's movement (described as constant in the screenplay) leads back to the gym, giving the audience a fairly good sense of the neighborhood. The long shot shows the church-like stained glass windows of the gym—a sort of YMCA clubhouse—seen previously only from the inside. Tony's final close-up covers the words "Say it soft and it's almost like praying," and the gym's tall windows in the background are indeed reminiscent of church architecture. (In fact, there are no fewer than four references to praying in the film, including this one. María is seen praying in her bedroom twice, and in the first bridal shop scene, Anita warns María that "with these boys you can start in dancing and end up praying.") The last shot of the song is a high angle on Tony looking up into the night sky as he stands on a hard, wet, checkered cement floor—a quick return to reality that arguably grounds Tony back in his urban context. A soft dissolve transitions the scene to María's bedroom; she is in close-up, at the window, holding on to the curtain and staring out while vaguely listening to Bernardo's stern warnings. In other words, the word "Maria" dissolves into the close-up of María standing dreamily at the window, "perhaps thinking of Tony," while her name, sung by Tony, still rings in the sound track.[19] As with the transition between "Something's Coming" and the close-up of María in the bridal shop, María and Tony are formally connected in this editing transition. A woman at a window is typically a symbol of longing and desire in classical cinema, and that is María's position in this shot.

Following the "Maria" number is the first of three song order changes. In the play, "Maria" is followed by the "Tonight" duet between María and Tony, whereas in the movie, it is followed by the new "America" number, rewritten as a joyous, farcical confrontation between the Puerto Rican boys and girls. This is a change that Robbins strongly objected to, fearing that it would disrupt the romantic mood and perhaps break the continuity of the "I want" and the courtship scenes that conclude with Tony's solo number declaring his affection for María. However, Lehman and Wise's decision to change the order of these numbers allows the unfolding of alternating moods in the nearly consecutive musical numbers: "Maria" (romantic), "America" (humorous), "Tonight" (romantic), and "Gee, Officer Krupke" (humorous). Thus, rather than the mood disruption sensed by Robbins, the four musical numbers, which take place in less than twenty-three minutes of screen time, actually provide some mood balance.

The setup for "America" in its new narrative place starts in the tenement hallway and stairway to the roof, as Anita argues with Bernardo over his scolding of María after the dance. This is especially poignant because they are arguing about gender roles, and in the movie, the song is turned into an argument along strict gender lines. Also, the setting changes to the rooftop, as opposed to a nondescript alley in the play. This too is relevant, in light of Lehman's observations about the importance of rooftops to youth and gang life in 1950s New York. (Interestingly, Wise's last film, also a youth gang drama about poverty and prejudice set in New York City, was the much-maligned *Rooftops* [1989].) Here, Lehman writes: "A lot of living goes on up here among the Puerto Ricans. Right now, a bit of loving is going on."[20] It is significant that although the Sharks are repeatedly denied access to the "streets," they have taken over the rooftops of their own tenement buildings.

Entangled in amorous embraces, among bottles of Coca-Cola and empty cans of Budweiser (the only evidence of teenage alcohol consumption in the movie), the boys and girls become involved in the "America" argument much as they do in the play. The boys, especially Bernardo, express their desire to go back to Puerto Rico after their disappointing "immigrant" experience in New York.[21] Their hopes and dreams have come at a price—that is, the realization that however much they struggle, they will remain second-class citizens. The girls, led by Anita, are perfectly happy and hopeful and see the material conveniences of living in the United States as a realization of the American Dream. In the play, after the boys leave for their war council, the girls resume the argument, with Rosalía as the sole dissenting voice. In the movie, however, the two sides are defined strictly by gender (and there are significant lyrics changes, as noted in chapter 2). All the girls defend and love the America they think they know; all the boys blow the whistle on its inequality, prejudice, violence, and resentment. When, in new dialogue written for the movie, Anita asks Bernardo, "Why would you want to go back to Puerto Rico? We had nothing," Bernardo sharply replies, "Ai! We still have nothing, only more expensive." As I discuss in chapter 5, the new "America" is the anchor of a much sharper social critique that emerges from the *West Side Story* film.

The song starts with a rare return to the classic audio dissolve, when Pepe is seen and heard rhythmically beating two sticks together. This sets up the basis for the dialogue to turn rhythmic as well, and for the orchestral score to swell up in the sound track.

This is the Sharks' signature song and is perhaps the most recognizable one from the score. The rooftop setting—now associated with the Sharks—is both intimate and expansive: removed from "the rest of the world," so to speak, it is a place where the Sharks can express themselves freely. It also becomes an important showcase for the dancers, especially George Chakiris and Rita Moreno. Like the "duel" of the couples and gangs in the "Dance at the Gym" sequence, this argument allows each side its own segregated segment in which it commands the dancing space, repeating the pattern of the gangs seen in the "Mambo" scene. Though less theatrical than the gym setting, the rooftop set (on stage 5 at the Goldwyn Studio) is also somewhat artificial. However, the controlled environment allows for a visibly mobile camera that seems to dance along with the performers. This dancing camera—used in the gym, on the rooftop, and later in the garage set during the "Cool" number—brings to mind some of the most elaborate dancing ever seen on film: Fred Astaire, Gene Kelly, Bob Fosse. But the song's lyrics and its abrasive style are among the most visible revisions of the classical musical style to date. In September 1960 *Los Angeles Mirror* columnist Erksine Johnson was allowed to visit the set during a camera rehearsal for the "America" number. After listening to the song's new "sharp, satirical" lyrics and watching some of the choreography, Johnson declared that *West Side Story* was "a departure" from the classical musical and that previously it would have been "unthinkable" as a film property; he predicted that the film would be "a rumble, a rumble in movieland."[22]

The sing-off and dance-off between Anita and the girls and Bernardo and the boys are comical, yet poignant. The dance-off gives each performer and his or her group apparently equal screen time and use of space. Unlike the gym "duel" though, the "America" number is joyful and playful, with a perceived spontaneity that is quite infectious. Low-angle shots—achieved by lifting the set floor—give the dancers a seemingly theatrical presence even when other dancers, by mistake or by design, get in the way of a shot, temporarily blocking the camera's view. Presumably, this is one of the shots that Robbins would have objected to, yet the slight imperfection suggests realism and spontaneity. Furthermore, unlike the "Mambo" duel, the finale of the "America" number brings the couples together, as the dancers run toward each other and the boys lift the girls up over their heads. They end in a celebratory communal laugh, some clapping their hands, more unified than ever. In fact, we never see the Sharks this happy again.

Yet, as is usually the case in *West Side Story*, reality interferes with the momentary joy. After the dance-off, the Sharks must leave to meet the Jets for their scheduled war council, the reality of prejudice and violence imposing itself on the fantasy of happiness. As she says good-bye to Bernardo, Anita reasserts her identity and reminds us of their disagreement that began the whole boys-versus-girls argument. Bernardo wants Anita to agree to see him later that night, but she replies, "I'm an American girl now. I don't wait." Like María in the bridal shop, Anita's ambition to be "an American girl" seems somewhat at odds with her Puerto Rican identity, something the "America" song, as rewritten for the movie, emphasizes. Bernardo reminds her that "back home, women know their place," perhaps longing for the more traditional gender roles that their cultural, ethnic, and religious background supposedly favors.

Tellingly, we next see María in her bedroom, kneeling in front of a makeshift altar to the Virgin Mary. She is wearing the same white slip with the gold medal and the crucifix around her neck. She makes the sign of the cross as she says her prayers before going to bed. In contrast to Anita, María is still assuming the "traditional" role of women "back home." Yet María's personality dissolve, already started on the way to the dance ("a real lady of America"), resumes with Tony's arrival at her window.

"See Only Me": The "Tonight" Duet

As noted earlier, rather than coming between "Maria" and "America," the "Tonight" duet follows "America" and precedes the "War Council" scene in the movie. This allows for some mood elasticity—for a shifting rather than a sustained tone. While running through an alley, Tony looks around and calls for María, presumably guessing which building is hers. This detail makes the duet's placement here more plausible, since some time has evidently elapsed since Tony's "Maria" solo. The fire escape and the alley below are recognizably realistic, with soft lighting and the suggestion of a recent light rain. After preliminary "sweet nothings" are exchanged between the would-be lovers, María sings the first lines: "Only you / you're the only thing I'll see." The camera setups are intimate at first, favoring medium two-shots of the couple, close shots, and "choker" close-ups of the actors in slightly soft focus. Here again, as in "Something's Coming," the editing is noticeably softer and slower than in the energetic "Mambo" and "America" numbers. After all, this is the movie's major love song, the conventional love duet that cements the relationship and brings the courtship to its conclusion.

In spite of the initially realistic setting, by the beginning of the second stanza ("the world is full of light"), the two actors, in a medium close shot from the waist up, are gradually surrounded by the special effects Dunn and Wise finally settled on (see chapter 1). Slowly, roughly, the left and right quarters of the screen become diffused, bathed in a visibly "unnatural" light and a softer focus, with hints of purple, red, and yellow—the gangs' colors—yet with a soft innocence reminiscent of the "oil" effect at the gym. Indeed, it seems that the conflict has been "defused" by Tony and María's desire and their singing. However, they are wearing the gangs' colors: Tony in a mustard yellow jacket, María in a light purple robe over her white slip. Regardless of the dreamy atmosphere, they are still attached to the two respective gangs—their personality dissolves not yet completed. This particular effect is sustained through most of the scene, regardless of Dunn's initial suggestion to use different special effects with every line of the song (no doubt abandoned because of budget, scheduling, and technical concerns). As late as 18 August 1961, Dunn was still testing this specific design but had not yet settled on its final look: "subtly brightening and diffusing the area surrounding" the lovers.[23]

At the end of the second stanza, the light effect actually fades back to "natural" cinematographic lighting, returning the scene to its "realistic" mode. The shot shifts to an over-the-shoulder close-up of María as the two are about to kiss. María's father's voice is then heard offscreen, gently calling her back into the apartment and interrupting the imminent kiss. María replies that she will be inside in a moment. The spoken part of the "song" thus reverts to the "realistic" mise-en-scène, as Wise and Dunn had discussed in the early stages of design. They agreed there would be visible but not disruptive transitions between dialogue and drama, songs and dance. The spoken part of the scene sets up the meeting between Tony and María the next day at the bridal shop and provides such basic information as Tony's proper name, before returning to the final sung segment and the last verse of the song: "Good night, good night." After the last note, Tony excitedly runs away, back up the alley, while María momentarily reaches her hand out to him and is last seen in close-up, with an expression of apparent concern on her face. It is as if she knows that their unlikely romance is doomed, "star-crossed." It is notable that although Dunn proposed many complicated special effects for this number, the more subtle approach falls in line with Wise's desire to minimize the shock between realistic settings and theatrical effects.

"Understand Them": "Gee, Officer Krupke" and the "War Council"

A stark reminder of the accuracy of María's concern comes when the scene immediately cuts to a close-up of Action, waiting impatiently outside Doc's store and angrily, rhetorically asking, "Where the devil are them Sharks!" At this point, the screenplay introduces the second significant change in song order, adopted by Lehman for purposes of mood continuity later in the "second act." The Jets seem either anxious or bored as they wait for the Sharks, and in the play, this is where the "Cool" number is placed—a dark jazz tune at odds with the comical "America" that it follows onstage. As I have argued, the reordering is justifiable for two reasons: it adds a more comfortable balance of drama and comedy, and it helps establish the movie's clear turn to a somber mood after the rumble. (For the same reason, "I Feel Pretty" was moved up in the movie narrative to the bridal shop scene—before "One Hand, One Heart," before Tony and María's mock wedding, and before the tragic rumble. "I Feel Pretty" constitutes, in fact, María's "I want" song.)

In the setup to "Gee, Officer Krupke," Lehman retains or slightly adapts the play's dialogue (leading up to "Cool"), all the way to Ice telling the typically hotheaded Action to "cool." The scene then changes to Officer Krupke arriving in his patrol car and harassing the Jets (with dialogue similar to that used in the play when, after the rumble, he fails to arrest A-Rab and Baby John in an alley). The new setup is still perfectly plausible: Krupke is patrolling his beat while the Jets are standing around "blocking the sidewalk," simply occupying or perhaps defending their turf. After Krupke has to leave suddenly in response to a "1013" (code for a police officer in trouble, as Lehman learned during his 1959 research trip), Tiger play-acts, in a mock Krupke voice, the policeman's admonishing of the gang. Riff leads the Jets in the comical, vaudeville-style "Gee, Officer Krupke"—Russ Tamblyn does his own singing here—as the gang needs to blow off some steam in anticipation of the war council.

"Gee, Officer Krupke" is the Jets' communal song—what the rewritten "America" is to the Sharks. Like "America," it is a critical satire of a number of social failures in Eisenhower's America, and it is filmed in a dynamic editing style with a fluidly mobile camera to match its playful tone and Tamblyn's acrobatics. Composed of twenty-eight shots in four minutes and two seconds, it is one of the liveliest numbers in the movie. (In contrast, the "Tonight" duet runs five minutes and fifteen seconds with thirty shots; shot number ten, containing the special effects, is sustained longer than any other.) "Gee, Officer Krupke" mocks social fears and failed policies to deal with "cruddy JDs" (juvenile delinquents), and it includes some of the raciest lines in the movie, despite a few lyrics changes, courtesy of Lehman (including the substitution of "Captain Marvel" for "Superman," after the owners of the latter brand protested).[24] Whereas Lehman kept lyrics such as "Our mothers all are junkies" and the mention of marijuana, he removed the words "bastard," "SOB," and "plastered" and substituted lines like "My Daddy beats my Mommy / My Momma clobbers me" and "My Grandpa is a commie." Equally telling is the substitution of the word "slob" in the movie for "schmuck" in the play; perhaps this was done in the interest of using more neutral slang and avoiding the Yiddish term for "penis," considered quite offensive in the 1960s context.

When the Sharks finally arrive for the war council, the Jets' girls Graziella and Velma (Carole D'Andrea) are impolitely asked to leave; presumably, they are a threat to the gang's homosocial sphere and have no say in "men's business." Even Anybodys, the tomboy who was allowed to fight in the free-for-all, is not permitted in the war council. She leaves, but not before a lively and convincing threat to the arriving Sharks. This is men's stuff, satirically treated as a political or social engagement. Once they are seated at the negotiating table, a medium shot of the Jets (Riff, Ice, and Action) over Bernardo's shoulder reveals the wall behind. It is full of Jets' chalk graffiti, a few scribbled names, and, screen right over Action's left shoulder, a (bad) reproduction or copy of John Trumbull's popular painting *Presentation of the Declaration of Independence* (1817–1819). Its presence in this context is too ironic to be ignored, especially with the poignancy of the "America" and "Gee, Officer Krupke" numbers. It certainly adds to *West Side Story*'s running commentary that all men are not, in fact, created equal and that for these poor urban kids in 1950s America, the "pursuit of happiness" is not a "self-evident" truth. The picture on the wall quietly overlooks the escalating argument that ends with a series of ethnic epithets spat at each other ("Spics!" "Micks!" "Wop!") that almost leads to a fight (in the movie, not the play) right there and then. The Jets' and Sharks' "gentlemen's agreement" over the rumble terms is a further mockery of the perceived solemnity of the historical moment as pompously imagined by Trumbull.

Even as the gangs agree to a "fair fight" under the grave shadow of the painting, Lieutenant Schrank arrives on the scene, and for the second time, the gangs make a momentary truce to confront their mutual enemy: the Law. Schrank's presence in this scene (longer in the movie than in the play) poses him as the true antagonist: a corrupt cop who cannot hide his own prejudices. He insults both the Sharks ("As if this neighborhood wasn't crummy enough") and the Jets, calling their parents "immigrant scum" and suggesting that Action's mother is a prostitute, among other name-calling. Schrank, however, takes personal responsibility for his feelings, likely to satisfy the censors. Lehman's rewrite of Schrank's monologue includes various new lines of dialogue, such as: "Oh, sure. Understand them. That's what they keep telling me down at headquarters. Understand them." This seems to be responding directly to the MPAA's rule that the police or any other official state apparatus cannot be portrayed as an antagonist or painted in a negative light. Theatrical audiences

Trumbull's *Declaration of Independence* irreverently presides over the "War Council," top right of the frame. ©1961 Metro-Goldwyn-Mayer Studios Inc. All rights reserved.

may have been allowed to see the shortcomings of the NYPD, but in the movie, Schrank takes full responsibility for his failure to "understand" the context of this particular turf war; he becomes the active antagonist or villain to the gangs. Although Schrank has no real authority to do so, he makes the Sharks leave Doc's store with a spiteful remark, pointed at Bernardo: "Sure, it's a free country an' I ain't got the right. But I got a badge. Whadda you got?"

With the reference to "a free country" and the Trumbull painting on the wall, Schrank's words resonate within the social critique of *West Side Story*. This becomes especially evident when, as they leave Doc's store, the Sharks whistle a mocking rendition of "My Country 'Tis of Thee"—surprisingly, listed as a "musical number" in Stanley Scheuer's working script. It is arguable that, with the rewritten "America" lyrics, the satire of "Gee, Officer Krupke," and the conspicuous placement of a venerable reference to American history aligned with the war council, *West Side Story* makes a genuine, if generally harmless, critique of contemporary American society—more so than any musical film of its time. Recall that the Mirisch brothers initially approached Wise because he had experience with "gritty subject matter," and the Cinerama corporation shied away from any involvement with the movie, fearing it might be "controversial." After all, up to this time, the social function of the classical musical had been, for the most part, to avoid and ignore controversy, not embrace it.

Following Schrank's angry exit—the Jets have refused to cooperate or reveal the site of the rumble—Tony is left alone with Doc. Infused with enthusiasm after his meeting with María, Tony helps clean up the store and, as he had done with Riff in the "Something's Coming" sequence, opens up to Doc and confesses his love for María. Doc (Ned Glass) asks Tony, "Aren't you afraid?" But Tony sees no reason for fear. "I'm frightened enough for the both of you," Doc concludes, seemingly resigned to "fate"—in the tragic sense of the word. The "first act" of the movie closes with Tony wishing Doc "*Buenas noches*" and walking out into the street pensively, dreamily, to an instrumental rendition of a few bars from "Maria." He walks past the handball court again, which will reappear in the film's tragic final scenes. Then, at one hour, twenty-one minutes, and two seconds, a slow fade to black indicates the placement of the intermission, as originally conceived. Eventually, the intermission was withdrawn from the published screenplay and the general-release prints; it was optional for exhibitors during the road-show engagements.[25]

"Too Much Feeling": "I Feel Pretty" and "One Hand, One Heart"

The beginning of the "second act" of the movie finds María in the bridal shop again. In a close-up similar to her earlier introduction, she is playfully trying on hats and other bridal headwear in front of a mirror. The narcissistic setup is quite appropriate to the upcoming "I Feel Pretty," but it is also consistent with the first bridal shop scene where, for the first time, María sees herself as both desirable and desiring. "I Feel Pretty" is the third of the reshuffled musical numbers; it and "Gee, Officer Krupke" are the two songs Lehman decided to move up, before the rumble and the deaths of Riff and Bernardo (in the play, the song comes after "Cool," the "Tonight" quintet, and the rumble). In the movie, it is positioned to be the setup for Tony and María's "mock wedding." The joyfully vain "I Feel Pretty" makes more sense here and is perfectly justifiable in light of María's excitement at the prospect of seeing Tony at the end of her workday. María is wearing Jet colors in the scene: an orange smock over a light yellow dress; her personality dissolve is in progress but not yet completed. She is, however, framed in Shark colors, especially the deep purple satin fabric seen the day before behind Anita. In contrast to Doc's Candy Store or the rooftop, this is a particularly "feminine" space, with soft pastels and silky fabrics dominating the background—like Tony's "Something's Coming" setting. The bridal shop is the Puerto Rican girls' own homosocial space (rewritten for the movie from the more intimate, less social setting of María's bedroom).

María is self-absorbed in front of the mirror when her friends and workmates start to quiz her about acting differently and being "up to something." María replies excitedly with the song's title and first verse: "I feel pretty," leading to the song. In fifteen shots and a short two minutes and forty-one seconds, the number is lively, yet it seems intimate in the spatially limited setting of the sewing room in back of the bridal shop. The camera is mostly static in various setups, but it dances with the girls toward the end of the song, with one visibly jerky camera movement reframing the girls for the number's finale. "I Feel Pretty" functions as María's "I want" song, and it is also an expression of desire. She sings about being loved by a "pretty wonderful boy" and suggests usurping the title of "Miss America"—a clever political commentary, as I argue in chapter 5. The number is not particularly elaborate, especially compared with the sets, the number of performers, and the formal complexities of the "America" and "Cool" numbers. It is also one of the last numbers that Jerome Robbins was involved in to some extent, as we know from the November 1960 *Los Angeles Examiner* article that described, somewhat flippantly, the "heap of people" surrounding Natalie Wood at the time of the shoot. In addition to providing comic relief and functioning as an "I want" song for María, it allows her to show some sexual initiative and desire—the "excitement" she has longed for since the beginning of the film.

With her excitement exercised and expressed, María readies herself to see Tony while Madame Lucía and the rest of the girls make hasty exits. Appropriately, María expects to meet Tony in the prophetic space of the bridal shop itself, not the sewing room in the back where she typically works. Anita, more jaded and more knowledgeable than María, refers to the bridal shop, perhaps also prophetically, as a "jail." We see María once more in front of a mirror, where she fixes her hair and nervously prompts Anita to leave. We have already seen María standing at a window, which typically represents longing in classical cinema, and especially in musicals (think of Judy Garland singing "The Boy Next Door" in *Meet Me in St. Louis* or Jane Powell singing "When You're in Love" in *Seven Brides for Seven Brothers*), but a woman standing before a mirror signifies that she is not only a desirable object but also, and more important, a desiring subject: María is at the brink of sexual and romantic maturity.

The perceptive Anita seems suspicious of María's desire to stay behind and finish some work. While the childish María anticipates an encounter with the object of her as-yet chaste desire, Anita is eagerly anticipating a sexual encounter with Bernardo after the rumble. "After a fight," she tells María, "that brother of yours is so healthy." In the movie, this is the first time María learns that the Sharks and Jets are going to fight that night; in the play, she is already aware.[26] This detail makes María seem a bit more childish and innocent than she has already been portrayed. When María asks Anita, naïvely, "Why do they fight?" Anita's response makes the precise parallel between dancing and fighting that Robbins so insistently sought. Just like their dancing, says Anita, they fight as if they "need to get rid of something fast . . . too much feeling."

Tony arrives before Anita's exit, and María pleads for sympathy. Surprisingly, the Shark alpha female agrees, however reluctantly, to allow María to see Tony, but only for "fifteen minutes." Anita shows an understanding of María's feelings and enters into an unspoken alliance with the would-be lovers that leads to the traumatic "taunting" at the film's climax. This is the only scene where María, Tony, and Anita are seen close together, and it is notable that Anita is also wearing Jet colors: when she takes off her purple smock, there is a bright orange dress underneath—the only time in the movie Anita does not wear Shark colors. It is equally conspicuous that Tony's tones are shifting. When he arrives just after six o'clock, he is wearing a tan windbreaker with a visible purple lining and black jeans:

Shark colors. María, Anita, and Tony form a brief, tenuous alliance that allows Tony and María to imagine that their romance will survive and, as in the classical Hollywood musical, perhaps even resolve the social conflict. "She likes us!" says Tony, hopeful.

The bridal shop is the obvious lyrical setting for Tony and María's mock wedding, surrounded symbolically by their family and friends, in the form of the shop dummies. The mock wedding, their improvised vows, and the consummation duet "One Hand, One Heart" set up and justify their imminent sexual activity. The entire bridal shop sequence—from "I Feel Pretty" and the storefront to the mock wedding and "One Hand, One Heart"—constitute the last scenes in *West Side Story* that follow, to a certain extent, the conventions of the classical Hollywood "folk" musical. The entire sequence suggests that music can indeed resolve the conflicts that have thus far prevented the couple's happiness. But as we know, that is not the case in *West Side Story*.

The mock wedding begins with María and Tony setting up the dummies to represent characters from the movie, seen and unseen: Anita, Riff, María's parents, Tony's mother. They hold hands and kneel next to each other, in front of the camera, making the audience both witness and minister. They recite vows, traditional and improvised, surrounded by the dummies in a symmetrical composition behind them, a sign of harmony. As they say their vows, an unnatural ray of sunlight appears to "magically" preside over the scene at the top of the frame. The sun ray, described in Dunn's November 1960 progress report as "a gold ray . . . double exposed, coming from an offstage sky-light," was one of the special effects that had run into technical problems and was still in progress in mid-August 1961. It was evidently important for Wise's desired effect to add "magical," fantastic accents to most of the songs.[27] The improvised wedding thus seems to be a delicate illusion—like the "Tonight" duet—that can easily be shattered by reality (or realistic lighting). Also conspicuous in the shot is the shape of a cross seen high on a mock window, giving the heretical ceremony—recall that María is a devout Catholic— the look of a sacrament.

María and Tony naturally seal the act with a kiss and then proceed to sing "One Hand, One Heart." The simple number is filmed

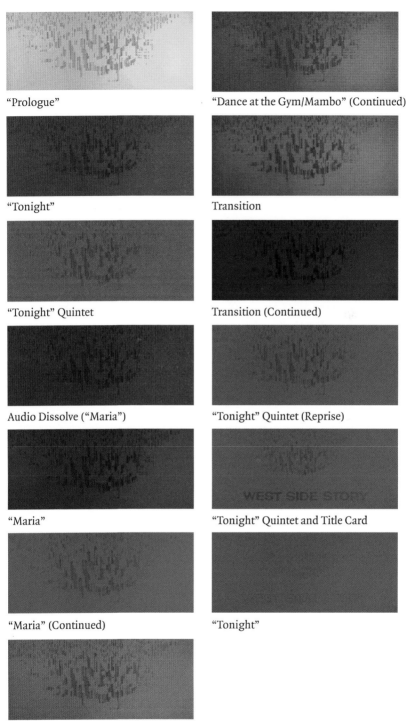

"Prologue"

"Dance at the Gym/Mambo" (Continued)

"Tonight"

Transition

"Tonight" Quintet

Transition (Continued)

Audio Dissolve ("Maria")

"Tonight" Quintet (Reprise)

"Maria"

"Tonight" Quintet and Title Card

"Maria" (Continued)

"Tonight"

"Dance at the Gym/Mambo"

©1961 Metro-Goldwyn-Mayer Studios Inc. All rights reserved.

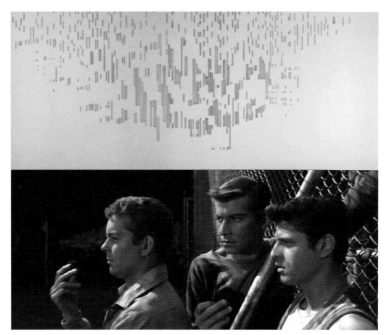

Overture and Jets' colors. ©1961 Metro-Goldwyn-Mayer Studios Inc. All rights reserved.

Overture and Sharks' colors. ©1961 Metro-Goldwyn-Mayer Studios Inc. All rights reserved.

Overture and "Dance at Gym/Mambo." ©1961 Metro-Goldwyn-Mayer Studios Inc. All rights reserved.

Overture and "Tonight" Quintet. ©1961 Metro-Goldwyn-Mayer Studios Inc. All rights reserved.

Bernardo and Riff at the Gym. ©1961 Metro-Goldwyn-Mayer Studios Inc. All rights reserved.

María and Tony at the Bridal Shop. ©1961 Metro-Goldwyn-Mayer Studios Inc. All rights reserved.

in four shots, with no camera movements, cutting classically from a medium shot to close-ups and back to a medium shot of the two actors. It has a peaceful, soothing quality, and it is the last time in the movie that we see María and Tony happy together, in contradiction of the song's promise, "Now it begins / Now it starts." Like the promise of escaping "Somewhere" later in the film, the quiet notes and passive look of "One Hand, One Heart" are dissonantly interrupted, derailed, by the reality of imminent violence. The shock created by the next scene, in fact, is particularly effective in the movie, since the editing and lighting design in the bridal shop contrast so sharply with the beginning of the "Tonight" quintet that follows.

"An Orange Sky": The "Tonight" Quintet and "The Rumble"

The quiet ending of "One Hand, One Heart," with its soft golden light and descending tones, is appropriately disrupted by the loud, high introductory notes of the "Tonight" quintet. The dim light of the sun ray is drowned in the shock cut to the reddish orange sun setting over the rooftops. Paradoxically, the shot is quite stylized, yet it indicates a return to the stark reality that María and Tony have momentarily left behind. Visually, the scene was designed by Dunn to show "an orange sky" and a "reddish stationary sun," a painted sunset shot by a tilting camera.[28] Aurally, the calm notes of the previous song are abruptly overtaken by the opening trumpet blast of the quintet. The entire sequence shifts between the Jets and the Sharks; Anita, Tony, and María are each in different settings, but the lighting and photographic effects sustain the motif of a slowly setting sun: dusk in New York City on a summer evening. Loud reds and oranges, trembling golds and yellows also evoke the emotions of the characters as each prepares for the night's events—a bit of mise-en-scène that melodramatically underscores the characters' different moods.

The Jets and the Sharks are first seen in an "angry" red light in an alley and on a rooftop, respectively—the spaces they command. Both gangs look directly into the camera in these shots, an uncommon practice in most fiction films but one that is often seen in the musical genre. In this case, however, the breaking of the fourth wall is aggressive; it looks like a challenge. By contrast, Anita is seen in a faint suggestion of a bedroom (originally imagined as a bath-room on the list of sets to be built) in dimmer red light with a dark, "romantic," nondescript background, against the silhouette of an elaborate brass headboard. She is barely dressed in a black silk slip and is putting on a pair of silk stockings, immodestly showing her thighs to the camera. The setting is conventionally "sexy" to match her mood as she sings about "getting her kicks" and Bernardo "hav-ing his way" tonight. Still, some of the movie lyrics were changed to be less suggestive.[29]

Meanwhile, Tony is leaning outside a window at Doc's store, also bathed in a cooler red light, longingly imagining his rendezvous with María later that evening. He sings a variation of the original lyrics of the "Tonight" duet to emphasize the anticipation. María is once again formally aligned with Tony, as she too is introduced by her window—always a symbol of desire—in identical, passionate red light. Like Tony, she sings her eager lyrics bathed in the apparent sunlight—in visible contrast to the gangs and Anita.

The changes to the lyrics are minor, but the different settings ren-der the sequence quite cinematic. Whereas in the play, spotlights highlight the characters in an otherwise entirely dark stage they all share, the movie adds clearly visible and different spaces for each. Also in the play, Tony is actually with the Jets during the strategic planning for the rumble; he is still playing the gangster role and is still attached to Riff to a certain extent. The movie places Tony in the more neutral candy store, removed from the Jets and aligned with María. As mentioned in chapter 1, the montage envisioned by Lehman included shots of Lieutenant Schrank and Officer Krupke in their patrol car, anxiously cruising the neighborhood in search of the imminent action. In fact, Schrank was supposed to "song-talk" a few lines during the montage—something about "clean out the gangs" and "stop the action . . . tonight," but evidently, this idea was not pursued.[30] Likewise, María's second stanza was shifted to immediately follow Tony's—a change from the play, where Riff and Tony sing together, briefly displacing María.

A final important element of the "Tonight" quintet's design comes in the second shot of María, who is now at the fire escape, as in the earlier "Tonight" duet. Also like the duet, she is framed in a similar special effects pattern and masked by soft purple diffused lighting. This slightly "unreal" treatment connects the two numbers visually.

The final sustained note of the song reviews the various settings and locations of each party, as the Jets and the Sharks walk in opposite directions toward each other: for the first time in the movie, they have slightly switched orientations. The final shot of the sequence dissolves melodramatically to a blood-red screen and fades into an extreme close-up of two attached diamonds of a chain-link fence, bathed in the red tint. The chain-link motif continues to represent the threat or certainty of violence, and nowhere is it more underscored or heavy-handed than in the transition between the quintet and the rumble.

The chain-link fence close-up widens to show a large segment of the fence and turns to natural colors, introducing the rumble site "under the highway" through the fence pattern. Bernardo is the first to arrive and enters from screen left, the Sharks' usual side. He is seen through the fence as well. The young men enter one by one, always emerging from their own side of the screen. The whole rumble set is surrounded by fences and hard cement walls, creating the sensation of a cage and literalizing the theme of being "trapped" throughout the movie. The set, designed by Boris Leven and built on stage 4 at the Goldwyn Studio, is beneath the ominous, bright red steel of the highway exit ramp, under which the gangs meet. Cinematographer Daniel Fapp uses the wide-screen composition here as effectively as in the reedited gym sequence, separating, stretching, and fanning out the gangs to opposite sides of the frame. Visible are the same "BOBBY" and "Lakers" graffiti seen earlier at the playground, suggesting that this territory has been the subject of gang strife in the past (and evidencing the need to cut production costs). The rumble is, of course, a repetition and another representation of the stylized dueling seen in the "Prologue," at the dance, and even during the "America" argument. Repetitions and dualities are common in the Hollywood musical genre, and they are generally intended to create a sense of familiarity for the spectator.[31] In West Side Story the motif that recurs most often is the duality and division between the gangs and the representation of those differences in wide-screen compositions and choreographed confrontations, as seen in the "Prologue," the free-for-all, the "Mambo," María and Tony's "love at first sight" shot, and "America." By contrast, compositions for the romantic, courtship, conciliatory, and "I want" numbers mostly range from medium long shots to close-ups, as in the courtship pas de deux and the "Tonight" duet.

As Ice and Bernardo get ready for the final conflict, Bernardo kneels down, says a prayer, and makes the sign of the cross. He refuses, however, to shake Ice's hand before the fight because this is "always done," and he rejects the hypocrisy of American "gracious living" and the protocol the Jets follow. Just as the "fair fight" is beginning, Tony suddenly arrives, jumping over a fence and yelling for everyone to stop. Tony makes a brief, sincere effort to stop the fight, claiming that there is nothing to fight about. Bernardo's provocation, however, soon reveals Tony's true nature: he finds himself making his hands into fists and assuming a fighting position; he is a gangbanger after all. Tony is then "taunted" by the others, foreshadowing the Jets' "taunting" of Anita barely two hours later. In defense of Tony, Riff loses control and attacks Bernardo, throwing a punch that starts the real fight. All previous agreements from the war council are tossed aside when switchblades are drawn simultaneously by Bernardo and Riff—twin motions occurring on opposite sides of the screen. The following close-up of Bernardo's blade was one of Dunn's special effects shots: a blinding flash of light reflecting off the blade for about a second, for dramatic detail. The censors objected to promotional lobby cards showing the switchblades too conspicuously, yet in the film, Bernardo's knife is the only object to get an extreme close-up.[32]

Obviously, things go wrong at the "rumble that is no rumble," and Riff dies first, at Bernardo's hand. It is treated almost like an accidental event: Riff charges Bernardo, blade in hand, and runs into Bernardo's ready knife. In his final gesture, Riff reaches out with his arm and hands the weapon to Tony. In a moment of blind rage, Tony knifes Bernardo in the abdomen, avenging his friend's death. Belts, chains, bricks, and other makeshift weapons suddenly appear in the men's hands, and the rumble, a new free-for-all, begins. The whole scene is covered in six shots and less than one minute of screen time, all in oblique Dutch angles for dramatic effect—the only such treatment in the movie. Soon police sirens can be heard approaching, and one by one, the Jets and Sharks disappear over the fences and walls, leaving the two dead bodies and Tony in the center of the frame. Tony cries out María's name, which no longer sounds like music or a prayer. Tony is last seen physically trapped between the concrete walls and chain-link fences, which finally take on the literal meaning they have thus far symbolized. Appearing out of the shadows, Anybodys leads Tony away. As in the play (this scene ends the first act), the sequence ends with the dead bodies in the center of the frame, overwhelmed by the ominous scenic design, the flash of "searchlights cutting into the darkness," and the angular perspective created by the underside of the highway ramp. Then, "a distant clock begins to boom."[33]

"No Sides, No Hostility": "Somewhere" and "Cool"

The sounds of the distant clock act as a bridge to the next setting: María is sitting on the rooftop in a light purple summer dress, dreamily waiting for Tony. Inexplicably, the clock booms only four times—even though it is supposed to be 10:00 PM—but the two scenes appear to be temporally connected. Whereas in the play this scene occurs in María's bedroom and is the setup for "I Feel Pretty," the movie's rearrangement retains the somber mood following the rumble. The rooftop provides a peaceful place for María to indulge her illusions. She is "enjoying the very last moments of pure happiness that she will ever know."[34] She revisits the courtship pas de deux she had with Tony at the dance—now, paradoxically, a solo—and swirls around the rooftop to a rearranged instrumental version of "Maria" in a promising crescendo. Her peace and exhilaration are interrupted by Chino's sudden arrival, and she briefly mistakes him for Tony in the dark doorway.[35] Noticing Chino's bruised, flustered face, she asks a question that is also an assertion: "You have been fighting Chino?" The following exchange (which several actresses performed when they tried out for the part) is the most dramatic scene for both Chino and María. He, disappointed and heartbroken by María's concern for Tony, angrily tells her, "He killed your brother!" She, desperately hopeful but unconvincing, responds,

"Chino, why do you lie to me!?" She runs after Chino, crying and screaming.

María winds up in her bedroom, where she immediately kneels in front of her makeshift altar to the Virgin Mary. Crossing herself, she begins a bilingual prayer to the Virgin: "*Santa María*, make it not be true, please make it not be true. *Madre de Dios*, I will do anything. Make me die! Only, please make it not be true. *Le soopliko* [sic]. *No puede ser.*" The Spanish lines were added in pencil in Wise's working script, some of it in phonetic spelling. The lines augment Laurents's original, since the book states only that she prays, "some of it in Spanish, some of it in English."[36] Outside in the hall, we hear a child confirm in Spanish, "*Mamá, Mamá Bernardo está muerto!*" In her moment of desperation, María (as well as the neighbors) reverts to her native language, belying her aspirations, stated only the night before, of becoming "a young lady of America." All illusions—romantic, social, and political—are broken upon hearing the news of the night's tragic events.

Tony's furtive entry through the window behind her triggers María's collapse and her acknowledgment of Tony's new identity. She strikes his chest as she screams at him: "killer killer killer killer." Tony's apology and his account of the chain of events momentarily sound logical: nobody meant for it to happen. Yet he wants María's forgiveness and intends to go directly to the police. Thus, the setup for the new "Somewhere" number is complete, with María and Tony alone in her bedroom, broken and desperate, making one last appeal in the movie's final—and saddest—"I want" song. Recall that in the play, "Somewhere" is a fantasy ballet scene in which Tony and María, a resurrected Riff and Bernardo, and all the Jets and Sharks and their girls appear on an empty, brightly lit stage—a "big white set." All are dressed in white or very light pastels, and they briefly live in a world of "space and air and sun" where there are "no sides, no hostility."[37] Robert Wise's and Stanley Scheuer's working scripts, with revisions up to 26 October 1960, still describe "Somewhere" as a "ballet" scripted by Lehman, in nearly identical terms to the original text. Lehman describes a world of "space, air, sun and friendship," adding that "it is a dream, a vision of a world that should have been, could have been, might have been."[38]

At the time of *West Side Story*, the "dream ballet" sequence was not unusual in either stage or film musicals. Examples include Rodgers and Hammerstein's *Oklahoma!* on stage (1943), Minnelli's *Yolanda and the Thief* (1945), the movie version of *Oklahoma!* (Fred Zinnemann, 1955), and the "Gotta Dance/Broadway Rhythm/Cyd Charisse" sequence in *Singin' in the Rain*, among many others. Evidently, at some point, Wise and Lehman decided to drop the dream ballet idea entirely. There are several plausible reasons for this decision. For one thing, the courtship pas de deux during the dance at the gym already serves the purpose of a dream ballet. More important, the movie was dangerously behind schedule and over budget, and a new sequence would have required new choreography, new costumes, and new sets. But there was also the issue of "mood": a dream ballet, with its lighter tone, would have been a distraction and a visual oddity, not to mention disrupting the tragic, dark tone of the movie's last forty-five minutes. Instead, Wise and Lehman rewrote the scene (as late as 29 December 1960), adopting a new, more realistic, and more tone-appropriate approach: the tragic "Somewhere" duet between María and Tony.[39]

Cinematographer Daniel Fapp lit the scene emphasizing an unrestrained, theatrical filter and gel colors in the background: blood red and Shark purple. The lighting and color design still allow that "not quite real" look, while delivering one of the movie's most "realistically" dramatic moments. "Somewhere" thus emerges as a new, but not quite, "I want" song. "I'll take you away," Tony promises, "where nothing can get to us, not anyone or anything." Then the bedroom setting suddenly acquires a "fantastic" look, with impossible pink, purple, orange, and blue light reflected through María's window and tinted glass doors. Even the lace curtains and bedspread soften the scene, stylized in a slightly soft focus, while Tony and María sing the poetically ironic lyrics, "There's a place for us." Momentarily appeased, Tony and María lie back on the bed, disappearing offscreen, while the camera tracks into the bright colors on the wall behind them.

Outside in the real world—in fact, in one of the downtown Los Angeles locations passing for New York City's West Sixty-Eighth Street—patrol cars are cruising the streets in search of answers and suspects. Hiding in a succession of alleys and rooftops, A-Rab finds Baby John (in what was originally the setup for "Gee, Officer Krupke" in the play). Teary-eyed and desperate, the two youngest members of the Jets console each other, confessing earnestly that they "wish it was yesterday." The gang gathers by the side of a building—presumably, a previously agreed on rendezvous point—in front of the sliding doors of a ground-level parking garage; in the background, a large, bright red cargo truck peers at them ominously through dead headlights. This is the new setting, setup, and narrative position of the "Cool" number. The context works as the Jets rearrange themselves under Ice's emerging leadership. Although Action had been Riff's lieutenant, in this new scene he is dangerously close to losing control, irrationally calling for retribution against the Sharks. But Ice takes over and calls for the gang to "cool." The action moves into the garage set, on stage 3 at Goldwyn, where a prophetic "No Exit" sign once again underscores the gang's situation. Early on, Lehman and Robbins had described the new setting (as opposed to the non-descript alley of the play) as a place where tensions could blow: "[a] garage [or] boiler room (any place that has a lid on and becomes a pressure cooker) and seems 'cool' to them." In these early conferences, Lehman and Robbins had also decided to make Diesel (appropriately renamed Ice—who is "cool") the heir apparent. Lehman describes the "Cool" number as "a frenetic DANCE in which the boys and girls release their emotions and learn how to get 'cool' under Ice's guidance."[40]

As the other gang members are losing control of their emotions and the situation, Ice gets their attention by flashing a truck's headlights at them—a mob of proverbial "deer in the headlights." The bright light shines directly into the camera, washing out the frame in one of Dunn's last special effects shots and blinding the audience, demanding their attention for the upcoming number. The choreography and lyrics are similar to the stage original. However, the setting better imparts the sense of entrapment, the need to get "cool," and the shift in the Jets' leadership from the hotheaded Action to the cool Ice. The headlights and bare overhead lightbulbs of the garage also infuse the number with a stark realistic tone that contrasts sharply with the melodramatic colors of "Somewhere." And even though the garage is closed and the Jets are "trapped" in it, it does not seem claustrophobic. Wise and Fapp employ various lenses, set-ups, and camera movements that open up the choreography.

This is arguably the Jets' signature music and dance number—their showstopper—what "America" is to the Sharks. Led by Ice, the Jets return to their distinctive finger snapping to keep the rhythm, like the Sharks' clapping and Spanish-influenced *taconeo* did in "America." The classic jazz score and arrangement highlight the cultural clash between the gangs, standing in direct opposition to the Latin breezes and instrumentation (including Afro-Caribbean percussion instruments like the güiro, marimba, and maracas) of the Sharks' parallel number. The finger snapping and hand clapping also work here as therapeutic practices, contrasting with the occasional bursts—accentuated by the loud, high notes of the score—of the slowly cooling Jets. One by one, Action, Baby John, A-Rab, and others blow up and calm down. The shots vary from wide angle to normal, sometimes revealing ceilings, floors, cars in the background, a back wall. Like the gym earlier, the closed setting expands to give the dancers space to move dramatically and energetically and to give the camera room to lead, follow, or join the actors' movements. Low-key lighting emphasizes shadows and contrast, while the car headlights create lens glare, giving the number an apparent "noir" quality, in keeping with the dark tone sustained after the "Tonight" quintet. Somewhere between "sweet" jazz and big band, the music and dancing reflect the Jets' mercurial emotions: a premature dénouement specific to the Jets that is much more necessary after the rumble than before the war council, where it occurs in the play.

By the end, the Jets are exhausted, sweaty, and out of breath but visibly relieved, "cool," and ready to reassemble as they plan how to "get by the cops" when the investigation into the deaths of Riff and Bernardo inevitably leads to them. As the Jets gather back on the street, Anybodys, who has been spying around "PR territory," brings them the news of Chino's intent to kill "that Polack" Tony. The Jets plan to find Tony and help him escape. Acknowledging Anybodys's contribution, Ice sends her to look for Tony "in and out of the shadows," a task she accepts with a grateful, dreamy, "Thanks, Daddy-O."[41] When the Jets disperse, Ice runs across the street in front of a car whose headlights, like in the garage minutes before, wash out the frame and momentarily blind the audience. On the sidewalk, Ice runs by a campaign poster for a political candidate in the upcoming election, reminding us of the context—summer of 1953. He also passes a doorway suspiciously bathed by a bright red light, possibly suggesting prostitution activity in the low-income neighborhood. As he runs by these objects, Ice barely misses Chino, who is "in the shadows" looking for Tony.

Te adoro, Anton": "A Boy Like That"/"I Have a Love," the "Taunting," and the Finale

The scene dissolves from Chino's angry, sweaty, menacing face to a low-angle shot of the fire escape outside María's bedroom—a reminder of the "Tonight" duet and of Tony and María's brief happiness. As far as the passage of time is concerned, it is possible that Tony and María were here together only twenty-four hours ago. The action returns to María's bedroom, where the lighting has mysteriously reverted to "normal." The scene now reveals the tinted glass doors that created the artificial bursts of colors bathing the lovers in the earlier scene. The lighting is now conspicuously "realistic," unobtrusive. Napping together in bed, it seems that María and Tony have "cooled" too, and the emotional, erotic energy symbolized by the previous lighting scheme is now out of place. The lovers' last moment of peace is interrupted by Anita's arrival.

Anita is visibly devastated after learning of Bernardo's death, but she seems ready to resume her protective role of the mourning María. She goes confidently to María's bedroom door—obviously a regular event—and is genuinely surprised to find it locked from the inside. In the bedroom, María now takes the leadership role, telling Tony to go and wait for her at Doc's store. After Tony exits out the window and onto the fire escape, María allows Anita into the bedroom. Anita's eyes scrutinize María from head to toe, her accusing gaze stopping around the navel: the sexual Anita is quickly aware of the new, sexual María. Pushing María aside, Anita goes directly to the window and sees Tony running away with Anybodys. In the play, Anita inspects the bed for evidence of sexual activity; in the movie, she just "knows," and María immediately acknowledges that she is right. "And you still don't know," cries Anita, pointing out the window where Tony has escaped. "He is one of them!"

"A Boy Like That" is Anita's angry appeal to María to "stick to [her] own kind" and abandon Tony. The scene, lit in slight low key, is edited with very few cuts and has an overly dramatic, nearly operatic (or operetta) tone that is dark and distinct, different from any other song in the score. The song starts as an "argument"—like the "Mambo" and "America" numbers—a recognizable pattern in the *West Side Story* structure. However, its tone is decidedly, perceptively tragic, in opposition to the energetic "Mambo" and the playful "America." Unlike the other "arguments" in the score (including the "Prologue"), "A Boy Like That" transitions directly into the conciliatory words and softer lyrical mood of "I Have a Love," which is initially María's response to Anita's reproach. In this second song—as in the bridal shop sequence—Anita again yields and agrees, however reluctantly and implausibly, to be María's ally in her romantic pursuits. "I Have a Love" ends in a duet: María and Anita not only make peace but also resolve their personal conflict—a function of singing and dancing in the classical musical that comes too late, and only to these two women, in *West Side Story*. Their final lines, sung together—"When love comes so strong / There is no right or wrong / Your love is your life"—characterize romantic love as something tragic, final, and fatal.

Anita, now aligned with María, reveals Chino's plan to kill Tony when Lieutenant Schrank arrives at the door. As always in *West Side Story*, reality interferes with the temporary comforts of a song. This time, it is the arrival of the Law, however ineffectual it may be, that brings the women back to the night's tragic events. So far, Schrank has not been able to prevent violence or bring order to his tumultuous beat. Like the Jets and the Sharks after the free-for-all and the war council, Anita and María resist Schrank's authority, stonewalling when he asks his questions. In response to Schrank's rude, invasive presence, Anita agrees to take a message to Tony, who is waiting for María at Doc's store. María eventually lies to Schrank about her knowledge of events at the rumble. Like the gangs earlier, the women are wary and distrustful and offer a united resistance to the policeman.

Meanwhile, the Jets have gathered at Doc's store, while Tony hides in the cellar. He is waiting for Doc to return with some money so that he and María can escape to the country, "somewhere." Doc is yet another reluctant ally who is genuinely concerned about the unfortunate couple's trajectory, announcing at the end of the "first act" that he is "frightened" for Tony and María. Anita arrives at the candy store bearing the message for Tony to wait for María, just as Action is warning the Jets to keep vigilant for "those stinkin' PRs." Recalling the Trumbull painting on the wall of the war council room and the mocking rendition of "My Country 'Tis of Thee," Anita's entry—with Action's words still resonating in the room—is underlined by a large poster of the US flag hanging behind Doc's counter—another essential symbol of America that the movie treats ironically. Incongruously, upon Anita's entrance, Gee-Tar (Tommy Abbot) begins to whistle "La Cucaracha," a traditional Spanish song made popular during the Mexican Revolution; this detail (not seen in the play) personifies the Jets as genuinely culturally insensitive.

After a tense moment of silence between the parties, the jukebox starts playing the "Mambo," announcing—as it did in its previous appearance during the dance at the gym—an imminent confrontation. The "Taunting" of Anita is arguably the movie's climax, and the "Mambo" helps raise the tension. The Jets hurl epithets and insults, some in Spanish, to the increasingly terrified Anita, whom they accuse of spying for Chino. She is called "pig" and "tramp" and "lyin' spic" as the Jets slowly but resolutely surround her. As in the earlier "taunting" of Bernardo in the "Prologue," the Jets occupy about two-thirds of the screen space; Baby John, Snowboy, Action, Mouthpiece, A-Rab, and Anybodys trap Anita, her back to the camera, in the remaining third of the frame. She is eventually surrounded by seven Jets and Anybodys, and with the US flag still conspicuous at the top right of the frame, the music suddenly turns into a faster arrangement of "America" as the taunting escalates to an attempted sexual assault. The irony is quite poignant, as Anita's innocent dream of assimilation—"OK by me in America"—turns into the nightmare of prejudice and sexual violence. When the "Taunting" takes its most sexually threatening turn, Anybodys quietly retreats to a corner and adopts a visibly worried, scared look. The only other woman in the room, Anybodys reacts like her true self: she too is terrified by the thought of gang rape. When the scene and the camera move from the counter to the sitting room below, we again see the Trumbull reproduction in the background, accentuating the irony of Anita's experience in a way that is largely absent from the stage play. Finally, Anita is forced down to the floor, and Baby John, carried by some of the others, is dropped on top of her: she will be raped.

Doc, the reluctant ally, arrives just in time to stop the mayhem— a poor man's deus ex machina who saves Anita from certain rape but cannot resolve the overarching conflict. Anita's blouse has been pulled below her shoulders, her skirt lifted over her thighs. She composes herself with an air of nervous dignity, but she too is now beyond redemption. Collecting her shawl and herself, she heads to the door and insults the Jets, recognizing that Bernardo "was right," a reference to the "America" argument. Indeed, the sentence is much more powerful in the movie, given the new, more politically effective "America" song. In her final vengeful act, Anita offers the false news that Chino has killed María in revenge for Tony's alienation of her affection. She calls Tony a "murderer" and uses the word "American" as if it were an insult.

The Jets disperse after a scolding from Doc. Down in the cellar, Doc reluctantly conveys the (false) news to Tony that María is dead. The dark, dank cellar presents an example of a symptomatic use of mise-en-scène. During the "Something's Coming" number, in the sunny, soft, colorful setting of his "I want" song, Tony is seen carrying cases of Coca-Cola into this very space. In fact, a stack of Coca-Cola stands directly next to the door as Tony exits and darts into the street, challenging Chino to kill him too. The setting is the same as for the "Something's Coming" number, but now it looks dark, ominous, even expressionistic, conveying Tony's current state of mind. All the soft colors and fabrics, the light breeze and sunny setting of the previous afternoon, have disappeared, along with Tony's illusions: nothing is coming, nothing good.

Outside, Tony goes around the building and into the playground, giving a complete tour of the neighborhood and definitively connecting its familiar spaces. He continues into a maze of chain-link fences, some of them containing only more fences. This constant

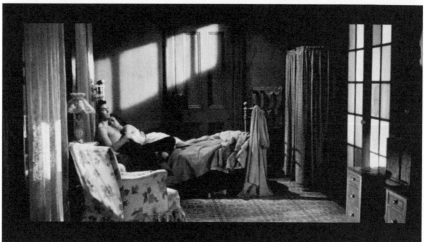

The lighting pattern in María's bedroom changes colors and intensity before and after their consummation to mimic the characters' emotions. ©1961 Metro-Goldwyn-Mayer Studios Inc. All rights reserved.

motif has been announcing the tragic end of this story since the Jets' introduction in the second scene of the movie: "No Exit" indeed. In one shot of Tony against the fence, we see the names "RIFF" and "ICE" graffitied in the background, trapped inside the cage-like pattern. Then Tony notices something offscreen, and the eye-line match reverse shot shows María, in a red dress and black shawl, behind three layers of chain-link fence. Tony is momentarily freed; he swings open a gate in front of him and runs offscreen toward María. Chino, gun in hand, appears in another shot behind yet another fence and fires, striking Tony in the chest. The gangs gather around María and Tony's final embrace, the fences more visible than ever. Under the dry light of a streetlamp, in the same handball court where he sang her name like "music," like "praying," Tony agonizes as María pleads, "Hold my hand and I'll take you there / Somehow / Somewhere." Tony dies in her arms, denying the most reliable convention of the classical musical: that conflict and sorrow and differences can, in fact, be sung away; that, as the singer Björk put it, "in a musical, nothing dreadful ever happens."[42]

Possessed of a sudden strength that is really hate, María resolutely walks up to Chino and, with a single gesture, takes possession of the gun. Her speech to the gangs about how "hate" killed the three victims sounds trite and contrived and probably worked better in the theatrical setting than in the movie: it is based on theater and Shakespeare, after all. Schrank arrives, too late again, and Chino quietly turns himself in. There is one moment of peace left for María: "*te adoro*, Anton," the last line of dialogue in the film and her sendoff to Tony (actually spoken by Marni Nixon). In a moment of apparent reconciliation, both Jets and Sharks help carry Tony's body to the patrol car, Baby John ceremoniously covers María's head with her shawl, and the gang members quietly file out. It is an implausible yet appropriately tragic theatrical finale. In the play, Laurents writes that this is "the same procession" seen in the "dream ballet" sequence, suggesting that the Jets and the Sharks have learned a lesson. But Lehman's screenplay is less optimistic. He writes that a few Jets and Sharks "have not joined the procession" and notes that they are "not yet ready . . . perhaps never will be ready" to give up their violent lifestyle.[43] In the last two shots of the movie, in fact, while

María walks expressionless behind Tony's body, the last remaining Jets and Sharks slowly walk away in opposite screen directions—Sharks exit to the left, Jets to the right, as is always the case in the film—leaving the conflict unresolved. The screen fades to black.

The words "The End" are followed by five minutes of end credits, as Wise warned his exhibitors. The contentious credits for Jerome Robbins appear as finally agreed on, after so much negotiation back in the spring of 1961. Besides his shared "Directed by Robert Wise and Jerome Robbins" credit, Robbins gets the extra card "Choreography by Jerome Robbins," appearing after "A Robert Wise Production" but before the cast. The credit sequence is accompanied by new instrumental arrangements of the main themes "Somewhere," "Tonight," "I Feel Pretty," another short phrase from "Somewhere," and "Maria." Paradoxically, even Bobby Tucker, Natalie Wood's vocal coach, gets onscreen credit, while "ghost singers" Marni Nixon, Betty Wand, and Jim Bryant do not. Robbins gets yet another separate credit when the acknowledgments for the original stage production appear at the end of the sequence, as is customary in the case of film versions of stage plays: "Play conceived, directed and choreographed by Jerome Robbins." Notably, the credits designed by Saul Bass are a mix of conventional screen titles optically superimposed on shots of neighborhood surfaces, randomly combined with handwritten graffiti, "Sharpie" marks, chalk, and even finger writing directly on motifs of the scenic design: brick walls, glass windows, unhinged doors, and traffic signs. Significantly, the word "End" is the last image seen in the film, on top of an "End of Street" traffic sign. The image is quite similar to and evocative of the last shot of Robert Wise's *Odds against Tomorrow* (1959), which he directed just before turning his attention to *West Side Story*. This subtle citation of his own work—a reference likely missed by many spectators—can arguably be interpreted as an authorial signature of sorts, like the "BOBBY" graffiti that appears twice in different settings in the film. It may be Wise's final claim to the film's authorship, which remained a rather prickly issue even after the departure of Jerome Robbins.

Of Wise's subsequent films, *The Sound of Music* (1965) was the most commercially successful, and many members of the creative team from *West Side Story* worked on it, among them Ernest Lehman,

Boris Leven, Saul Chaplin, and Irwin Kostal. Yet in 1978 Wise told an interviewer that West Side Story was "artistically" his personal favorite of all the films he had directed.[44] West Side Story is ultimately "Bobby's" film.

"Listen to Me, and Hear Me": Some Notes on Music and Design

As I have argued, the sets, costumes, narrative structure, color, cinematography, special effects, visual motifs, and overall mise-en-scène of West Side Story have a visual flair and a logical design. Musically, the new elements of the score composed by Leonard Bernstein and the orchestrations by Sid Ramin and Irwin Kostal were also coordinated with the film's visual patterns, creating even more complex relationships between image and music than may first be apparent to the eyes and ears. Bernstein's notoriously difficult score incorporates compound time signatures, polyrhythms, juxtaposing melodic lines, harmonies, tritones, and repetitions that are woven into the movie's pictorial and formal elements.[45]

Bernstein's new twenty-two-page "Overture" for the movie, dated 29 March 1961, offers a musical map, or forecast, of the rest of the film, as overtures always do.[46] It contains a revue of the major themes from the film, including the "Prologue," "Tonight," "Maria," and "Dance at the Gym," and it ends with a repetition of various phrases from the "Tonight" quintet. The color selections onscreen coincide with each song in the "Overture," and these accent colors are revisited as each song appears over the course of the film.

Another notable characteristic of this musical selection is the meter in which each song is composed. Meter, in music as in poetry, refers to the organization of the piece into measures—or bars—that appear in a regularly repeated pattern, creating bars of stressed or unstressed beats. The "Prologue" has a tempo defined as l'istesso, meaning that the beat remains constant when the meter changes. It has a 6/8 time signature that changes to a 2/4 time signature, creating a compound duple meter. Thus, the measures are divided into what the listener perceives to be groups of two beats. In the "Overture," the first segment of music heard is the "Tonight" quintet, which has a fast, rhythmic tempo conducted in common times of

4/4, 2/4, and 3/8, with a cut time of 2/2 when the melody makes its appearance. This too creates a sense of two-beat groupings that follow the lyrics "To-night, to-night." Next in the "Overture" are "Maria," in a cut time 2/2; the "Mambo," in 2/4; and then a reprise of the "Tonight" quintet. Most of these have tempo markings of a quarter note, equal to or greater than 120 beats per minute. The sole exception is "Maria," which is marked "*moderato con anima*," or "lively."[47] While each song appears to have distinct qualities because of the meter markings and conducting directions, the songs meld together as the "Overture" transitions seamlessly through the different musical movements, allowing the disharmonies to coexist.

Yet another example of Bernstein's innovations in the *West Side Story* score is the use of a discordant tritone as a musical motif. A tritone is a musical device consisting of a three-note interval, such as going from C to F sharp, creating a dissonant tone. This atonal sound is mediated by the final third note, which resolves the original dissonance. The ending notes of the film's "Overture," however, are the first two unresolved notes of a tritone; they lack the final "passing" tone that would resolve the dissonance created by the first interval. This leaves the "Overture" with an unresolved ending—a remaining conflict, so to speak. Arguably, this characteristic, specific to the film's "Overture," is a forewarning of the film's own conclusion, which leaves the major gang conflicts unresolved.

The revue of musical themes in the "Overture" also establishes the music's correlation with costumes and mise-en-scènes. The Sharks are often in deep purples, and the Jets are in oranges and mustards, but by the time of María and Tony's mock wedding scene, the lining of Tony's jacket has turned Shark purple, and María is wearing Jet yellow and orange. This serves in part to establish the convention of the "personality dissolve," wherein the main couple's apparent conflicts are gradually resolved to ensure their successful coupling by the film's end. This convention, as we have seen, is ultimately subverted in *West Side Story*.

Besides the "Overture," many of the film's other musical numbers show parallels among music, color, and mise-en-scène. For illustration purposes, I will briefly readdress the design of "Maria," which incorporates the personality dissolve, color coordination for narrative purposes, and the dangerous tritone, which Bernstein was so fond of in the *West Side Story* score.[48] As described earlier, "Maria" begins in the gym when Tony, upon learning the name of his newfound object of desire, declares it, in sing-talk, "the most beautiful sound I ever heard." Tony's walk during the first few lines of the song are accompanied by an inconspicuous, almost imperceptible change in the background, which dissolves from the gym's predominantly ocher and reddish tones to the notoriously artificial purple and magenta sky at dusk. This background color change announces and affirms the personality dissolve, as Tony is gradually leaving behind his Jet persona and acquiring María's Shark hues, en route to a successful coupling. The color change occurs precisely when Tony first "sings" the word "Maria," with an accompanying swell in the musical score, illustrating his personal change. In short, the music, lyrics, and visuals are exactly coordinated to underscore the narrative element: the man is in love. The audio dissolve and personality dissolve are both graphically exemplified in the musical score.

Significantly, the devilish tritone is used in this musical arrangement as well, as the word "Ma-ri-a" is broken down into the three notes of the discordant interval. As mentioned earlier, this interval is exemplary of musical disharmony, and for centuries, it was practically taboo for composers. In fact, the Catholic Church forbade the use of the tritone in medieval times, believing it to be the work of the devil because it denied God's harmony: it was called *Diabolus in musica*.[49] Arguably, the harsh, jarring tone of this interval makes the listener apprehensive and uneasy—an effect that violates the song's purpose as a courtship serenade. Instead, at least to the knowledgeable, the tritone in "Maria" takes on the quality of a warning. In fact, police sirens in Europe and the United States in the 1950s used a similar tritone.

This analysis of the "Overture" and "Maria" is intended to illustrate that the visual style sought by Robert Wise, Jerome Robbins, and the rest of the creative team of *West Side Story* was concerned not only with the specifics of mise-en-scène, cinematography, and other filmic components but also with the alignment of musical elements within that particular design. In addition to the "Overture," Bernstein's score included new musical phrases and cues composed between the spring of 1960 and the summer of 1961, such as "extensions" to the "Tonight" quintet; a new ending for the "Tonight" duet; the "I Feel Pretty" entr'acte; a "Kid's song" (never finished) to introduce A-Rab, Baby John, and Anybodys as childish characters; and all sorts of "cues" and "inserts" typical of a dramatic movie musical score.[50] All the music, whether new or reorchestrated by Ramin and Kostal, is an integral part of the film's overall effect vis-à-vis color, editing, cinematography, special effects, and even costume design. Besides looking at or watching *West Side Story*, the movie seems to be begging its audience, like María pleads with Tony, "Listen to me, and hear me."

Along with its revisionist approach, political commentary, and social satire, these visual and aural elements make the movie experience of *West Side Story* richer, more provocative, more progressive within its genre, and politically more daring not only than its original source material but also than most other musical films of the late classical era. In the last chapter, I provide more detailed examples of how the political and social commentary of *West Side Story* sometimes subtly, sometimes openly subverts conventions of the musical genre by presenting a demonstrably more radical message than many critics observed or dared to admit.

4 "Long, Long Runs":
Assessing *West Side Story*

 In their correspondence during the spring of 1962, as *West Side Story* was gathering mostly superlative reviews, receiving eleven Oscar nominations, and making box-office history, Robert Wise and Jerome Robbins set aside their differences and extended their respective olive branches. They wished each other good luck at the Oscars and with their current projects and optimistically predicted great success for their first and only collaboration. "In view of the way the picture has been received," Wise wrote, "I feel we both can be proud of our contributions to it." He signed off with an enthusiastic postscript reporting that the movie's openings in major European capitals (Paris, Brussels, Amsterdam, and Stockholm) had been "just sensational" and that "long, long runs" were "predicted for each engagement."[1] The excitement was justified, for the trajectory of *West Side Story* from stage to screen had not been particularly smooth. The relationship between the two directors had been contentious at best, leading to the firing of Robbins and the ensuing screen credits dispute involving agents and lawyers on both sides.

Furthermore, controversy over lyrics and suggestive content sometimes interfered with the production's progress. Rewrites and revisions were mandated and made through the last day of shooting and the final stages of editing. For the most part, the writers, Wise and Lehman in particular, accepted the script changes suggested by the censors. The film was first shown to the censorship committee, composed of Eugene Dougherty, Albert Van Schmus, and Jack Vizzard, on 12 April 1961. On 17 April Geoffrey M. Shurlock of the Motion Picture Association of America informed Wise that the board had found some of the lyrics from "Gee, Officer Krupke" "offensive" and "in bad taste." Shurlock argued that the movie was "one of the most outstanding pictures to come out of Hollywood this, or any other year" and insinuated that the song's references to "social disease" were inappropriate in light of the film's "superb good taste."[2] On this point, the writers disagreed, and the offensive lyrics were not eliminated. On 25 April 1961 the movie received approval from the Motion Picture Association of America and the Production Code Administration.[3]

The cut of the film presented to the censorship board ran 12,870 feet, or about 143 minutes. Opening and end credits, as well as various special effects shots, were still in progress, accounting for the longer final running time of 151 minutes. In its report, under "Significant Story Elements," the board checked the box for a "racial" angle. In the "Portrayal of Professions" section, Lieutenant Schrank was marked as a "minor" role and "unsympathetic," but with a "strong" characterization. In the "Portrayal of Races and Nationals" section, the board deemed the "prominent" Puerto Rican characters María and Anita "sympathetic" and Bernardo and Chino "sympathetic & unsympathetic," respectively. All the "Puerto Ricans" were noted to have "strong" characterizations. In terms of the description and treatment of crime, the board said the picture showed "murder" by shooting and knifing, and it labeled the two major fights "free-for-alls," just as the writers had defined them. "Violence" and "Prayer by a laywoman" were checked as miscellaneous but significant "sociological factors." Surprisingly, the censors marked "No" on the questions of whether the film showed or "indicated" elements of "illicit sex," "seduction," and "rape."[4] Although María and Tony's lovemaking occurs offscreen, and the "taunting" of Anita stops short of gang rape, it is arguable that they constitute the objectionable elements of "illicit sex" and "rape." Regardless of concerns about bad taste in the lyrics, the representation of violence, or the implication of sexual activity, reviews and box-office receipts soon indicated that West Side Story was destined to be a phenomenon.

"A Triumphant Work of Art": Contemporary Reviews

After previews in the summer of 1961, United Artists and the Mirisch Corporation planned to release *West Side Story* as a "road-show" attraction. This practice, designed for certain "prestige" pictures, allowed a film to be rolled out gradually in major cities and venues, with limited engagements and higher ticket prices, programmed intermissions, printed brochures, and only a handful of shows per week. (In this case, inclusion or exclusion of the much-discussed intermission would be left to the discretion of the road-show exhibitors.) At a cost of approximately $6,000 per wide-screen color print, *West Side Story* was a particularly expensive investment for both UA and the exhibitors. A special clause in all exhibition contracts, both domestic and foreign, required theater owners to agree to periodic inspections of the prints as well as all projection and sound reproduction equipment. Special 70mm Panavision lenses were ordered, and new equipment was installed in several theaters, including New York's Rivoli and Hollywood's Grauman's Chinese. If the film was going to be an event, Wise demanded that it have "high-quality" picture and sound.[5]

On 23 August 1961, while the film was still awaiting final certification from the Production Code Administration, Mirisch and United Artists announced that *West Side Story* would begin its road-show tour on 18 October. By that date, advance sales were already the largest "ever racked up . . . so far ahead of opening dates." Harold Mirisch and Arnold Picker, an executive vice president at UA, made the announcement during a press conference at UA headquarters. According to Mirisch and Picker, sales amounted to $250,000, with nearly half of that amount presold at the Rivoli Theatre in New York City, site of the world premiere. First-run theaters in Philadelphia, Washington, Los Angeles, and Boston completed the tally, with openings projected between early November and mid-December. The executives also claimed that *West Side Story* had been the subject of "the most extensive promotional campaign" ever designed for such an attraction, with publicity beginning back in August 1960. The trade journal *Film Daily* reported on 24 August that a special advertising budget of $1 million had been approved to flood radio and television markets. The distributors also planned to appeal to youth groups

and organizations throughout the country by direct mail, in anticipation of high degrees of interest among that demographic.[6] An album of the movie's songs and a selection of singles were released in
early September by Columbia Records as part of the "extensive campaign" to promote the film, specifically targeting the radio-listening,
record-buying youth market.[7] The album was a *Billboard* hit and won
the Grammy Award for best motion picture recording in 1962.

Special press preview screenings took place in Los Angeles during the second week of September 1961, leading to overwhelmingly
but not unanimously positive reviews. Industry observer and com-
mentator Stanley Skolsky of *Hollywood Citizen News* wrote on 15 September that the movie was "very good, but not great," while Hedda
Hopper of the *Los Angeles Times* declared it "a minor atomic bomb"
and a "triumph for the brothers Mirisch."[8] On 22 September the *Hollywood Reporter* headline read, "'West Side Story' Great Film Work."
Reviewer James Powers praised the joint direction in particular.
"The film musical, the one dramatic form that is purely American
and purely Hollywood," Powers emphasized, "has never been done
better." Mandel Herbstman of *Film Daily* wrote on 27 September that
the film was "brilliant" and had the "mark of commercial success."
The influential trade journal *Variety* ran a detailed critique of the film
by Dennis Harvey, proclaiming it "a beautifully mounted, impressive . . . and violent musical," as well as "powerful and sometimes
fascinating." Harvey also wrote that the movie was "technically superb," highlighting elements of mise-en-scène, color, and camera
as "dazzling" and "thrilling." He made special mention of Robbins's choreography, calling it "probably . . . the most spectacular
ever devised" for a motion picture, and he was relieved that although
the film "preached" about the evils of juvenile delinquency, it was
not a "message" film. A second review in the *Hollywood Reporter* by
Jim Heneghan came out on 2 October; he declared the film "technically flawless" and "artistically magnificent" and praised it as a
"moral play with no petty, mundane message." On 4 October *Motion
Picture Herald* named it "big, rich, lush" and "pulsing with youth and
vitality," while blaming Shakespeare for its "sentimentality" flaws.

Praise for the film's technical achievement was also common.
Frank Leyendecker's 4 October review in *Boxoffice* singled out Daniel

Fapp and the film's camera work and cinematography as "magnificent and breath-taking...stunning," favorably contrasting the movie's look to the "drab, sketchy" stage design. Leyendecker praised Natalie Wood's performance as "remarkably good" but belittled her dancing as "a few simple steps"; he also mentioned Marni Nixon by name as María's singing voice. Jack Holland of Limelight dedicated his entire 5 October commentary on the film to Fapp's cinematography, which he called "a real advance in camera technique." Holland pointed out that in West Side Story the camera takes on "new scope, new importance." Employing some technical language, Holland argued that the use of perspective, hazy backgrounds, and camera movements had helped "penetrate" characters' emotions and create new expressive effects. He concluded by stating that Fapp's cinematography had made his experience of watching West Side Story "like seeing a motion picture for the first time." Famously, in his 19 October review in the New York Times, the day after the world premiere at the Rivoli, mercurial critic Bosley Crowther called West Side Story, in language appropriate for advertising copy, "nothing short of a cinema masterpiece." He described the film as achieving "an artistic whole" and was particularly affected by the way the wide-screen Panavision 70 cinematography had "reconstructed" the theatrical source into "a true sense-experience." Renowned critic Paul V. Beckley of the New York Herald Tribune praised the film as "the best of its breed," ventured that it was "five years ahead of its time," and judged that the makers of West Side Story had made history.

Arthur Knight—film historian, former curator at the Museum of Modern Art (MoMA), author of the popular 1957 film textbook The Liveliest Art, and critic for the Saturday Review—wrote the most erudite review by any contemporary critic that I have come across. Knight had visited the film's New York locations and seen a camera rehearsal of a street number in February 1960, when Wise, Robbins, and Saul Chaplin were still scouting locations and testing actors in the city, and he was probably acquainted with Robbins through New York theatrical circles. In his critique, published in the 14 October Saturday Review, Knight compared the film's visual style to the Manhattan scenes by noted artist and photographer Benjamin Shahn and named it "a triumphant work of art" precisely because of its effective blending of realist and theatrical techniques with "real and seemingly real" settings. He remarked on the way the dances and camera work created "patterns that shape, dissolve, and regroup," commenting on the intricacies of framing and angles of vision. Adding dramatic authority, Knight observed how the dances and musical numbers contributed to the narrative structure, and he looked favorably on Ernest Lehman's rearrangement of the song order, specifically "Officer Krupke" and "Cool." Like Holland, Knight singled out Fapp's color cinematography, and he mentioned Saul Bass and Boris Leven by name, giving them shared credit for making the movie "as pictorially exciting as it is musically and dramatically."[9] Knight's final assessment was characteristically sharp and provocative: "Beyond any individual credits, there is a sense of dedication in 'West Side Story' that is all too rare in American pictures. It refuses to compromise, to make it easier for some nice old ladies in Dubuque to understand, or for some superpatriots in California to stomach." With his potential insults to the sensibilities of middle-American audiences and "superpatriots," Knight was one of the few critics who saw past the moralizing simplicity of the film's superficial stand on juvenile delinquency and speculated about its political sting. Knight's closing verdict was that the movie had not only succeeded; it had "exceeded" the original material.

Many other publications both big and small, such as *Harrison's Report*, *Cue*, *Show Business*, the Catholic journal *Commonweal*, the Catholic weekly *Our Sunday Visitor*, *Dance*, and *Life*, gave the film generally favorable reviews in the weeks and months following its release, although most found Richard Beymer's Tony weak or unconvincing. Other important critics included the *New Republic*'s Stanley Kauffmann, whose 23 October review called *West Side Story* "the best film musical ever made," despite its flaws in construction. He called the dialogue "pedestrian" and the premise of the story "utterly false." Significantly, while acknowledging that Robbins did not direct much of the film, Kauffmann gave him most of the credit for the "alchemy" that had turned the movie into "an even finer art" than its source; he called Wise "uncommonly qualified." Kauffmann also reported, incorrectly, that Wise had "replaced" Robbins as director.

Yet another Catholic weekly, the Jesuit magazine *America*, published a review by Moira Walsh on 28 October. She wrote that the film was one of "extraordinary power and beauty and impact," and "despite its faults," she labeled it "a brilliant film musical." Walsh was one of several critics who blamed Shakespeare for the lead characters' lack of depth, and she singled out "America" and "Gee, Officer Krupke" for a "pungency and satiric bite seldom found in the popular arts." Walsh stopped short of giving the film the Catholic publication's highest score; she was worried about the implications of sexuality, the absence of parental figures, and the "hateful" depiction of Lieutenant Schrank. She gave *West Side Story* the National Legion of Decency's rating of A-III, "suitable for adults only."

Not all critics were as kind, or as polite, as Walsh. Notorious negative reviews included the one by the influential Pauline Kael, published in *Film Quarterly* in 1962. She famously called the movie "frenzied hokum ... hyped up, slam bang"; she referred to the musical score as "distorted sounds" and dismissed the film as "a piece of cinematic technology." The critic for the *New Yorker* described the film, in a 21 October review, as "very long, very loud, and very brightly colored ... gigantic." Objecting to the "discrepancy" between stylized dance settings and naturalistic settings, the writer virtually accused Arthur Laurents of not having read Shakespeare and had only minimal praise for Daniel Fapp and Jerome Robbins, naming them the show's "stars." The *Newsweek* review of 23 October, under the dramatic title "Tragedy in Overdrive," accused the filmmakers of being out of control and claimed that the film went "full throttle" when the story called for restraint. The reviewer called Robbins's choreography "original and vivid" and Leonard Bernstein's score, paradoxically, "subtle." The writer then veered off course into a gossip-style feature "about the star," Natalie Wood, speculating about her separation from Robert Wagner, her imminent breakthrough, and her smoking on the set. The columnist concluded that with the release of *Splendor in the Grass* and *West Side Story* within a week of each other, Wood would soon be "the brightest young talent in Hollywood."

In his review for *Esquire* in early 1962, Dwight MacDonald began with the disclaimer that although many of his colleagues, "even the normally perceptive Stanley Kauffmann," had given *West Side Story* "terrific and colossal" notices, he begged to differ. He described the plot as "romantic schmaltz," Bernstein's score as an incongruous "pastiche" of better composers, the lyrics as simple and repetitive, and the social message of the film as "dishonest." Furthermore, as other critics had pointed out, MacDonald found many details of the plot unrealistic at best and totally implausible at worst. He concluded that the film was artistically flawed as well, failing to properly "modulate between stylization and realism." Like many before him, MacDonald praised the choreography but felt it was out of place and "discordant" within the film's shifting realistic and stylized moods. In his opinion, the filmmakers, in wanting to "have it both ways," had failed.[10]

On balance, the contemporary reviews were decidedly positive, and the commercial success of the film was historic.

"Unprecedented Enthusiasm": Box Office and Accolades

On 26 October 1961 the *Hollywood Reporter* cited "unprecedented enthusiasm" at the Rivoli, where the film was reportedly drawing "double lines" at the box office and selling a record number of advance tickets by mail, reaching all the way to April 1962. After the "extraordinary" opening in New York, United Artists decided to accelerate the rate of release, speeding up opening dates, expanding the number of domestic theaters, and exporting the movie to foreign markets earlier than previously planned.[11] Back in August, Wise had determined that the foreign release of *West Side Story* would be accompanied by subtitled song lyrics, in contrast to the frequent practice of letting the songs run in English or cutting out the musical numbers due to language barriers and technical difficulties. Accordingly, UA contracts with foreign exhibitors insisted that the picture run complete and uncut. On 4 August *Daily Variety* announced that Wise's decision marked "the first time" subtitles would be used for the translation of lyrics, constituting "a milestone" in the foreign release of musical films.[12] It was a gamble, since it was generally believed that language barriers were partly responsible for the comparatively modest box-office receipts for Hollywood musicals in foreign countries. The bet paid off, however, as the numbers from abroad came in through the winter and spring of 1962.

West Side Story opened in Japan, Brazil, Italy, and Sweden between

December 1961 and February 1962, and it had a gala premiere in London's Odeon Theatre in Leicester Square on 27 February. Robert Wise, on a press tour for the European openings, personally inspected the projection and sound equipment at the Odeon and determined it to be "excellent."[13] Her Majesty Queen Elizabeth II was in attendance, as well as members of Parliament, lords, reporters, actors (among them Russ Tamblyn, Peter Sellers, Yul Brynner, and Leslie Caron), and other celebrities. According to one report, the critics gave the movie "a bum rap," flippantly referring to it as "Love among the Switch Blades," and were distracted by the unseasonable snow and the queen's presence.[14]

Nevertheless, on 27 March *Daily Variety* broke the news that *West Side Story* was already being touted as "the strongest box-office hit in United Artists' history" in many overseas markets. Calling the film "as American and as musical as they come," the anonymous staff writer pointed out that although Hollywood films typically fared well in foreign markets, American musicals had been "dying" overseas. *West Side Story* was reversing that trend. Also notable was that the film was being publicized under its original English title and with "no dubbing (titles only)" in all its foreign engagements. Arnold Picker of United Artists, according to *Daily Variety*, was having "difficulty" believing the figures and refused to offer further projections. Picker hinted, however, that marketing the film to younger audiences was paying off, particularly by bringing together "the younger generation and the oldest story [in] the world." A feature in the *Hollywood Reporter* on the same day noted that *West Side Story*, in its thirteenth week of release in Japan, was the "biggest grosser of all films, in all languages, ever released" in that country. Long engagements were expected, and record-breaking advance sales had been tallied in Tokyo, London, Paris, Stockholm (where one particular theater could not handle the volume), Brussels, and Amsterdam. The *Reporter* also pointed out the rarity of an American musical, with subtitled lyrics, delivering such an "extraordinary" performance and even went so far as to declare the movie "the first American musical to achieve blockbuster success in the non-English speaking world."[15]

In October 1962 Rita Moreno went to Japan on a promotional tour for the film. Upon her return, she told the *Los Angeles Times* that the film's setting and racial differences were lost on the Japanese audience, yet they saw it as a "tuneful musical based on hopes of two young people." Thus, Moreno philosophized, the younger audiences abroad were "seeing the beauty" beyond the "squalor" of the film's setting.[16] Whether international audiences were seeing the film differently or not, they embraced it enthusiastically, bestowing accolades and storming the box office for several years. In June 1963 in Helsinki, Finland, the Filmiaura Society gave *West Side Story* a special honorary Jussi Award in the best foreign film category. In France it won the *Victoires du Cinéma Français* prize as the best foreign-language film of 1962, based on a national poll of movie fans.[17] In Great Britain it was nominated for the BAFTA award as best film "from any source." Even in the Soviet Union, where *West Side Story* was shown at the Moscow Film Festival on 7 July 1963, an anonymous reviewer in the youth-oriented *Komsomolskaya Pravda* demurely praised the film as presenting "a great theme in an interesting, artistic form."[18]

During the previews and the first months of its release, leading to the awards season of 1961–1962, Robert Wise and company received hundreds of congratulatory letters at the Mirisch offices from enthusiastic fans, literati, professional peers, actors, and hopefuls. Henry Grunwald, future managing editor of *Time* magazine, wrote to Wise in August 1961 to say that he thought the film was better than the original stage show, and UA records executive Harry Goldstein called it "one of the greats."[19] Doris Daniels Kaufman, who was related to Leonard Bernstein, wrote to Wise that she thought the movie was "great"; Harold Mirisch surmised this was Bernstein's way of passing on his own opinion indirectly.[20]

Oscar-winning director Fred Zinnemann sent a congratulatory note, warmly addressed to "Bobby," dated 14 September. Robert Aldrich, who was in Rome directing *The Last Days of Sodom and Gomorrah*, wrote in an ambiguous telegram to Wise that *West Side Story* was "a wonderful, wonderful picture. The first thirty minutes are perhaps the best movie it's ever [been] my pleasure and honor to watch, and the last almost as good." On 18 September Richard Beymer sent a telegram that included an apparent jab at Robbins, simply stating that the movie was "absolutely wise." Bit player Maria Jimenez, who played Teresita in the movie, thanked Wise for the opportunity and asked him to write her a letter of recommendation. Carole D'Andrea, who played Velma onstage and in the film, also thanked Wise for the experience in a handwritten note and signed it with Velma's characteristic exclamation, "Ooblee-oo." Actor Pat Colby, a bit player in movies and occasional guest on *The Andy Griffith Show*, wrote to ask for a part in Wise's next film, *Two for the Seesaw*. Novelist and screenwriter Leon Uris, whose *Exodus* had recently been adapted by Otto Preminger into an epic film, wrote to Wise in January 1962 that *West Side Story* was "the greatest motion picture I have ever seen. I really don't know what else I can say or add to that." Even former first lady Eleanor Roosevelt wrote to Wise directly at one point, asking him to consider a benefit premiere for an antibigotry teen organization she mentored. As the awards season approached in the winter and early spring of 1962, the pace of these congratulatory notes, telegrams, and letters became nearly frantic, numbering in the hundreds. Yet another note from Zinnemann came with the Academy Awards nominations. On a piece of yellow cardboard dated 12 February, Zinnemann scribbled, in black and red marker, "CONGRATULATIONS."[21]

To court Academy voters, *West Side Story* had its West Coast gala premiere at Hollywood's Grauman's Chinese Theater on 13 December 1961. Nine days earlier, as part of the publicity storm, Natalie Wood had become the 136th celebrity to leave her footprint and handprint "cemented" in the theater's famous forecourt.[22] One thousand people, including all the film's principals and the Hollywood elite, attended the premiere, which was a benefit for the Women's Guild of Cedars of Lebanon–Mount Sinai Hospitals. Rubbing elbows with the Mirisch brothers were Sammy Davis Jr. and May Britt, Ernie Kovacs and Edie Adams, Audrey Hepburn and Mel Ferrer, and Dean and Jean Martin. The benefit reportedly netted more than $100,000.[23]

Over the course of the awards season, the film was nominated for almost every major honor given by critics' polls, religious organizations, social clubs, and professional guilds. Among them were the Gold Owl given by *Playboy's Show Business Illustrated*, with a note from Hugh Hefner himself; a commendation by the Motion Picture Arts Club of Flushing, New York; the Institute of High Fidelity Manufacturers title for "Outstanding Presentation of a Motion

Picture"; the "Blue Ribbon" award from *Boxoffice* magazine; and best picture, technical, and artistic prizes from organizations such as the National Screen Council, the Screen Directors Guild, the Producers Guild of America, the Motion Picture Sound Editors, and the Japan Press Club. It was also nominated for five Golden Globes and eleven Oscars, winning three and ten, respectively.

At the Academy Awards ceremony on 9 April 1962, Ernest Lehman was the only *West Side Story* nominee to go home empty-handed, losing to Abby Mann for *Judgment at Nuremberg*. Oscars went to the entire principal creative team: Robert Wise for producing and directing, Jerome Robbins for codirecting, Daniel Fapp for cinematography, Boris Leven for production design, Thomas Stanford for film editing, and Irene Sharaff for costumes. Awards also went to the music scoring team of Saul Chaplin, Johnny Green, Irwin Kostal, and Sid Ramin and to the sound technicians of the TODD-AO and Samuel Goldwyn Studios team. Outside the Santa Monica Civic Auditorium, a crowd of teenagers loudly cheered for *West Side Story* and waved homemade banners and posters reading "Win 'Em West Side Story." Besides his codirecting award, shared with Wise, Jerome Robbins was given a "special" Oscar for achievement in choreography. The *West Side Story* Oscars "sweep," which included wins for Rita Moreno and George Chakiris, upset some Academy voters and industry analysts. Some critics had speculated that Judy Garland and Montgomery Clift, bigger stars in more dramatic roles, would win in the supporting categories for Stanley Kramer's *Judgment at Nuremberg*, considered a more serious drama. The final verdict came on 1 August when *Boxoffice* reported that *West Side Story*, which had been named "Best Picture" of 1961 by the New York Film Critics Circle, was the only commercial release of the year that had also made nine out of nine "ten best" lists, including the National Board of Review and the "seven New York daily" newspapers. *Judgment at Nuremberg* came in second, with seven "top ten" mentions.[24]

Perhaps more important, the film's success with critics and Academy voters may have ushered in a new trend in the history of the Oscars. *New York Times* reporter Murray Schumach speculated on 15 April that *West Side Story*'s Oscar sweep "cheerfully" predicted the beginning of a new era for independent productions: the big "Oscar

Bait" films of the major studios were no longer sure tickets to the Academy Awards ceremony. Schumach noted that the best picture winner and all the other best picture nominees—*Judgment at Nuremberg, The Hustler, The Guns of Navarone,* and *Fanny*—had been shepherded by independent producers. Schumach argued that the 1961 Oscar race proved that "the basic considerations [were] now artistic freedom and the subject of the movie."[25] While the end of the studio era was surely in sight, *West Side Story*'s historic sweep was further evidence of the real beginning of the end and the rise of the new independents.

"The Longest Run": The Afterlife of *West Side Story*

Less than two years after *West Side Story*'s road show and general release, the weekly issue of *Variety* announced on 26 August 1963 that it had reached the landmark sum of $15 million in the domestic market alone, making it the fifth highest-grossing film in American box-office history. Some engagements lasted for years. By the summer of 1964 it had played continuously in Amsterdam, Brussels, Copenhagen, Stockholm, and Paris. In May 1966 *West Side Story* made box-office history again by becoming the longest-running film in French history. After 218 uninterrupted weeks at the George V Theatre in the Champs Élysées (2 March 1962 to 10 May 1966) and "astronomical" grosses of nearly $2.6 million, the *Hollywood Reporter* and *Variety* announced that the film was ending its historic four-year run there and moving to the nearby Avenue Theatre.[26] Ten months later, in March 1967, *West Side Story* finally ended its "record-breaking" five-year run in Paris (after twenty-five weeks at the Avenue Theatre and another sixteen weeks at the Arlequine), with final grosses estimated at $2.8 million. The *Hollywood Reporter* confirmed that the five-year run and "blockbuster" grosses established a record in French motion picture history.[27]

In September 1966 the Mirisch Corporation rejected an offer from ABC-TV for the television rights to broadcast *West Side Story*. At $3 million, the offer would have broken the record of $2 million paid by ABC for the television rights to David Lean's *The Bridge on the River Kwai* (1957), which first aired on US television on Sunday, 25 September 1966. In an interview with *Daily Variety*, Marvin Mirisch revealed that his company and United Artists were planning to rere-lease the film in US theaters in 1969 or 1970 and were not yet ready to consider television broadcasts.[28] In March 1967, however, UA entered into a package deal with NBC-TV that included the rights to *West Side Story*, the first four James Bond movies starring Sean Connery, and other assorted properties. Though the film's share of the deal—$5 million—was not initially disclosed, according to the *Hollywood Reporter*, the deal allowed for as many as three showings of *West Side Story* over the course of nine years, starting after the September 1968 rerelease. The film would not air on US television for another four years.[29]

As usual, it was not all smooth sailing. In 1971 United Artists resold the TV rights to *West Side Story*, this time to CBS, again as part of a multipicture package deal that included domestic and foreign rights. In 1976 Jerome Robbins, Leonard Bernstein, Stephen Sondheim, and Arthur Laurents hired the auditing firm of Solomon & Finger to look into the picture's revenues. After an eighteen-month audit, the firm found "improper accounting" in United Artists' ledgers, and the four men filed a complaint with the American Arbitration Association. The action against United Artists did not name Robert Wise or the Mirisch brothers as respondents. The claimants alleged that they had been denied their share of more than $4 million UA had generated through the various TV deals. Of particular interest was the way United Artists had (mis)calculated the value of *West Side Story* in comparison to other, less desirable properties that were part of the same package deals. In an attempt to offset profit sharing and make up for box-office losses by commercial failures, *West Side Story*'s worth was undervalued. The Japanese box-office figures were offered as evidence of the unfair slant. In Japan, *West Side Story* had grossed more than $3 million, but it was sold to the country's major network in a package that included films never even released there (and therefore less valuable). *West Side Story*'s value was degraded in the package because the most successful film's share was capped at three times the fee for the smaller or unreleased films.

The arbitrators' final decision came on 24 October 1979, and *Variety* gave it a first-page headline: "Authors Win 400G from Film Audit." *Variety* reporter Stephen Klain even speculated that the ruling

would have a significant impact on how distributors sold properties to television networks in the future, both at home and abroad.
Although the arbitration panel determined that the 1967 deal with
NBC for $5 million was fair, it found that the contract with CBS and
the foreign TV rights sales had effectively "shortchanged" the original authors.[30] This decision marked the third time West Side Story set
a precedent for future practices in the US film industry (the others
being the credits and royalties dispute with the ghost singers and
the song subtitling decision).

It Grows "Younger": Longevity and Legacy

The 1968–1969 season saw the first rerelease of West Side Story in
US theaters. According to Chris Jones of Films and Filming, the film
did not need reviving because he had "never considered it to be
away" in the first place. He recalled that the impact of the original
release had been "immediate," and he described the choreography
as "the most balletic . . . that had been seen on screen" and the location settings as contributing "a powerful modern-day reality" rarely
seen in American musicals. About Bernstein's score, Jones said it
was a "work of art" capable of seizing the public's attention "without too much commercial pandering." And while acknowledging
the film's "schmaltz" factor, he predicted that new audiences would
still leave the theaters with "almost visible lumps" in their throats.
Finally, Jones concluded that, to his surprise, the film's topics were
"even more relevant" in the context of the late 1960s youth culture,
and the movie did not seem "at all dated."[31] Coincidentally, United
Artists' tagline in the rerelease theatrical trailer predicted that, "unlike other classics," West Side Story grew "younger."

On Sunday, 4 April 1971, West Side Story was aired for the first
time on American television by NBC, almost four years after the TV
rights agreement had been signed.[32] Another impressive rerelease in
France and Spain in April and September 1981, respectively, proved
that the film continued to be popular in foreign markets. The sixteen-
week French rerelease reported 400,000 admissions and more than
$1.5 million in box-office sales.[33] Through the 1980s and 1990s,
the film had multiple special screenings, one-night showings, and
limited rereleases in the United States and abroad. Typically, these

engagements were special events of some sort. The Los Angeles International Film Exposition, for instance, offered a free screening on 31 March 1982, publicized with quotes from the original reviews by Arthur Knight, Bosley Crowther, and Paul Beckley. The screening concluded with a sequence from *Brainstorm*, Natalie Wood's last film, introduced by director Douglas Trumbull. It was a tribute to the late actress, who had drowned on 29 November 1981 at age forty-three.[34] Many other screenings followed, often as alternative, tribute, or cult presentations: at the Pacific Cinerama Dome in Hollywood in October 1989; in a new 70mm print converted to THX sound in Los Angeles in 1990; at a tribute to Leonard Bernstein in June 1991 at the Pacific Film Archive, where the film was screened nearly annually throughout the decade; in Melbourne, Australia, in 1995; and in September 1995 as part of a program at the Long Beach Civic Opera.

In 1992 the American Film Institute hosted a screening at Jordan High School in Long Beach, California, as part of a "living literature" program for teenagers at risk of gang violence. Robert Wise was in attendance, as were former Los Angeles gang members, present in part to legitimize the film's story. In 1997 the Library of Congress designated *West Side Story* for preservation in the National Film Registry, in 1998 the American Film Institute named it one of the "Top 100" films of all time, and in 1999 it was inducted into the Producers Guild of America Hall of Fame.[35] On 9 October 2002 a "reunion" screening in Hollywood at Grauman's Egyptian Theatre was attended by Robert Wise, Rita Moreno, George Chakiris, Russ Tamblyn, Marni Nixon, and, according to the *Los Angeles Times*, "19 assorted Jets and Sharks."[36] In January 2003 the Academy of Motion Picture Arts and Sciences hosted a special screening, with printed programs, at the Samuel Goldwyn Theatre, with Wise, Moreno, Chakiris, Tamblyn, and Walter Mirisch all in attendance. Banking on the film's popularity with a wide audience, in the spring of 2003 MGM released the film for limited, "one night only" engagements in a much-maligned "sing-along" tour of San Francisco, Dallas, Chicago, Atlanta, Fort Lauderdale, Boston, Philadelphia, and Toronto. The purpose of the sing-along tour was to promote the "Special Edition" DVD release of the film by MGM Home Entertainment. A London theatrical rerelease in the summer of 2005 led to a *Time*

Out London review by David Calhoun, who wrote, "there's something thoroughly modern about the whole affair," confirming that the movie seems to "grow younger" or is, at least, ageless.[37]

The film was shown at the Los Angeles Film Festival on 23 June 2006 and (newly available on 35mm prints) at New York's Museum of Modern Art in December of that year. After the special screening at MoMA, a notice appeared in the arts journal the *Three Penny Review* in spring 2007. Founding editor Wendy Lesser called Bernstein's score "the best thing he ever wrote" and, emphasizing the film's formal structure, remarked, "I've never seen a movie that made me more conscious of its construction."[38] In 2008 the UCLA Film and Television Archive struck a new 70mm print that had a special screening in November 2008 at Grauman's Egyptian, with Chakiris appearing in person. And in April 2009 Chakiris and Tamblyn hosted yet another special screening at the Los Angeles Harbor Film Festival in San Pedro. The local newspaper, the *Daily Breeze*, made a big deal of the fact that the former screen gang "rivals" were appearing together. The event was a good-natured stunt, part of another anti–gang violence campaign targeted at teens. The show featured "Puerto Rican food" as an extra attraction.[39] Like the 1992 Long Beach screening attended by Wise and former gang members, the 2009 San Pedro screening suggests that the film still has considerable appeal to younger audiences and that its message against gang activity still resonates.

Even more recently, *West Side Story* had a special screening at the Seattle International Film Festival in 2010. It was rereleased in theaters as a special "one night only" digital screening on 9 November 2011 to commemorate the fiftieth anniversary of the film, touted in the promotion as "the most honored musical of all time." The special event, sponsored by Turner Classic Movies and Fathom Events, featured an introduction by TCM host Robert Osborne and interviews with Walter Mirisch, George Chakiris, and Marni Nixon. This event, like the 2003 "sing-along," was designed to coincide with the release of the film's first Special Edition Blu-Ray three-disc set. Reviewing the Blu-Ray release, distinguished dance critic Joan Acocella of the *New Yorker* reminded her readers that the movie is not about the romantic plot but about "the city, and immigration, and gang wars." She firmly praised the realistic location shooting, the "truth" of the score's "1950s melting pot," and the "bristling" detail of the camera work. Acocella concluded authoritatively that the film version of the "Prologue" is "the most thrilling film dance ever made."[40]

Given its long original engagements in the United States and Europe; its periodic, nearly continuous special screenings at film festivals; and its venues ranging from the popular Grauman's to the high-brow MoMA to the silly "sing-alongs," it seems that *West Side Story*'s longevity justifies the pronouncement that it is a classic. The stage show is ubiquitous as well, a popular property in regional, amateur, and school productions. The 2009 Broadway revival and US tour, directed for the first time by then ninety-one-year-old Arthur Laurents, was nominated for four Tonys (winning one) and two Drama Desk Awards; it also won the Grammy for Best Musical Show album. The play opened on 19 March and ran for nearly two years, with 27 previews and 748 performances, just slightly exceeding the original's 734 shows from 1957 to 1959. An important distinction in the 2009 revival was the translation of several lines of dialogue and some song lyrics into Spanish, specifically in "I Feel Pretty" and "A Boy Like That."

For the revival, Laurents and company engaged composer and lyricist Lin-Manuel Miranda, author of the 2008 Tony Award–winning hit *In the Heights*. Miranda's task was to adapt lyrics and segments of dialogue into Spanish, working with Laurents and Stephen Sondheim. Miranda was born in New York to Puerto Rican parents, and he and Laurents insisted on casting Latino American actors to play all the Puerto Rican roles. The part of María, however, went to Argentine-born musical theater actress Josefina Scaglione. There was some fear that the story might seem dated, but it was hoped that the inclusion of Spanish dialogue and lyrics would make the show more plausible and commercially viable among the contemporary public, an experiment that had been successful with *In the Heights*.[41] However, audiences were less receptive than the producers had imagined. Theatergoers also missed the dramatic meaning of "A Boy Like That," so the lyrics were changed back to English in the summer of 2009. The Broadway revival closed in January 2011, after grossing more than $7 million and making "a very nice profit" for its investors, according to producer Jeffrey Seller.[42] It went on to tour the nation and internationally for the next two years, premiering in Tokyo in August 2012.

On the occasion of the Broadway revival of West Side Story, Todd McCarthy of Variety (perhaps the second most prominent film critic in the nation, after Roger Ebert) revisited the 1961 film. McCarthy began by expressing his disappointment that the movie's critical esteem was not "what it once was," in great part, he wrote, because the surviving creators of the original show, Stephen Sondheim and Arthur Laurents, seemed eager to "bad mouth" the movie in public statements. McCarthy speculated that Sondheim and Laurents were probably most concerned about the specifically cinematic elements of the adaptation: the way the film form had "diluted" the theatrical experience; the voice dubbing; and, most likely, their partner Jerome Robbins's unhappy history with the production. Surely, they also resented that the public's "perception" of West Side Story—the model for most amateur and school theatrical productions and the collective memory of West Side Story—"is" the film. Judiciously yet unapologetically, McCarthy affirmed that Sondheim and Laurents were "simply wrong, dead wrong." He then proceeded point by cinematic point—design and mise-en-scène, camera movements, composition, editing, characterization, Lehman's rearrangement of narrative structure and additional dialogue—arguing that they all amount to a production that is "more powerful onscreen" than its source material.[43] Like his predecessors Arthur Knight and Bosley Crowther in 1961, McCarthy tried to understand the movie experience of West Side Story as a cinematic event, indebted but not subordinate to the original stage version.

West Side Story continues to be current. As recently as 2009, the film was still being shown to "at-risk" youth groups. The show is almost always being performed onstage by any number of regional, amateur, and school theater companies that draw on the film for guidance, inspiration, and Robbins's choreography. It was "remade" as the 2006 Oscar-winning musical short West Bank Story, about the romance between an Israeli soldier and a Palestinian girl (among rival falafel stands) in the midst of Middle Eastern tensions. It was remade again in 2007 as the Brazilian musical Maré: Our Love Story, setting the doomed romance in the slums of Rio de Janeiro.

Most recently, on 11 November 2011, a New York City–based group of professional dancers, under the name "Dance On," produced a three-minute "flash mob" in the middle of Times Square, reproducing segments of the "Prologue" and "Mambo" numbers to celebrate (and promote) the release of the Blu-Ray package. The group of nearly fifty dancers used playback tracks recognizable from the movie score, including the longer "Prologue." They were cheered enthusiastically by hundreds of onlookers and received a long ovation as they dispersed.

Also in the fall of 2011, the popular Fox television show *Glee* centered several episodes on a production of *West Side Story* and a related narrative arc. The cast produced and performed versions of "Somewhere," "Something's Coming," "Tonight," "A Boy Like That"/"I Have a Love," "One Hand, One Heart," and "America." The choreography and camera work, and even the lyrics and gender division in the "America" number, were closely derivative of the movie. The other numbers and vocalizations also faithfully mimicked the film's score and choreography. Each of the episodes, which aired between 20 September and 8 November 2011, attracted an average of 7 million viewers. Some of the numbers from *Glee* have appeared illegally on the website YouTube. As of August 2012, the *Glee* cast's rendition of "America," recorded by digital camera from a high-definition television screen, boasted nearly 100,000 views on YouTube, in spite of the poor sound quality. Due to *Glee*'s appeal to younger viewers, it is possible that for many of them, this was their first contact with *West Side Story*. That may be unfortunate, but the producers' decision to air a *West Side Story* theme, however sanitized for contemporary network television and its YouTube afterlife, shows the film's continuous impact on and relevance to the current media landscape.

Likewise, illegal, copyright-infringing uploads of every single musical number in the film are available on YouTube. The most popular are "I Feel Pretty" and "Maria," with more than 6 million views combined. All the other numbers register "hits" between 1 million and 2 million each, and most are preceded by commercial advertisements.

West Side Story is an American cinema phenomenon—a rare combination of a highly regarded artistic achievement that is popular at

MoMA screenings and major film festivals and enjoys equal appeal among the public at large. Many critics, both cited and not cited in this book, have named it "one of the best" if not "the best" film of its genre ever produced. It has been legitimized in such lists from the American Film Institute, the National Film Registry, the Producers Guild of America, national and international critics' polls, and other historical, professional, technical, and even social organizations. Its themes have currency and social relevance, as demonstrated by its use in antiviolence and antigang campaigns. Its artistic accomplishments in cinematography, special effects, editing, and musical scoring are almost unanimously acknowledged. And, as critics Arthur Knight and Moira Walsh suggest in their respective 1961 notices, *West Side Story* has more political bite than any musical film of its time and offers a near-perfect example of a complex and visible relationship between form and content. It may very well be the musical film equivalent of the great American novel.

5 "Bernardo Was Right": Arguing Puerto Rican Representation in *West Side Story*

West Side Story's political and social implications were a topic of discussion and concern during the production and even preview stages of the film. Similar to the controversy surrounding the stage show's initial run, which has been documented in a number of works,[1] the film's potential positive or negative effects on the moviegoing public were debated. Shortly after the 18 October premiere, the offices of United Artists received a letter addressed to Robert Wise and Jerome Robbins and signed by R. Domínguez of Washington, D.C. Mr. Domínguez threatened the producers with a libel suit and vowed to use "every legal means" to call attention to the "insulting attitudes" about Puerto Rico and Puerto Ricans allegedly portrayed in the movie. Domínguez called the movie "the most powerful piece of anti–Puerto Rican propaganda to be released by any film studio," singling out its depiction of "delinquency" and "sexual looseness" as "irresponsible defamation" of a minority group. Reporting to Harold Mirisch on 3 November, Wise dismissed the letter as "completely wrong" and Domínguez's attitude as a "fallacy." He suggested that "someone in the organization" should reply to the letter, as he was too busy with correspondence to answer himself.[2] Ultimately, there is no evidence that any suit ever materialized.

Similar fears were expressed by others. Philip H. Coombs, President Kennedy's assistant secretary of state for education and culture, had attended the Washington premiere of *West Side Story* and met Wise there. In a letter sent to the director in care of the Mirisch Company, Coombs praised the film as "a first-class job" but then warned of possible political misinterpretations. He wrote: "Many people, including a number of foreign friends, expressed concern that the movie, partly because it is so well done and forceful would create an unfortunate impression among foreign viewers who did not understand its social context and would lend itself to exploitation by the Communists." Coombs suggested that this potential problem could be averted by "simply adding some lines at the beginning which would help indirectly to put the story in context." And, he added, "It might not be a bad idea to have the lines in even for United States audiences."[3] Coombs made a point of assuring Wise that the State Department was not intervening officially; rather, it was offering a friendly suggestion to avoid possible controversy. In an interoffice memo dated 29 November, Wise forwarded the letter to Harold Mirisch and stated that he "didn't concur" with the opinion that the film presented a negative image of the United States. However, Wise proposed a meeting with Mirisch to determine "whether we want to do anything about it."[4] Whether that meeting ever took place, we have no way of knowing. What we do know is that the film was released, both domestically and internationally, without the suggested narration or text scrawl proposed by Coombs.

Even in the early stages of production, the film's potentially positive and pedagogical uses with regard to gangs, gang violence, and Puerto Rican youths in particular were already being discussed in some influential circles. In a letter to Harold Mirisch dated 26 September 1960, former first lady Eleanor Roosevelt appealed to the producers on behalf of a project called the Encampment for Citizenship.[5] Mrs. Roosevelt explained that the project's purpose was to "equip young people with the knowledge of the major issues before our American community" and to promote democratic action. She asked the producers to make West Side Story's premiere—which would not occur for another year—a benefit for the organization. Encampment for Citizenship, she wrote, planned to have camps in New York, California, and Puerto Rico that year, hoping "to involve the youth of the Caribbean and to make a bridge between Latin American and North American youth."[6] Mirisch forwarded the letter to Wise, but any follow-up on Mrs. Roosevelt's request was ultimately unfruitful. In the end, the gala premiere of West Side Story was a benefit for the Women's Guild of Cedars of Lebanon–Mount Sinai Hospitals, as announced by the *Hollywood Reporter* in December 1961. In any case, Eleanor Roosevelt's interest in the movie as a potentially positive piece of propaganda, as a "bridge-building" tool between the United States and Puerto Rico and Latin America, suggests that *West Side Story* was expected to be politically and socially constructive, if somewhat controversial.

Perhaps paradoxically, some form of official vindication came on 11 April 1962, two days after *West Side Story*'s historic sweep of the 1961 Academy Awards, when the *Hollywood Reporter* ran a story quoting Senator Clair Engle, a Democrat from California. Engle had praised *West Side Story* in Washington, calling it "American in type, character, and in spirit." He had affirmed to the Senate that "the locale was America, the theme was America, the music was America, and the young people who gave it charm, style and distinction were American. . . . I believe this film is an outstanding tribute to American motion-picture making." Given the oddity of a Washington politician publicly praising a popular Hollywood movie, the senator's gesture underscores the apparent lingering anxiety that the film's controversial content might stir anti-American or even anti–Puerto Rican sentiments.

The "American Way": *West Side Story* in Sociopolitical Debates

There is no doubt that in artistic and even scholarly circles, *West Side Story* is considered a turning point in the representation of Puerto Ricans in Hollywood cinema. Cultural critic Frances Negrón-Muntaner writes that "there is no American cultural product that haunts Puerto Rican identity discourses in the United States more intensely than the 1961 film *West Side Story*."[7] This bombastic (but arguably true) statement situates *West Side Story* as a cultural event, a polymorphous text about which Puerto Ricans often feel ambivalent. They might be attracted by the film's aesthetic achievements but repelled by its invention of an abject Puerto Rican identity forever marked by gang violence, hatred, poverty, colonialism, vibrant colors, and energetic dance. Latino actors in general, but Puerto Ricans in particular, often tell and retell their personal stories about

West Side Story. On the occasion of a reunion screening in Los Angeles in October 2002 attended by Robert Wise, George Chakiris, Russ Tamblyn, Marni Nixon, and other members of the cast, Rita Moreno told the *Los Angeles Times* that "every Hispanic actor" owed a great debt to *West Side Story*. "It meant a great deal to every Hispanic actor I have ever met," she said.[8] Singer and actress Jennifer López, born in New York to Puerto Rican parents, dreamed of playing Anita and María alternately and described the movie not only as her childhood favorite but also as an inspiration to her professional ambitions. In contrast, singer Ricky Martin, born and raised in Puerto Rico, publicly condemned the film's representation of Puerto Rico and Puerto Ricans and rejected any suggestions that he headline a proposed remake with all Latino actors.[9] From participants in every high school or amateur theater production to professional entertainers, most Latino performers have had to think about, deal with, or assimilate *West Side Story* at some point. The film has also been the focus of intense criticism and close critical readings, especially about its depiction and treatment of Puerto Rican identity and the creation of a particular type of masquerade—in other words, about "brown-facing" Puerto Ricanness.[10]

Alberto Sandoval-Sánchez, a theater critic and professor of Spanish at Mount Holyoke College, once wrote that, as a young student in the United States, *West Side Story* "was imposed upon [him] as a model of/for [his] Puerto Rican ethnic identity."[11] This traumatic experience informed Sandoval-Sánchez's oft-quoted article about the film, in which he lists a series of misconceptions, or misrepresentations, created by its "ethnic, social, and racial stereotypes about Latinos" and its idealization of some sort of "American way of life."[12] According to Sandoval-Sánchez, the political discourse of *West Side Story* is not only racist and colonialist but also denigrating in its definition of Puerto Ricans "only in their criminal potentiality, as carrying weapons that the Jets will have to face and to deem equal."[13]

Nevertheless, it is not only *West Side Story*'s status as a cultural marker, or "maker," of Puerto Ricanness for white, dominant audiences that needs to be addressed. Equally important is its generic specificity: the Hollywood musical is a fantasy-making mode of representation. In all its iterations and three main types (backstage,

fairy tale, and folk), the musical operates—like most classical Hollywood genres—as a mythmaking archetype. *West Side Story* "creates"
Puerto Rican identity within the confines of a particularly performative genre in which references to reality are extremely mediated
at best and, more often than not, respond only to its own generic,
formal, and structural rules. *West Side Story* arguably fits into the
subgeneric category of the folk musical, which, according to Rick
Altman, aspires to create the illusion of a unified "community." This
imagined community in the classical form—that is, before *West Side
Story*—creates homosocial and homoerotic bonds among youths
that must be broken to offer the promise, or the fantasy, of heterosexual coupling.[14] However, the genre is associated with camp, gay,
utopian, "drag," and marginal sensibilities, and historically, it has
been created by gay talent because it offers a "place" where sexual
repression (especially in classical Hollywood) can be channeled into
"sexual substitutions" that, more often than not, re-dress heterosex-
uality itself as a camp fantasy.[15] Matthew Tinkcom has argued that in
the classical musical (in particular, those created at the Arthur Freed
unit at MGM, but equally applicable to the genre's entire canon),
"camp excess, masquerade and performance" hide a gay sensibil-
ity that ultimately serves to self-consciously mock the realism of
heterosexual coupling narratives.[16] In "the world of the musical,"
writes Tinkcom, "a man and a woman meet and find initial attraction . . . their union is frustrated . . . and ultimately the prohibi-
tions to heterosexual bonding are overcome through the mediation
of song and dance."[17] This is not the case in *West Side Story*, which
might well be one of the original "revisionist" musicals, since Tony
and María's conflicts are never resolved. The revisionist thread that
runs through *West Side Story* rewrites not only the camp fantasy of a
heterosexual "happy ending" but also the utopian "somewhere" created by the folk musical.

In his work on the articulation of utopia in the classical musical,
Richard Dyer has argued that the depiction of the "ideal" is presented through "emotion" and "affect" rather than psychology or
social concerns. The musical addresses some social anxieties while
purposely neglecting other needs and concerns, especially those
related to "class, race [and] patriarchy."[18] Typically, the dominant

ideology of the classical musical denies the validity of such social problems. However, the end of the classical era is predicted in West Side Story, a film that provides a dystopian conclusion to the generic utopian (or fantastic) concept of social reality typical of the classical musical. Surprisingly, West Side Story acknowledges some of these conflicts (particularly in its treatment of sexual, class, and ethnic tensions in 1950s urban America), while suggesting that the "reality" of the film world is already a crumbling dreamland. What is most unusual is that, contrary to some perceptions of West Side Story, the "utopia" it puts forth is not that of the "values, beliefs, and ideals of the Anglo-American national subjectivity"; nor is it the Jets' "sociopolitical and personal superiority," as Sandoval-Sánchez argues. Rather, it is the search for a stable Puerto Rican American identity that comes under aggressive attack. The Puerto Rican fantasy in West Side Story is a camp performance as well, a form of "drag," yet one in which it is arguably the Sharks, not the Jets—the Puerto Ricans, not the "Americans"—whose sense of identity is better delineated. In fact, if there is any claim to an identity that is somewhat cohesive, it is the fantasy of a Nuyorican identity.

"In America Now": Must We Burn West Side Story?

Frances Negrón-Muntaner has argued that the film is not "about" Puerto Ricans, that it was never intended to be "real," and that it does not "seem real to Puerto Rican spectators."[19] Furthermore, she convincingly claims that West Side Story is "the most cohesive product of American culture to 'hail' Puerto Ricans as U.S. Puerto Ricans." Even though that subjectivity is certainly problematic (men-as-criminals and women-as-victims), Negrón-Muntaner declares, "Puerto Rican spectators have not been able to resist the command to turn around and respond to the film's shameful hailing."[20] It is significant that Negrón-Muntaner's example of "hailing" has to do with an individual's "encounter with a police officer and the Law," which is essential to the relationship among the Jets, Sharks, Lieutenant Schrank, and Officer Krupke.[21] In spite of the persuasive assertion that the Sharks are depicted "only as criminals,"[22] it is clearly the Jets who begin the cycle of violence that leads the Sharks down the path to delinquency. In the lengthy music and dance prologue that sets up the first narrative act, the spectator is first introduced to the leader of the Jets, Riff, who refers to his gang as "juvenile delinquents," and later to Bernardo, leader of the Sharks, who is harassed by the Jets with no visible provocation, apart from his "otherness." Later, at the war council held to set the rules for the rumble, it is confirmed that the Jets "jumped" Bernardo the first day he moved into the neighborhood. Thus the movie establishes that criminality and lawlessness are not initially associated with the so-called immigrants but rather with the perceived "natives."

Lieutenant Schrank and Officer Krupke are continually represented as operating somewhat "outside" the law in trying to make deals with the Jets. But they are also the common enemy, and the only visible truce between the Sharks and the Jets occurs in the context of a joint rebellious gesture against these ineffectual—and possibly corrupt—authority figures. The "State" is represented only by Schrank and Krupke, who in fact "hail" the Jets outside Doc's Candy Store with the words, "Hey, you!"[23] Naturally, the Jets reply, knowing themselves to be, in fact, criminals. Represented by Schrank and Krupke, all authority in *West Side Story* ultimately appears fragile, incompetent, and characterized by bigotry and dishonesty.

In contrast to the lawlessness of the "natives" and the impotence of the "Law," the Sharks—especially the Shark women—are productive, law-abiding, and apparently bound by ties that constitute some sense of community. María, Anita, Rosalía, and Consuelo all work in Madame Lucía's bridal shop and apparently live in the same tenement building; they speak Spanish to one another occasionally and visit one another's homes (the "I Feel Pretty" number is sung in María's bedroom in the original stage version, although it is set in the bridal shop in the movie). Among the Jets, there is no real reference to "home" or community; with the exception of their gang identity, their social or national identity is amorphous. Tony refers at one point to his mother at home, but he is finished with gang life; he works (which provokes scorn among his former fellow gang members) and tells María that he "goes to church." In contrast, we know that Riff lives with Tony's family because he hates "living with his bugging uncle." And, in the "Gee, Officer Krupke" number, Riff explains the Jets' social dysfunction in these terms:

Our mothers all are junkies
Our fathers all are drunks . . .
My parents treat me rough . . .
My Daddy beats my Mommy
My Mommy clobbers me
My Grandpa is a Commie
My Grandma pushes tea
My sister wears a mustache
My brother wears a dress.
Goodness Gracious that's why I'm a mess![24]

As comical as the number is, it illustrates a great contrast with what we know about the Sharks and their community and family lives.

Bernardo and María live with their parents, and their neighbors seem to know and respect them (recall that after the rumble, we hear offscreen in the hall, "Bernardo está muerto!"). We know that María has a loving relationship with her parents, especially her father, as evidenced by their exchange at the fire escape during the first "Tonight" number. Although they are absent from the immediate space of the narrative action, we know that María and Bernardo's parents are just offscreen. It is also evident that María has been brought up properly, in an environment that encourages a work ethic and the Catholic religion, an important cultural identity symbol for many Puerto Ricans on and off the island (among the questions María imagines her parents asking Tony is whether he goes to church). Besides the Shark women, we know that Chino also works—as does Tony, who has openly rejected the Jets and their lifestyle—and the movie and play suggest that María's parents own or work at the local bodega (María announces at one point that her parents are "at the store" and she does not expect them back for quite a while, implying they are working).

More important, the only "domestic" space represented in West Side Story is María's family's apartment, which exists in the community within the "Puerto Rican" neighborhood. As comedian Robert Wuhl once joked, "The most fantastic thing about West Side Story is that Tony runs through the Puerto Rican neighborhood yelling 'Maria!' and only *one* girl comes to the window." Jokes aside, there is a sense of community in the space shared by the characters, and it is a space of diversity and integration, however undesirable this might be to the assorted "Anglos." As demonstrated in chapter 3, in the "Prologue" sequence we see two prophetic signs in opposition: one stating "KEEP OFF," presiding over the assorted Jets, and the other one behind the Sharks announcing, "*Se Habla Español.*" These signs suggest the inevitable integration of this part of the city and acknowledge the Puerto Rican presence in the neighborhood's changing cultural profile. By contrast, Schrank refers to the Jets as a mixture of other "immigrant scum" with no discernible cultural background. (Bernardo calls Tony "the American" before dismissively correcting his own statement, saying, "He's really a Polack.") With no "home" other than Doc's Candy Store and the streets, no "family" other than the gang, no social ambitions other than reclaiming their indistinct "turf," the Jets are unquestionably the group with no real "national, territorial, [or] racial . . . identity" in *West Side Story*, in spite of Sandoval-Sánchez's assertion. The block, the tenement building, and the apartment where María and Bernardo live with their parents constitute the only "homemaking" in the movie at all.

Seven important narrative sequences take place in María and Bernardo's family's apartment and its immediate surroundings—more than in any other social or private space in the movie. They are: (1) Bernardo, Anita, and María in the apartment after the dance at the gym; (2) Tony and María on the fire escape, where she speaks to her father through the window; (3) the "America" number sung on the rooftop of the building; (4) Chino's announcement that Tony has killed Bernardo at the rumble; (5) Tony and María's utopian ("I want") song, "Somewhere," followed by the lovemaking scene in María's bedroom; (6) María and Anita's confrontation in the "A Boy Like That"/"I Have a Love" duet, also in María's bedroom; and (7) Lieutenant Schrank's interview with María, after the deaths of Riff and Bernardo, in the living/dining room of the apartment. This unique domestic space in *West Side Story* is somewhat problematic, given the conspicuous absence of parental figures, its "colorful" design, and the shrine to the Virgin Mary in María's bedroom, all of which expand on certain stereotypes about Latinos. Yet it is the only domestic space seen in the film, and it offers glimpses of cultural identity: a bowl of tropical fruit on the table, a guitar propped up against a corner.

Besides the superficial references to food, music, and Catholicism as cultural identity signs, there is a fleeting but clear image of a small Puerto Rican flag—along with the US flag—on top of a television set in the apartment. The two flags seem to catch Schrank's attention, and he stops, for a moment, to observe. The Puerto Rican flag shows up occasionally in films and television series featuring Puerto Rican characters, including Abel Ferrara's *Bad Lieutenant* (1992), various episodes of Dick Wolf's *Law & Order*, and the infamous "Puerto Rican Day" episode of *Seinfeld*, which first aired on 7 May 1998. In that episode, Cosmo Kramer (Michael Richards) accidentally sets the Puerto Rican flag on fire and steps over it, triggering an angry, near-violent reaction from the parade spectators around him. What is far less common is to see the Puerto Rican flag together with the US flag, although this display is the official practice in Puerto Rico. It is as if most US media representations prefer not to acknowledge Puerto Rico's unusual political relationship with the United States. As Bernardo reminds Anita in the "America" counterpoint, "Puerto Rico is in America now," referring to the island's status as a "free associated state." María's family has apparently adjusted to this new status and welcomes their "US–Puerto Rican" political and social (if not ethnic and cultural) identity.

Puerto Ricans have been US citizens since the 1917 Jones-Shafroth Act, and its "commonwealth" status (which it shares with the Northern Mariana Islands) was approved by a popular referendum in 1952, ratified by Congress, and signed into law by President Harry S. Truman. Puerto Rican "migration" to the US mainland began in earnest in the 1920s and increased over the next three decades. It is estimated that between 1950 and 1960, some 45,000 Puerto Ricans, or as much as 20 percent of the island's population, came to the United States, settling mostly in New York City but also in places such as Philadelphia, Chicago, and Boston.[25] This migratory wave peaked in 1954. The movie establishes that the action takes place in an election year—based on the fictional "Vote Al Wood" for city council posters seen in the film—possibly 1953. Thus, María's arrival ("one month have I been in this country") coincides with this

Lieutenant Schrank is curious about the US and Puerto Rico flags in María's family apartment. ©1961 Metro-Goldwyn-Mayer Studios Inc. All rights reserved.

migratory peak and with the period when Jerome Robbins, Arthur Laurents, Leonard Bernstein, and Stephen Sondheim began in earnest to conceive, write, and score *West Side Story*. Nevertheless, it is the definition of María's family as "Puerto Rican American" that is most significant, giving them, more than any other characters in the film, a sense of identity. It is a dual identity, and possibly problematic, but it is also, to a certain extent, "real." María's family would be considered examples of "good" immigrants and good Americans: hardworking, law-abiding, churchgoing, and respectful of Puerto Rico's political and constitutional status vis-à-vis the United States, however awkward it might be.

In this context, Bernardo's statement that "Puerto Rico is in America now," delivered with ironic gusto, also acquires a double significance. On the one hand, it acknowledges Puerto Rico's new political status, which coincides with the film's temporal context (most likely, the summer of 1953). On the other hand, it emphasizes the slippery, sardonic definition of that status by Bernardo. As the male-female "counterpoint" of "America" foregrounds so well, "Puerto Rico is in America now," but Puerto Ricans remain trapped between unofficial second-class citizen status and the genuine desire to assimilate.

"Queer for Uncle Sam": The Controversy of "America"

Within the improbable narrative world of *West Side Story* and the history of its trajectory—1949 concept, 1955 creation, 1957 Broadway debut, 1961 movie version—the focus on Puerto Ricans (as opposed to other marginalized groups) has been well documented and criticized. All four principal creative minds behind the show were of Jewish descent, and Stephen Sondheim acknowledged that he was not qualified to write for these characters. "I can't do this show," he reportedly said. "I've never been that poor and I've never known a Puerto Rican."[26] Yet in the process of adaptation, and after considerable criticism, Sondheim and screenwriter Ernest Lehman made significant changes to the lyrics and format of the song "America," transforming it into a polyrhythmic "controversy" that, as discussed earlier, employs two time signatures repeatedly altered, emphasizing specific syllables. The tempo is maintained, yet it creates an "argument" between time signatures that is mimicked by the argument between the men and women onscreen. The dispute oscillates between definitions and revisions of the immigrant experience and the fallacy of the American Dream.

In the early stages of adaptation, Robbins proposed setting "America" around the Sharks and showing them from an entirely different perspective. He wrote to Lehman in early 1960:

> The Puerto Ricans are at home, relaxed, at ease without any outside pressures . . . not on guard. The Scene should have a feeling of warm, relaxed affection . . . [and] should bring out the warmth and kidding qualities of the humor of the song "America." If possible the material should serve as some tie-in with the Balcony Scene [sic] . . . and that is a variation on "love feelings." It is also one of the few scenes in which we get to see Bernardo other than in his "chip on the shoulder" attitude and in this scene, we can possibly see his sensitivity, hurt, longings and his early dreams, which were slapped out of him.

Significantly, in these same notes, Robbins proposes the change to the original theatrical version that came to characterize the "America" number in the movie. He suggests that the song depict one of "three different attitudes" Puerto Ricans have about the United States: (1) Rosalía wanting to go back to Puerto Rico but being mocked by her girlfriends (as in the stage version), (2) Anita wanting to stay in New York because "it's a great life," and (3) Bernardo voicing his dissent: "Sure it's a great life if you want to pay the price . . . all the strings and red tapes that are connected to the dazzling promise of America."[27] It was a combination of Anita's and Bernardo's confronting "attitudes," along with the addition of the gender split, that became the signature of this particular musical number.

The film version of the song significantly softens the "prejudiced" content that led to such criticism and controversy during the play's initial run from 1957 to 1959.[28] The biggest change involved reworking the song's structure from an argument among four of the girls (Rosalía, in favor of returning to Puerto Rico, against Anita and the others, wanting to stay in New York) into the gender-divided counterpoint in which the boys, led by Bernardo, and the girls, led by Anita, passionately discuss the immigrant experience from two completely opposite points of view. In the play, the song "America" is emphatic in its lampooning of Puerto Rico as an underdeveloped, third world, poverty-stricken, overpopulated, violence-infested, disease-riddled country, and as contrast, it cites almost exclusively the material advantages of the American experience:

> Puerto Rico . . . you ugly island
> Island of tropic diseases
> Always the hurricanes blowing
> Always the population growing
> And the money owing
> And the babies crying
> And the bullets flying . . .
>
> Everything free in America . . .
> Automobile in America
> Chromium steel in America . . .
> Comfort is yours in America
> Knobs on the doors in America
> Wall-to-wall floors in America . . .

The movie version of "America" emphasizes quite sharply the social disadvantages, the ethnic and racial prejudice, and even the violence to which the immigrant is exposed. Bernardo and the Sharks thus ridicule Anita's "Americanization" as a sign of weakness, and Bernardo quips (only in the movie), "Look, instead of a shampoo, she's been brainwashed . . . and now she's queer for Uncle Sam." The movie's prologue to the musical number is faithful to the play, stating Bernardo's disappointment at the contradictions between his naïve immigrant desires ("We came eager, with our hearts open") and the cruel reality of prejudice ("Lice! Cockroaches!"). But that is as far as the play goes, so it is especially meaningful that the movie version goes to such lengths to dramatize Bernardo's disillusion and, later, gives him the final word—agreeing, in essence and in no uncertain terms, with Bernardo's miserable prophecy of "America."

As noted in chapter 1, it was Lehman who asked Sondheim to change the song's lyrics. Lehman reportedly said, "I looked at it and I said to myself . . . they're singing about Puerto Ricans in Puerto Rico. This is ridiculous. This is a show about Puerto Ricans coming to America and what they go through."[29] Yet the movie's gender counterpoint still emphasizes the women's shallow view of "assimilation" as something strictly related to conspicuous consumption: it suggests that *being* American means spending visibly and extravagantly. The men, however, have a decidedly dystopian—or perhaps just more realistic—view of the immigrant experience:

Girls: Everything free in America.
Boys: For a small fee in America.
Girls: Buying on credit is so nice.
Boys: One look at us and they charge twice.
Girl: Skyscrapers bloom in America.
Girl: Cadillacs zoom in America.
Girl: Industry boom in America.
Boys: Twelve in a room in America!
Anita: Lots of new housing with more space.
Bernardo: Lots of doors slamming in our face.
Anita: I'll get the terrace apartment.
Bernardo: Better get rid of your accent.

> Girls: Life can be bright in America.
> Boys: If you can fight in America.
> Girls: Life is all right in America!
> Boys: If you're all white in America.
> Girls: Here you are free and you have pride.
> Boys: 'Long as you stay on your own side.
> Girls: Free to be anything you choose.
> Boys: Free to wait tables and shine shoes.
> Bernardo: Everywhere grime in America.
> Bernardo: Organized crime in America.
> Bernardo: Terrible time in America.

Surely the result is imperfect but nothing short of subversive, especially since Anita, the most vocal champion of the American experience, later recants her "Americanization." Tellingly, it is after the attempted rape by the Jets that Anita has a change of attitude about the immigrant experience and the promise of America. Her near-final words in the movie serve as a redemption for her character: "Bernardo was right. . . . If one of you [Jets] was bleeding in the street, I'd walk by and spit on you!" Before delivering the false news of María's death, she prefaces it by saying, "I have a message for your *American* buddy," pronouncing "American" as if it were an insult or as if she were spitting. Anita realizes that "Bernardo was right" about the fallacy of the American Dream, even though it takes sexual violence to open her eyes to this reality.

Although the Sharks are certainly portrayed as patriarchal and exhibit stereotypical "Latin" machismo in their treatment of women, they are also affectionate (especially Bernardo's interactions with María and Anita), whereas the Jets are consistently and plainly misogynistic. ("Anh, whadda we poopin' around wit' dumb broads?" Action asks before the war council.) The Jets' women, Anybodys, Graziella, and Velma, are treated in an openly hostile manner, manifested most violently in the racially and sexually charged assault against Anita.

Anita's attempt to make peace, prompted by María's desire to escape with Tony, leads to the attempted rape, which is arguably the most violent scene in the movie. All the fight action between the

Jets and the Sharks is "stylized" dancing rather than stunt-fighting choreography, and within the context of the classical musical, it is also highly homoerotic. Even the killings of Riff and Bernardo—one seemingly accidental, the other happening quickly—are notorious for their lack of graphic violence. But Anita's confrontation with the Jets at Doc's Candy Store is verbally and dramatically aggressive. While trying to reach Doc and Tony, Anita is harassed by the Jets:

> Will you let me pass?
> She's too dark to pass.
> Don't. . . . Listen, you . . . I've got to give a friend of yours a message. I've got to tell Tony. . . . Don't you understand I want to help!
> Bernardo's girl wants ta help!
> Even a greaseball got feelin's.
> Bernardo's tramp!
> Bernardo's pig!
> Ya lyin' spic!
> Don't do that! [after a Jet tries to lift her skirt]
> Gold tooth!
> Pierced ear!
> Garlic mouth!
> Spic! Lyin' spic!

The screenplay and libretto describe the rest of the scene—referred to as "the taunting"—quite graphically, implying that the Jets are animals, like a pack of wolves: "The taunting breaks out into a *wild, savage* DANCE, with epithets hurled at Anita, who is encircled and driven by the whole *pack*. At the peak she is shoved and falls in a corner. The Jets lift Baby John up high and drop him on top of her."[30] Ultimately, for Anita as much as Bernardo, the phrase "terrible time in America" turns out to be a prophetic, emphatic truth.

Considered subversive for 1961, the "antidominant" discourse in *West Side Story* is subtle yet persistent. It is also relevant that in Laurents's play, Lehman's screenplay, and the Wise-Robbins movie, all the Puerto Rican characters speak better English than the Jets, whose slang, a sort of early "Nadsat," is infected by and peppered with neologisms, misappropriations, word fragments, and phonetic spelling.

The Jets sound distinctly "lower" working class or even illiterate.[31] In contrast, the English spoken by the Puerto Rican characters—particularly Bernardo, Chino, Anita, and María—sounds much cleaner; it is grammatically and syntactically correct and, though accented, is virtually devoid of slang. In other words, the Puerto Rican "reading" of America as a failed utopia is also much more "articulate" than the Jets' fantasy.

Though certainly not as violent as the assault against Anita, I see María's desire to usurp the "Miss America" title as an act of resistance and rebellion against that ultimate celebration of white female Americana. In the 1950s, the idea of naming an "ethnic" Miss America was nothing short of unthinkable; even African Americans were not allowed to compete until 1970, and to this date, there has yet to be a Hispanic winner of the pageant. While some critics may see the "I Feel Pretty" number as a sign of María's submission to the gaze of a white man—as if she becomes visible only when desired by Tony—I argue that she is also exhibiting an unusual degree of subjectivity. She rebels against Bernardo's patriarchal assumptions: "Why did my brother bring me here? To marry Chino. When I look at Chino nothing happens." And she expresses her desire to experience more of life: "One month have I been in this country. Do I ever even touch excitement? I sew in this place all day, I sit at home all night." Granted, she immediately falls in love with the first man she sees outside the confines of her work and domestic spheres, but the important thing is that the "choice" of Tony is her only expression of sexual and romantic desire. "I Feel Pretty" and the Miss America claim extend this manifestation of María's desire and subjectivity, while expanding on the movie's consistent questions about Puerto Ricans' Americanness.

Finally, another relevant signifier in the Puerto Rico–America "controversy" is the Sharks' whistled rendition of Samuel Francis Smith's 1831 song "America." Recall that Lieutenant Schrank bans the Sharks from Doc's Candy Store with the politically charged verdict: "I know, it's a free country and I ain't got the right. But I got a badge. What do you got? Now beat it." The Sharks' farewell statement is a whistled phrase from Smith's song, invoking the lyrics, "My country 'tis of thee / Sweet land of liberty / Of thee I sing." The last note is rendered in a lowering turn, as if deflating or exhausting, thus subverting the fallacious lyrics. Like María's claim to the title of Miss America, Bernardo and the Sharks' appropriation of this other "America" song comes across as an act of rebellion—an ironic use of a cultural symbol whose lyrics insist on the "native" profile of the "real" American ("Land where my fathers died," "My native country thee," and so forth).

With these three visions and revisions of the word "America" in three distinct musical moments, Anita, María, Bernardo, and the Sharks are constantly calling our attention to the dystopia of this immigrant experience.

Masquerade, Identity, Folk

In his landmark history and theory of the genre, Rick Altman has defined the "folk" variation of the classical Hollywood musical as one that "presents us with a mythicized version of [culture]," one that creates or invents "tradition, folklore [and] Americana." Its function, like all classical genres, is to create and uphold the illusion of social stability. The folk subgenre, argues Altman, is usually set in either small-town America (Vincente Minnelli's *Meet Me in St. Louis*, Stanley Donen's *Seven Brides for Seven Brothers*, Morton DaCosta's *The Music Man*) or "coherent neighborhoods" (or even New York City itself, as in Donen and Gene Kelly's *On the Town*) populated with people and language that are or become familiar to the spectator. According to Altman, such settings are required because "love is only possible when we are in familiar territory."[32]

The classic folk musical seeks to create utopia out of things we know, people we recognize, and places we are familiar with. *West Side Story*, in contrast, works as a "revisionist" musical, in that it subverts, ever so slightly, many of the conventions of this particular genre. *West Side Story* insists on showing us people, places, and things we do not want to see: poverty, prejudice, corruption, violence, death. It also purposely derails all concepts of utopia, romantic or otherwise, upheld by the musical genre in general—and the folk variation in particular—by emphasizing that love does not conquer all, none of the characters will live happily ever after, and the social anxieties surrounding them will never be resolved. In fact, the ending in the screenplay suggests (unlike the stage libretto) that the gangs are "not yet ready, perhaps never will be ready, to give up war as a way of life."[33] The movie's finale is equally bleak, with most of the Jets and Sharks, except for those carrying Tony's body, remaining on opposite sides of the screen. The gap between them, it seems, will never be closed.

Most conventions of form, narrative, and structure in the classical musical are ultimately revised in West Side Story, not in a groundbreaking way, perhaps, but certainly in the reflexive acknowledgment of the imperfections and fissures of the heterosexual WASP utopia. None of the four creators of West Side Story was Puerto Rican, of course; according to Negrón-Muntaner, they were Jewish and homosexual.[34] Thus, West Side Story is a way to address many manifestations of prejudice and conflict by centering on sympathetic characters (mostly, the Puerto Ricans) who are abused by the mainstream, dominant culture because of something they cannot deny or escape—because of who they are. Arthur Laurents wrote in his last memoir that being gay affected his writing the same way being Jewish did, declaring, "I often write about outsiders."[35] This makes the show, and particularly the movie, a metaphor for "the closet." The Puerto Rican characters in West Side Story serve as a vehicle, a narrative tool, to make a point about a "terrible time in America," a time of prejudice and despair. The characters were never meant to be taken for "real" Puerto Ricans. But they are demonstrably favored by the narrative, made into protagonists for the first time in film history, and better articulated as characters than their white gang rivals. The musical is a world of fantasy, and West Side Story is no exception, but this fantasy is not entirely escapist or completely shallow.

It may be fair to condemn West Side Story for its cultural stereotypes, for "brown-facing" a white actor to play Bernardo, or for casting a white woman, the daughter of Russian immigrants, in the key role of the Puerto Rican heroine. Yet, as Steven Cohan has pointed out, the narrative and formal structure of the classical musical typically results in "heightening, disrupting, revising, or multiplying the codes of cinematic realism."[36] In other words, the musical cannot be measured by "realism," even in the conventional cinematic sense of the word; the musical creates its own sense of realism, and in that way, it is unlike any other genre (with the exception of "fantasy" films à la *Star Wars* or *The Lord of the Rings*). Sociologists might like to see the Hollywood musical abide by other rules, but that would negate the functions of performance and representation, and it would limit the range of any actor to suggest that he or she should not "play" a character of a different race, ethnicity, or nationality. Natalie Wood and George Chakiris are performing a type of "drag" show in *West Side Story* (as Negrón-Muntaner suggests), but it is no different from any other performative function of the musical specifically or of narrative Hollywood fiction in general.[37] Arguably, there are many other types of "drag" in *West Side Story*, such as the dubbing of the singing voices of four of the five principal actors. Yet performance is what actors do, and performance in the musical is self-reflexively foregrounded: performance is what reality *becomes* in the Hollywood musical. The juxtaposition between performance and identity, and between the real and the fantastic, is present in many aspects of *West Side Story*'s production design, costume color coordination, music, dance dueling, and other contrasts, as I have argued. To judge *West Side Story* by the conventional criteria of cinematic realism negates the generic specificity that characterizes this most capricious of Hollywood genres. Years ahead of its time, unlike any other musical film, *West Side Story* continues to explore ethnic, sexual, and social anxieties and to underscore dystopian polyrhythms within a fantastically utopian genre.

NOTES

A Note on Sources

Many of the primary research materials for this book came from the Robert Wise Collection in the Special Collections room of the Cinematic Arts Library at the University of Southern California in Los Angeles. Memos, personal letters, notes, budgets, schedules, interoffice communications, general correspondence, and research notes from Robert Wise, Jerome Robbins, Ernest Lehman, the Mirisch brothers, and their associates are held there. Facsimiles of the Ernest Lehman Papers are also available there. The Lehman Papers contain numerous handwritten comments by Lehman—on legal pad sheets, index cards, and even on the document pages themselves— presumably as context to the originals. Most of these are undated, added as Lehman was preparing the documents for donation to the University of Texas Libraries.

The staff at USC Special Collections also allowed me to see originals of the *West Side Story* movie score arranged by Sid Ramin and Irwin Kostal and to consult both Stanley K. Scheuer's and Robert Wise's original hand-annotated shooting scripts.

Many other materials came from the Core Collection and the *West Side Story* clippings and photographs folders, on microfiche and microfilm, at the Margaret Herrick Library, located in the Douglas Fairbanks Center for Motion Picture Study at the Academy of Motion Picture Arts and Sciences in Beverly Hills. The Herrick Library also provided me with Robert Wise's oral history, compiled from interviews conducted by Ronald L. Davis in 1979, as well as access to the Boris Leven, Linwood Dunn, and George Stevens Collections.

The following periodicals were consulted from the clippings and microfilm collections at the Margaret Herrick Library: *America, Boxoffice, Citizen News, Commonweal, Daily Breeze, Dance Magazine, Esquire, Film Daily, Film Review, Films and Filming, Harrison's Report, Hollywood Citizen News, Hollywood Reporter, Life, Los Angeles Herald Examiner, Los Angeles Mirror, Los Angeles Times, National Review, New Republic, New York Herald Tribune, New York Times, New Yorker, Newsweek, People, Redbook, Saturday Review, Seventeen, Theatre Arts, Three Penny Review, Time, Time Out London, TV Guide, Our Sunday Visitor, Variety,* and *Youth*. Reports, reviews, publicity, and articles from these publications are identified in the text or referenced in the endnotes.

Film and theater histories, scholarly articles, published memoirs, biographies, chronicles, interviews, critical and theoretical volumes, and other secondary sources were consulted and relied on for general background facts, framework, and historical information. These are referenced in the text when appropriate and are listed in the bibliography.

Abbreviations
AMPAS
Academy of Motion Picture Arts and Sciences
USC CAL
University of Southern California Cinematic Arts Library

Introduction. "My Heart's Devotion": Finding *West Side Story*

1. Sondheim and Bernstein collaborated on most of the lyrics and intended to share credit for the songs. By the time the show previewed and premiered, however, Bernstein had removed his name from the lyrics—presumably to aid Sondheim's budding career—but continued to take the larger share of the profits. See Elizabeth A. Wells, West Side Story: *Cultural Perspectives on an American Musical* (Lanham, MD: Scarecrow Press, 2011), 45.

2. Keith Garebian, *The Making of* West Side Story (Oakville, ON: Mosaic Press, 2000), 29–31.

3. Arthur Laurents, *Original Story By: A Memoir of Broadway and Hollywood* (New York: Applause Theatre Books, 2000), 338.

4. Wells, West Side Story, 32–33. See also Garebian, *Making of* West Side Story, 36–37.

5. Garebian, *Making of* West Side Story, 41–42.

6. Ibid., 42–43.

7. Arthur Laurents, "Growth of an Idea," *New York Herald Tribune*, 4 August 1957.

8. Misha Berson, *Something's Coming, Something Good: West Side Story and the American Imagination* (Milwaukee: Applause Theatre and Cinema Books, 2011), 31.

9. Wells, West Side Story, 44–45.

10. *West Side Story* was touted as such in publicity materials handed out during the film's previews in the summer of 1961. Publicity materials from the Margaret Herrick Library Core Collection, Academy of Motion Picture Arts and Sciences, microfiche reels.

11. Garebian, *Making of* West Side Story, 134.

12. Contemporary reviews quoted in Garebian, *Making of* West Side Story, 134–135, and Wells, West Side Story, 217.

13. Quoted in Berson, *Something's Coming*, back flap, and Joan Peyser, *Bernstein: A Biography* (New York: Beech Tree Books, 1987), 254.

14. Wells, West Side Story, 218.

15. Ibid.; Berson, *Something's Coming*, chap. 15.

16. There are several books on the history and impact of the stage version of *West Side Story*. The most comprehensive book on the show itself is Garebian's *Making of* West Side Story. The most complete work on its cultural impact and musical complexities is Wells's West Side Story. I recommend them both to interested readers.

17. Frances Negrón-Muntaner, *Boricua Pop: Puerto Ricans and the Latinization of American Culture* (New York: New York University Press, 2004), 61.

18. Ibid., 60.

Chapter 1. "Not a Photographed Stage Play": Creating *West Side Story*

1. Walter Mirisch, *I Thought We Were Making Movies, Not History* (Madison: University of Wisconsin Press, 2008), 305. At the time, United Artists had a distribution arrangement with Mirisch.

2. Ibid., chaps. 3–5, 7, 8.

3. Ibid., 114–115.

4. Curiously, Lehman had written *North by Northwest* for Alfred Hitchcock in 1958. The protagonist of that film, played by Cary Grant, is abducted in New York City by Soviet spies on 24 or 25 November 1958. He protests to his abductors that he had plans to go to the Winter Garden Theatre to see a show he was "looking forward to." In November 1958 *West Side Story* was playing at the Winter Garden.

5. Notably, Gene Kelly and Stanley Donen combined studio shooting and location shooting in New York in their 1949 version of *On the Town* for MGM's Arthur Freed unit.

6. Robert Wise to Willard Morrison, 22 January 1960, box 37, "General Correspondence" folder, Robert Wise Collection, USC CAL. Morrison was from the Audio Film Center in San Francisco, where Wise had rented the print of *Gang War*.

7. Robert E. Wise, oral history interview by Ronald L. Davis, 26 June 1979, Margaret Herrick Library, AMPAS.

8. Ernest Lehman, "Some Notes Taken during Police Car Tour of West Side," "Early Materials" folder, Ernest Lehman Collection, USC CAL. The Ernest Lehman Papers are actually in storage at the Harry Ransom Center at the University of Texas at Austin. Photocopies of material related to Robert Wise and *West Side Story* are also in the Robert Wise Collection, USC CAL, where I consulted them.

9. Elizabeth A. Wells, *West Side Story: Cultural Perspectives on an American Musical* (Lanham, MD: Scarecrow Press, 2011), 100–103.

10. Interview with Judy Sloane, *Film Review*, June 1994.

11. By the time of the New York City location shoot, the producers had hired a Puerto Rican neighborhood leader, John Gómez of 238 East 116th Street, to help recruit extras and assist with crowd control. Gómez later thanked Wise for using his services. John Gómez to Robert Wise, 28 December 1961, box 37, "General Correspondence" folder, Wise Collection.

12. "Bob Wise N.Y. Bound to Seek 'Side' Streets," *Variety*, 27 November 1959; "Jerome Robbins Co-Directs Mirisch 'West Side Story,'" *Hollywood Reporter*, 26 December 1959.

13. Mirisch, *I Thought We Were Making Movies*, 123.

14. Memo from Robert Wise, "West Side Story: The Problems of Style," 21 January 1960, box 27, folder 1, p. 1, Lehman Collection.

15. Ibid., pp. 1–2.

16. Sergio Leemann, *Robert Wise on His Films: From Editing Room to Director's Chair* (Los Angeles: Silman-James Press, 1995), 165.

17. Wise memo, "West Side Story: The Problems of Style," p. 3.

18. Interdepartmental memo from Bob Relyea to Boris Leven, 23 May 1960, box 37, folder 9, "Production Memos," Wise Collection.

19. Memo from Boris Leven to Robert Wise, undated, box 37, folder 11, "West Side Story-Material," Wise Collection. The memo is hand-signed "Boris Leven"; emphasis in original.

20. Boris Leven to Patrick Downing, 16 November 1982, file 172, "Correspondence A–L," Boris Leven Papers, Special Collections, Margaret Herrick Library, AMPAS.

21. Memo from Robert Relyea to Boris Leven, 23 May 1960, box 37, folder 9, "Production Memos," Wise Collection.

22. "West Side Story New York Location List," undated, box 37, folder 9, "Production Memos," Wise Collection.

23. Mirisch, *I Thought We Were Making Movies*, 123.

24. "The Changing Faces of New York," box 37, folder 12, "Miscellaneous Notes," Wise Collection.

25. Robert Wise to Ziff Davis Publishing Co., 3 February 1960, box 37, "General Correspondence" folder, Wise Collection.

26. Anonymous, untitled typescript, 1 February 1960, box 37, folder 11, "West Side Story Story Materials," Wise Collection.

27. Keith Garebian, *The Making of West Side Story* (Oakville, ON: Mosaic Press, 2000), 52–56.

28. Wells, West Side Story, 37–38.

29. Letter from Cinerama, 5 October 1959, box 37, "General Correspondence" folder, Wise Collection.

30. Robert Wise to Sidney H. Levin, Stillman & Stillman, 7 January 1960, box 37, "General Correspondence" folder, Wise Collection.

31. Internal memo, 11 April 1960, file 160, "Miscellaneous Notes on WSS," Linwood Dunn Collection, Margaret Herrick Library, AMPAS.

32. Report from Linwood Dunn to Mirisch Studios, 16 May 1960, file 160, "Miscellaneous Notes on WSS," Dunn Collection. The heading reads "EXPERIMENTAL EFFECTS BY OPTICAL PRINTING FOR 'WEST SIDE STORY.'"

33. Dunn's notes, undated, file 161, "Production West Side Story," Dunn Collection.

34. Linwood Dunn, "Rough Estimate of Optical Effects Costs," 30 June 1960, folder 159, "West Side Story—Legal," Dunn Collection.

35. Linwood Dunn to Marvin Mirisch, 25 August 1960, folder 159, "West Side Story—Legal," Dunn Collection.

36. Memo re "Lin Dunn and West Side Story," 26 February 1962, file 1792, "TGSET mattes; opticals," George Stevens Collection, Margaret Herrick Library, AMPAS.

37. Pat Kirkham, "Reassessing the Saul Bass and Alfred Hitchcock Collaboration," *West 86th: A Journal of Decorative Arts, Design, History, and Material Culture* 18, 1 (Spring 2011): 50–85, http://www.west86th.bgc.bard.edu/articles/kirkham-bass-hitchcock.html#.

38. Core Collection, Margaret Herrick Library, AMPAS.

39. Untitled notes, 7 April 1960, box 37, folder 11, "West Side Story Material," Wise Collection.

40. Undated note from Jerome Robbins to Ernest Lehman, "West Side Story Early Materials" folder, Lehman Collection; emphasis in original.

41. Ernest Lehman, undated notes re "Step Outline," box 27, folder 1, "Early Materials," pp. 1–2, Lehman Collection; emphasis in original.

42. Ernest Lehman, "Step Outline," undated, box 27, folder 1, "Early Materials," Lehman Collection.

43. In his memoirs, Walter Mirisch describes Jerome Robbins's fear of the "stylized" approach. Mirisch, *I Thought We Were Making Movies*, 123.

44. Lehman, "Step Outline."

45. The description of the song's "fast, vaudeville style" comes from Irwin Kostal and Sid Ramin's orchestration notes, which I consulted at the Special Collections, USC CAL.

46. Ernest Lehman, "Notes, West Side Story," undated, box 27, folder 4, "Early Materials," p. 4, Lehman Collection.

47. Arthur Laurents, *West Side Story* (1965; reprint, New York: Bantam Doubleday, 1996), 193.

48. In the same notes cited earlier, Lehman mentions that at one point the movie was intended to have an intermission—not uncommon at the time, for films of a certain length—but this idea was dropped in favor of a better narrative construction. Leonard Bernstein even composed an "I Feel Pretty" entr'acte to summon moviegoers back to their seats. Eventually, during the film's road-show engagements, exhibitors were given the option of showing it with or without the intermission. I saw copies of the musical score as adapted for the movie, including this entr'acte, at the Special Collections, USC CAL.

49. Robert Wise, undated note, box 37, folder 12, "Miscellaneous Notes," Wise Collection.

50. Laurents, *West Side Story*, 186.

51. Lehman, undated notes re "Step Outline," p. 5; emphasis in original.

52. In his memoir, Mirisch notes that they brought in Saul Chaplin, "who had a great deal of experience at the MGM musical department . . . to help [them] organize the musical elements of the picture." Mirisch, *I Thought We Were Making Movies*, 122.

53. Raymond Kurtzman, head of the Legal Department at the Mirisch

Company, to Sidney H. Levin of Stillman & Stillman, 4 March 1960, box 37, folder 10, "Jerome Robbins," Wise Collection.

54. Robbins's unusual credit for *The King and I*—"Dance and musical numbers staged by"—later became a source of contention on *West Side Story*, as discussed in chapter 2.

55. Jerome Robbins to Robert Wise, 4 April 1960, box 37, folder 10, "Jerome Robbins," Wise Collection.

56. Memo from Lynn Stalmaster, "Preliminary Thoughts," undated, box 37, folder 13, "'West Side Story' Hollywood Casting Interviews," Wise Collection.

57. Interoffice memo from Jerome Robbins to Robert Wise, 25 May 1960, box 37, folder 9, "Production Memos," Wise Collection.

58. The original Broadway production of *West Side Story* lists a cast of thirty-nine: eleven Jets, ten Sharks, fourteen "girls"—including María, Anita, and Anybodys— plus four "adults." Garebian, *Making of* West Side Story, 154–155.

59. Note, 16 June 1960, box 37, folder 12, "Miscellaneous Notes," Wise Collection.

60. Undated note, box 37, folder 10, "Jerome Robbins," Wise Collection.

61. For films such as *Whoopee!* (Thornton Freeland, 1930), Berkeley received separate screen credit as "dances and ensembles staged by." By the time of *42nd Street* (Lloyd Bacon, 1933) and *Gold Diggers of 1933* (Mervyn LeRoy, 1933), Berkeley's credit, still separate from and smaller than that of the "director," read "dances and ensembles created by" and "numbers created and directed by," respectively (Internet Movie Data Base).

62. Leemann, *Robert Wise on His Films*, 164–165.

Chapter 2. "A Different Medium": Making *West Side Story*

1. Walter Mirisch, *I Thought We Were Making Movies, Not History* (Madison: University of Wisconsin Press, 2008), 127.

2. Tubelle cites $6 million, but Mirisch's $6.75 million figure is more reliable.

3. Larry Tubelle, "The Feature Story," *Daily Variety*, 7 December 1960.

4. "West Side Story Work Script," Stanley K. Scheuer Papers, Special Collections, USC CAL.

5. Memo from Lynn Stalmaster, "West Side Story Preliminary Thoughts," box 37, folder 13, "Casting Interviews," Robert Wise Collection, USC CAL.

6. Ibid.

7. Memo from Robert Wise to Jerome Robbins, 10 June 1960, box 37, folder 12, "Miscellaneous Notes," Wise Collection.

8. Memo from Ray Kurtzman to Robert Wise, 8 July 1960, box 37, "General Inter-Office" folder, Wise Collection.

9. Bill Becker, "Director Robbins' Dance Rehearsals Whip 'West Side Story' into Shape," *New York Times*, 3 July 1960.

10. Casting list, 16 July 1960, box 37, folder 12, "Miscellaneous Notes," Wise Collection.

11. Mirisch, *I Thought We Were Making Movies*, 45, 124.

12. Barry Monush, West Side Story: *Music on Film* (Milwaukee: Limelight Editions, 2010), 87; Marni Nixon and Stephen Cole, *I Could Have Sung All Night: My Story* (New York: Billboard Books, 2006), 131–132.

13. Misha Berson, *Something's Coming, Something Good:* West Side Story *and the American Imagination* (Milwaukee: Applause Theatre and Cinema Books, 2011), 170–171. See also Nixon and Cole, *I Could Have Sung All Night*, 132.

14. Mirisch, *I Thought We Were Making Movies*, 45, 124.

15. Nixon and Cole, *I Could Have Sung All Night*, 133.

16. Robert Wise to Eugene Dougherty of the MPAA, 24 June 1960, *West Side Story* photos and clippings microfilm, Margaret Herrick Library, AMPAS.

17. Geoffrey M. Shurlock to Walter Mirisch, 28 June 1960, *West Side Story* photos and clippings microfilm, Margaret Herrick Library, AMPAS.

18. Geoffrey Shurlock to Walter Mirisch, 3 August 1960, *West Side Story* photos and clippings microfilm, Margaret Herrick Library, AMPAS.

19. Memo from Robert E. Relyea to Allen K. Wood, 6 June 1960, box 37, folder 9, "Production Memos," Wise Collection.

20. New York production schedule, 7 June 1960, box 37, folder 12, "Miscellaneous Notes," pp. 1–3, Wise Collection.

21. As late as 28 July 1960, the screenplay indicates scenes taking place "day and night" and "flowing continuously." By the time production started in New York, this had been revised so that the entire "Prologue" could be shot in the daytime.

22. About the substitution of Los Angeles sets for nighttime New York locations, Wise said in a 1995 interview: "You can't tell the difference, because you light just what you want to be seen." Sergio Leemann, *Robert Wise and His Films: From Editing Room to Director's Chair* (Los Angeles: Silman-James Press, 1995), 166. See also New York production schedule, 7 June 1960, pp. 4–5.

23. Recording schedule, box 37, folder 9, "Production Memos," Wise Collection.

24. Memo from Bob Relyea to Al Wood, 6 June 1960, box 37, folder 9, "Production Memos," Wise Collection.

25. Leemann, *Robert Wise on His Films*, 166. See also Mirisch, *I Thought We Were Making Movies*, 124.

26. Monush, West Side Story, 88.

27. Bruce Austin, "An Interview with Robert Wise," *Literature Film Quarterly* 6, 4 (October 1978): 305, 308.

28. Mirisch, *I Thought We Were Making Movies*, 125.

29. Lehman's original version of "Somewhere" in the "Work Script" still included this elaborate fantasy sequence as of 26 October 1960. "West Side Story Work Script," Scheuer Papers. The screenplay published with the DVD and Blu-Ray editions of the film was the revised version, dated 29 December 1960, which describes the scene as it was produced for the finished film.

30. Memo on "Proposed sets and stage space," June 1960, box 37, folder 12, Wise Collection; memo from Bob Relyea to Boris Leven, 23 May 1960, box 37, folder 9, "Production Memos," Wise Collection.

31. Harold Mirisch to Robert Wise and Jerome Robbins, 12 September 1960, box 37, folder 9, "Production Memos," Wise Collection; emphasis in original.

32. Harold Mirisch to Wise and Robbins, 15 September 1960, box 37, folder 9, "Production Memos," Wise Collection.

33. TV Guide, 27 October 2001.

34. People Magazine, 8 April 2002.

35. Harold Mirisch to Wise and Robbins, 5 October 1960, box 37, folder 9, "Production Memos," Wise Collection.

36. Harold Mirisch to Wise and Robbins, c. 12 October 1960, box 37, folder 9, "Production Memos," Wise Collection.

37. Mirisch, I Thought We Were Making Movies, 126.

38. "West Side Story Work Script," Scheuer Papers.

39. Earl J. Hess and Pratibha A. Dabholkar, Singin' in the Rain: The Making of an American Masterpiece (Lawrence: University Press of Kansas, 2009), 92–93.

40. Al Wood to Herman Helgrath, 5 October 1960, box 37, folder 9, "Production Memos," Wise Collection.

41. Undated budget spreadsheet, box 37, folder 9, "Production Memos," Wise Collection.

42. Mirisch, I Thought We Were Making Movies, 126.

43. Monush gives Robbins's exit date as "around October 25" (West Side Story, 93). Although he does not cite a specific source, based on my analysis of the shooting log and the dates of the memos, I am inclined to agree with this approximation.

44. Mirisch, I Thought We Were Making Movies, 126.

45. In interviews with both Charles Champlin of the Los Angeles Times (31 July 1998) and Leemann (Robert Wise on His Films, 167), Wise offered the estimate of 60 percent.

46. Letters between Leonard Hirschman and Ray Kurtzman, 1 and 3 November 1960, box 37, "General Correspondence" folder, Wise Collection.

47. Technically, the movie features only twelve songs, plus a few bars of "Somewhere" at Tony's death scene; however, the list in Scheuer's "Work Script" includes the dances performed without songs, such as the "Gym Dance" and "The Rumble."

48. See p. 2 of the Ernest Lehman screenplay published with the 2003 DVD

edition (MGM Home Entertainment Inc.), which includes brief descriptions of the characters' temperaments.

49. Original copy of the screenplay belonging to Robert Wise, p. 6, Wise Collection. The screenplay published with the 2003 Special Edition DVD shows the identical page, but clean: without the strike-through of the word "Playground" or the penciled notation "Painting Out Sharks."

50. Ibid., 26.

51. There are hundreds of handwritten annotations, changes to lines of dialogue, continuity details, adopted ad-libs, character line changes, and even corrections to the Spanish spoken by the Sharks in the combined 252 pages of Wise's and Scheuer's original copies of the screenplay. I have picked only a handful for illustration purposes.

52. Letters and memos, file 161, "Production West Side Story," Linwood Dunn Collection, Margaret Herrick Library, AMPAS.

53. Memo from the Mirisch Corporation to Tom Andre of George Stevens Productions, "Re Lin Dunn & West Side Story," 26 February 1962, file 1792, George Stevens Collection, Margaret Herrick Library, AMPAS.

54. Undated memo from Bob Relyea to Al Wood, box 37, folder 9, "Production Memos," Wise Collection.

55. "West Side Story Work Script," Scheuer Papers.

56. Based on his incorrect description of the scene—María "alone in the shop" doing a "dance and song of joy"—it is likely that Rau saw only a rehearsal. Neil Rau, "Heap of People Make a Scene," *Los Angeles Examiner*, 27 November 1960.

57. Nixon and Cole, *I Could Have Sung All Night*, 133–135.

58. Ibid., 136.

59. Robert Wise to Paul F. Johnson, 18 September 1961, box 37, "Congratulatory Letters" folder, Wise Collection.

60. Nixon and Cole, *I Could Have Sung All Night*, 137.

61. "Singer Files Suit against Musical," *Citizen News*, 10 February 1963.

62. "Suit Charges Star Role Sung by Bit Player," *Los Angeles Times*, 9 February 1963.

63. "Call for a Ghost in a Hurry: Voice Dubbing a Tough Job—Ask Oscar," *Los Angeles Herald Examiner*, 17 February 1963. There are similar stories in the 15 February 1963 editions of *Variety* and the *Los Angeles Times*.

64. Memo from Raymond Kurtzman to Robert Wise, 10 October 1960, box 37, folder 10, "Jerome Robbins," Wise Collection.

65. Edward E. Colton, Esq., to Raymond Kurtzman, 21 December 1960, box 37, folder 10, "Jerome Robbins," Wise Collection.

66. Robert Wise to Jay Kanter, 21 March 1961, box 37, folder 10, "Jerome Robbins," Wise Collection.

67. Interoffice memo from Robert Wise to Harold Mirisch, 3 April 1961, box 37, folder 10, "Jerome Robbins," Wise Collection.

68. Jerome Robbins to Robert Wise, 12 April 1961, box 37, folder 10, "Jerome Robbins," Wise Collection; emphasis in original.

69. Though fairly common now, the use of an entire end-credits sequence in lieu of opening credits, as seen in *West Side Story*, was relatively rare in 1961. Robert Wise, as film editor for *Citizen Kane* and *The Magnificent Ambersons*, would have been familiar with the practice, since Orson Welles favored it in those two films.

70. Interoffice memo from Robert Wise to Harold Mirisch, 24 April 1960, box 37, folder 10, "Jerome Robbins," Wise Collection.

71. Raymond Kurtzman to Sidney H. Levin, 4 March 1960, box 37, folder 10, "Jerome Robbins," Wise Collection.

72. Interoffice memo from Robert Wise to Raymond Kurtzman, 24 May 1961, box 37, folder 10, "Jerome Robbins," Wise Collection; emphasis added.

73. Robert Wise to Jerome Robbins, 31 May 1961, box 37, folder 10, "Jerome Robbins," Wise Collection.

74. Interoffice memo from Robert Wise to Raymond Kurtzman, 1 June 1961, box 37, folder 10, "Jerome Robbins," Wise Collection.

75. Interoffice memo from Robert Wise to Raymond Kurtzman, 2 June 1961, box 37, folder 10, "Jerome Robbins," Wise Collection.

76. Robert Wise to Guy Biondi of the Michael Todd Corporation, box 37, folder 10, "Jerome Robbins," Wise Collection.

77. Jerome Robbins to Robert Wise, 1 March 1962, box 37, folder 10, "Jerome Robbins," Wise Collection.

Chapter 3. "You're the Only Thing I'll See": Watching *West Side Story*

1. These figures are from the publicity materials included with the *West Side Story* DVD (MGM Home Entertainment, 2003).

2. Quoted from the "Memos and Reviews" section of the publicity and screenplay booklet included with the *West Side Story* DVD (MGM Home Entertainment, 2003).

3. In a congratulatory telegram, director Fred Zinnemann used the nickname "Bobby." Zinnemann to Wise, 14 September 1961, box 37, folder 3, "Congratulatory Letters," Robert Wise Collection, USC CAL.

4. The image appeared on the cover of Barry Monush's *West Side Story: Music on Film* (Milwaukee: Limelight Editions, 2010) and, most recently, on the cover of a booklet included with the fiftieth anniversary commemorative Blu-Ray edition in 2011.

5. As I argue in chapter 5, there is evidence that the neighborhood store belongs to Bernardo and María's parents. At one point, María refers to her parents being "at the store," while in the play, Bernardo complains that the Jets have "stink bombed" his "old man's store." See Arthur Laurents, *West Side Story* (1965; reprint, New York: Bantam Doubleday, 1996),140.

6. Ernest Lehman, "Some Notes Taken during Police Car Tour of West Side," "Early Materials" folder, Ernest Lehman Collection, USC CAL.

7. Laurents, *West Side Story*, 137.

8. Jerome Robbins to Robert Wise, 12 April 1961, box 37, folder 10, "Jerome Robbins," Wise Collection.

9. The origin of the term *"I want" song* is unclear, but it is commonly used in theater and film to describe a song in which the main character expresses his or her desire to accomplish something, to change his or her current situation, or to find happiness and love. Examples include "Oh, What a Beautiful Mornin'" in Rodgers and Hammerstein's *Oklahoma!* (1943); "Wonderful, Wonderful Day" from Stanley Donen's film *Seven Brides for Seven Brothers* (1954); "Maybe This Time" from Kander and Ebb's original *Cabaret* (1966), as well as the Bob Fosse version; "Tomorrow" and "Maybe" from both versions of Charles Strauss and Martin Charnin's *Annie* (1977, 1982); and Alan Menken and Howard Ashman's "Part of Your World" from *The Little Mermaid* (1989).

10. Rick Altman, *The American Film Musical* (Bloomington: Indiana University Press, 1987), 80–89.

11. Ernest Lehman, West Side Story *Screenplay* (MGM Home Entertainment DVD, 2003), 43.

12. Laurents, *West Side Story*, 150.

13. For the conclusive word on the concepts of the "audio dissolve" and the "personality dissolve," see Altman's definitive study of the genre, *The American Film Musical*, especially chapter 4. See also Jane Feuer's *The Hollywood Musical* (Bloomington: Indiana University Press, 1993).

14. Letters and memos, file 161, "Production West Side Story," Linwood Dunn Collection, Margaret Herrick Library, AMPAS.

15. Robbins to Wise, 12 April 1961.

16. Internal memo, 11 April 1960, file 160, Dunn Collection.

17. Memo from Robert Wise to Al Wood, re "West Side Story Opticals," 29 June 1961, file 161, Dunn Collection.

18. Lehman, *Screenplay*, 33.

19. "Standing at her window, gazing out, perhaps thinking of Tony" is how Lehman describes María in this scene. Lehman, *Screenplay*, 35.

20. Ibid., 36.

21. As I explore in chapter 5, the term *immigrant* to refer to Puerto Ricans in New York, even in the 1950s, is something of a misnomer: since 1917, Puerto Ricans have been US citizens by birthright.

22. Erskine Johnson, "'West Side Story' Is a Departure," *Los Angeles Mirror*, 23 September 1960.

23. "Work in Progress" memo from Linwood Dunn to Robert Wise, file 161, Dunn Collection.

24. The publishers of *Superman* comics (National Publications) objected to the reference in Baby John's comic book, so it was changed to "Captain

Marvel" for the movie. Memo, 22 July 1960, "General Correspondence" folder, Wise Collection.

25. The new Blu-Ray and DVD editions of *West Side Story* released in October 2011 to commemorate the film's fiftieth anniversary restore the "Intermission" to its original place, with the "I Feel Pretty" entr'acte composed by Bernstein, adding one minute and fifty-two seconds to the film's original length.

26. Laurents, *West Side Story*, 181.

27. "Progress report" memo, 3 November 1960, file 161, Dunn Collection; memos, 11 April 1960, 29 June and 18 August 1961, files 160 and 161, Dunn Collection.

28. "Progress report" memo, 3 November 1960, file 161, Dunn Collection.

29. In the play, Anita sings: "He'll walk in hot and tired / So what? / Don't matter if he's tired / As long as he's hot." In the movie, the lyrics are changed to: "He'll walk in hot and tired / Poor dear / Don't matter if he's tired / As long as he's here."

30. Lehman, *Screenplay*, 84, with revisions dated 26 October 1960.

31. Altman, *American Film Musical*, 32, 331.

32. In the clippings and photographs collection at the Margaret Herrick Library of AMPAS, the lobby card shows a grease pencil mark around Riff's knife; on the back of the photograph a handwritten note in pencil states, "Shot killed by MPAA. See circled knife."

33. Lehman, *Screenplay*, 91; Laurents, *West Side Story*, 193.

34. Lehman, *Screenplay*, 92.

35. In the play, Chino arrives after María and the girls sing "I Feel Pretty" in her bedroom. As Lehman concluded, placing that number after the rumble would shift moods too violently for the movie's purposes. However, it can also be argued that Chino's visit to María's bedroom would be unlikely, given her strict Catholic upbringing.

36. Lehman, *Screenplay*, 95; Laurents, *West Side Story*, 199.

37. Laurents, *West Side Story*, 201.

38. Ernest Lehman, "West Side Story Work Script," 96–97, Stanley Scheuer Papers, Special Collections, USC CAL.

39. The book of the play assigns the song "Somewhere" to Consuelo as an "off-stage voice." In the versions I have seen in the theater—the 2009 Broadway revival, the 2008 Central City Opera production, and a 2007 University of Colorado Opera presentation—the singer has varied, being one of the Sharks' girls, Tony and María, and Anybodys, respectively.

40. Memo from Jerome Robbins to Ernest Lehman, undated, "Early Materials" folder, p. 3, Lehman Collection.

41. In the book of the play, Laurents incongruously directs that Anybodys has "fallen in love" with Action, who gives her the order in the original and hence assumes leadership of the gang (*West Side Story*, 211). It seems more logical, in the movie, that she has simply fulfilled the dream of becoming a Jet, in spite of her gender.

42. From *Dancer in the Dark*, directed by Lars Von Trier (Fine Line Features, 2000).

43. Laurents, *West Side Story*, 224; Lehman, *Screenplay*, 126.

44. Bruce Austin, "An Interview with Robert Wise," *Literature Film Quarterly* 6, 4 (October 1978): 301.

45. My research assistant Larissa Rhodes provided me with the correct technical vocabulary for this section of the chapter.

46. Musical Score of Motion Picture Play "West Side Story," Music by Leonard Bernstein, Lyrics by Stephen Sondheim, Orchestrated by Sid Ramin and Irwin Kostal, vol. 1, Special Collections, USC CAL.

47. Leonard Bernstein, *West Side Story* (New York: Leonard Bernstein Music Publishing Company LLC, 2000); Boosey & Hawkes Inc., agent for rental.

48. "Cool" and "Tonight" also rely on the tritone to create tension in the apparent harmonies.

49. Daniel J. Levitin, *This Is Your Brain on Music: The Science of a Human Obsession* (New York: Plume, 2007), 13. Levitin specifically refers to "the interval in Leonard Bernstein's *West Side Story* when Tony sings the name "Maria" as an example of this practice.

50. Musical Score of Motion Picture Play "West Side Story," vols. 1 and 2, Special Collections, USC CAL.

Chapter 4. "Long, Long Runs": Assessing *West Side Story*

1. Letters between Jerome Robbins and Robert Wise, 1 and 3 March 1962, box 37, folder 10, "Jerome Robbins," Robert Wise Collection, USC CAL.

2. Geoffrey M. Shurlock to Robert Wise, 17 April 1961, *West Side Story* photos and clippings microfilm, Margaret Herrick Library, AMPAS.

3. Motion Picture Association of America, Production Code Administration, "Analysis of Film Content" report, 25 April 1961, and Certificate of Approval #19949, signed by Geoffry M. Shurlock, *West Side Story* photos and clippings microfilm, Margaret Herrick Library, AMPAS.

4. Ibid.

5. "'West Side' Exhibition Pacts Call for Periodic Inspection of Projection," *Hollywood Reporter*, 7 March 1962.

6. Louis Pelegrini, "Record Advance Sales Claimed for 'Story,'" *Film Daily*, 24 August 1961.

7. "Musical Campaign on 'West Side' Launched," *Hollywood Reporter*, 7 September 1961.

8. Stanley Skolsky, "Movie of the Week," *Hollywood Citizen News*, 15 September 1961; Hedda Hopper, "It's a Winner!" *Los Angeles Times*, 19 September 1961.

9. Leven responded to Knight's review by specifically objecting to Knight's "assigning credit" to both Bass and Leven for the film's design. Leven writes, "Mr. Bass had absolutely nothing, and I repeat, nothing to do with either the

conception, or the design, or the color or the ideas for lighting of any of the sets or backgrounds—or with anything that had to do with the visual aspect of the film." He ends by asking Knight to correct his statement. Knight's review was published on 14 October with the line intact, giving shared credit to Bass and Leven. Boris Leven to Arthur Knight, 13 [sic] October 1961, file 172, Boris Leven Collection, Margaret Herrick Library, AMPAS.

10. Contemporary reviews from *America, Commonweal, Dance Magazine, Esquire, Life, National Review, New Republic, New Yorker, Newsweek, Redbook, Saturday Review, Seventeen, Theatre Arts, Time,* and many other publications are from the microfilm clippings collection, Margaret Herrick Library, AMPAS.

11. "'West Side' Release May Be Speeded up by United Artists," *Hollywood Reporter,* 26 October 1961.

12. Dale Olson, "'West Side Story' Lyrics Will Be Subtitled for Foreign Bookings," *Daily Variety,* 4 August 1961.

13. "'West Side' Exhibition Pacts."

14. Stan Delaplane, "Post Card from London," *Los Angeles Herald Examiner,* 15 March 1962.

15. "'Story' May Set New Musical Pattern in Foreign Sites as It Jingles at B.O.," *Daily Variety,* 27 March 1961; "'West Side Story' Setting Records," *Hollywood Reporter,* 27 March 1961.

16. "Orientals See Differently," *Los Angeles Times,* 21 October 1962.

17. "'West Side' Wins Finland Award," *Hollywood Reporter,* 13 June 1963; "'West Side' Voted Best by French Moviegoers," *Hollywood Reporter,* 2 July 1963.

18. "U.S. Film Is Noticed by Soviets—at Last," *New York Times,* 15 July 1963.

19. Henry Grunwald to Robert Wise, 30 August 1961, and Harry Goldstein to Robert Wise, 5 April 1962, box 37, folder 3, "Congratulatory Letters," Wise Collection.

20. Doris Daniels Kaufman to Robert Wise, 29 April 1962, box 37, folder 3, "Congratulatory Letters," Wise Collection.

21. All letters cited are in box 37, folder 3, "Congratulatory Letters," Wise Collection.

22. "Natalie Wood 136th to Do the 'Chinese' Bit," *Variety,* 4 December 1961. The *Hollywood Reporter* ran the story the next day.

23. "'West Side' to Have Gala on Dec. 13," *Los Angeles Times,* 30 November 1961.

24. "'West Side' Makes 9 'Ten Best' Lists," *Boxoffice,* 1 August 1962.

25. Murray Schumach, "Oscar Triumphs of 'West Side Story' Seen as Victory for Independents," *New York Times,* 15 April 1962.

26. "'West Side Story' Ends 4-Year Run," *Hollywood Reporter,* 12 May 1966; "'West Side Story' Ends 218 Weeks at George V; Continues at Avenue," *Weekly Variety,* 18 May 1966.

27. "'West Side Story' 5-Yr. Paris Run Makes History," *Hollywood Reporter,* 9 March 1967.

28. "Mirisch Rejects $3 Mil TV Offer for 'West Side Story,'" *Daily Variety*, 21 September 1966.

29. "NBC Gets Bond Pictures, 'West Side Story' for TV," *Hollywood Reporter*, 3 March 1967; "Mirisch '68 Slate to Have Budget Topping $20 Mil," *Hollywood Reporter*, 20 November 1967.

30. Two related stories were also published in *Variety* on 24 October 1979: "UA to Shell Out on 'West Side Story'" and "Price Formulas Challenged by 'Story' Authors," microfilm clippings collection, Margaret Herrick Library, AMPAS.

31. Chris Jones, *Films and Filming*, September 1969, microfilm clippings collection, Margaret Herrick Library, AMPAS.

32. *Hollywood Reporter*, 2 September 1970, microfilm clippings collection, Margaret Herrick Library, AMPAS.

33. "'West Side Story' Dances to 1,500,000 in French Re-Issue," United Artists press release, 24 June 1981, microfilm clippings collection, Margaret Herrick Library, AMPAS.

34. FILMEX press release, 16 March 1982, microfilm clippings collection, Margaret Herrick Library, AMPAS.

35. All notices are from the clippings collection at the Margaret Herrick Library, AMPAS.

36. *Los Angeles Times*, 11 October 2002, clippings collection, Margaret Herrick Library, AMPAS.

37. Clippings collection, Margaret Herrick Library, AMPAS.

38. Wendy Lesser, *Three Penny Review* (Spring 2007), clippings collection, Margaret Herrick Library, AMPAS.

39. *San Pedro Daily Breeze*, 21 April 2009, clippings collection, Margaret Herrick Library, AMPAS.

40. Joan Acocella, "Dance Notes: City Lights," *New Yorker*, 5 December 2011.

41. Patricia Cohen, "Same City, New Story," *New York Times*, 11 March 2009.

42. Patrick Healy, "Some 'West Side' Lyrics Are Returned to English," *New York Times*, 27 August 2009.

43. Todd McCarthy, "Jets Have Their Way Onscreen: 'West Side Story' Screen Version Underrated," *Variety*, 4 June 2009.

Chapter 5. "Bernardo Was Right":
Arguing Puerto Rican Representation in *West Side Story*

1. See, among others, Keith Garebian, *The Making of West Side Story* (Oakville, ON: Mosaic Press, 2000); Elizabeth Wells, *West Side Story: Cultural Perspectives on an American Musical* (Lanham, MD: Scarecrow Press, 2011); and Misha Berson, *Something's Coming, Something Good: West Side Story and the American Imagination* (Milwaukee: Applause Theatre and Cinema Books, 2011).

2. R. Domínguez to Robert Wise and Jerome Robbins, 31 October 1961, box 37, folder 2, "General Correspondence," Robert Wise Collection, USC CAL.

3. Philip H. Coombs to Robert Wise, 22 November 1961, box 37, folder 2, "General Correspondence," Wise Collection.

4. Memo from Robert Wise to Harold Mirisch, 29 November 1961, box 37, folder 2, "General Correspondence," Wise Collection.

5. The Encampment for Citizenship was a series of summer camps for underprivileged youth, founded in 1946. According to the alumni website (http://www.efcalumni.com/index.html), its aim was to instill the principles and responsibilities of citizenship in a liberal democracy and the values of tolerance and diversity. Joseph McCarthy reportedly attacked it for being "socialistic" in the 1950s.

6. Eleanor Roosevelt to Harold Mirisch, 26 September 1960, box 37, folder 2, "General Correspondence," Wise Collection.

7. Frances Negrón-Muntaner, "Feeling Pretty: *West Side Story* and Puerto Rican Identity Discourses," *Social Text* 18, 2 (Summer 2000): 83.

8. Susan King and Rachel Uslan, "Sharks and Jets: Musical History," *Los Angeles Times*, 11 October 2002.

9. López and Martin are cited in Frances Negrón-Muntaner, *Boricua Pop: Puerto Ricans and the Latinization of American Culture* (New York: New York University Press, 2004), 59.

10. See Berson, *Something's Coming*, especially chap. 12.

11. Alberto Sandoval-Sánchez, *José, Can You See? Latinos On and Off Broadway* (Madison: University of Wisconsin Press, 1999), 62.

12. Ibid., 63.

13. Ibid., 69.

14. Rick Altman, "The Folk Musical," chap. 8 of *The American Film Musical* (Bloomington: Indiana University Press, 1987).

15. Quoted in Negrón-Muntaner, "Feeling Pretty," 101.

16. Matthew Tinkcom, "Working Like a Homosexual: Camp Visual Codes in the MGM Freed Unit," in *Hollywood Musicals: The Film Reader*, ed. Steven Cohan (London: Routledge, 2002), 115–128.

17. Ibid., 121.

18. Richard Dyer, "Entertainment and Utopia," in Cohan, *Hollywood Musicals*, 19–30.

19. Negrón-Muntaner, "Feeling Pretty," 84.

20. Ibid., 85.

21. "Hailing" is a reference to Louis Althusser's widely anthologized essay "Ideology and Ideological State Apparatuses" (1970). It refers to the acknowledgment that one belongs to a national or social group by responding to the "hailing" of the police or other state representatives, as in "Hey, you!"

22. Sandoval-Sánchez, *José, Can You See?* 69.

23. Ernest Lehman, *West Side Story Screenplay* (MGM Home Entertainment DVD, 2003), 53.

24. According to the online *Urban Dictionary*, the expression "pushing tea" is a 1950s reference to selling marijuana.

25. Fernando Picó, *Historia General de Puerto Rico* (San Juan, PR: Ediciones Huracán, 1986), 270–271.

26. Craig Zadan, *Sondheim & Co.* (New York: Harper & Row, 1989), quoted in Garebian, *Making of West Side Story*, 37.

27. Notes from Jerome Robbins to Ernest Lehman, undated, p. 1, box 27, folder 1, Ernest Lehman Collection, USC CAL.

28. Garebian, *Making of West Side Story*, 134–137; Berson, *Something's Coming*, 213–217.

29. Interview with Judy Sloane, *Film Review*, June 1994. The changes to the "America" lyrics are dated 28 July 1960 in Wise's copy of the working screenplay at USC CAL. It includes handwritten notes, including "play change" and pointing to certain verses. Interestingly, in terms of the song's title and lyrics, no one in Puerto Rico refers to the United States as "America"; most say *Estados Unidos* or even "New York," which in Puerto Rican vernacular is typically a synecdoche for the United States.

30. Lehman, *Screenplay*, 117–119; Arthur Laurents, *West Side Story* (1965; reprint, New York: Bantam Doubleday, 1996), 217–219, emphasis added.

31. Action, for example, says, "C'mon, cut the frabbajabba; grab some readin' matter, turn on da juke, some of ya git outside an' if ya see Chino or any stinkin' PR. . . ." Lehman, *Screenplay*, 116.

32. Altman, *American Film Musical*, 272, 277.

33. Lehman, *Screenplay*, 126.

34. Negrón-Muntaner, "Feeling Pretty," 90, 101.

35. Arthur Laurents, *Mainly on Directing: Gypsy, West Side Story, and Other Musicals* (New York: Alfred A. Knopf, 2009), 175.

36. Steven Cohan, "Musicals of the Studio Era," in Cohan, *Hollywood Musicals*, 1.

37. Negrón-Muntaner, "Feeling Pretty," 100–101.

BIBLIOGRAPHY

Altman, Rick. *The American Film Musical*. Bloomington: Indiana University Press, 1987.

————. *Film/Genre*. London: British Film Institute, 1999.

————. *Sound Theory, Sound Practice*. New York: Routledge, 1992.

Austin, Bruce. "An Interview with Robert Wise." *Literature Film Quarterly* 6, 4 (October 1978): 295–313.

Babington, Bruce, and Peter W. Evans. *Blue Skies and Silver Linings: Aspects of the Hollywood Musical*. Manchester: Manchester University Press, 1985.

Banfield, Stephen. *Sondheim's Broadway Musicals*. Ann Arbor: University of Michigan Press, 1993.

Bernstein, Leonard. *Findings*. New York: Simon & Schuster, 1982.

Berson, Misha. *Something's Coming, Something Good: West Side Story and the American Imagination*. Milwaukee: Applause Theatre and Cinema Books, 2011.

Bordwell, David, Janet Staiger, and Kristin Thompson. *The Classical Hollywood Cinema: Film Style and Mode of Production to 1960*. New York: Columbia University Press, 1985.

Cohan, Steven. *Incongruous Entertainment: Camp, Cultural Value, and the MGM Musicals*. Durham, NC: Duke University Press, 2005.

————, ed. *Hollywood Musicals: The Film Reader*. London: Routledge, 2002.

Dunne, Michael. *The American Film Musical: Themes and Forms*. Jefferson, NC: McFarland, 2004.

Dyer, Richard. "Entertainment and Utopia." In *Hollywood Musicals: The Film Reader*, ed. Steven Cohan, 19–30. London: Routledge, 2002.

Feuer, Jane. *The Hollywood Musical*. Bloomington: Indiana University Press, 1993.

Garebian, Keith. *The Making of West Side Story*. Oakville, ON: Mosaic Press, 2000.

Goodhart, Sandor. *Reading Stephen Sondheim*. New York: Garland, 2000.

Hadley-García, George. *Hispanic Hollywood*. New York: Citadel, 1990.

Hess, Earl J., and Pratibha A. Dabholkar. *Singin' in the Rain: The Making of an American Masterpiece*. Lawrence: University Press of Kansas, 2009.

Hischak, Thomas. *Film It with Music*. Westport, CT: Greenwood, 2001.

Houghton, Norris, ed. *Romeo and Juliet/West Side Story*. New York: Bantam Doubleday, 1996.

Jowitt, Deborah. *Jerome Robbins: His Life, His Theater, His Dance*. New York: Simon & Schuster, 2005.

Kasha, Al, and Joel Hirschorn. *Notes on Broadway*. Chicago: Contemporary, 1985.

Kawin, Bruce. *How Movies Work*. Berkeley: University of California Press, 1992.

Keenan, Richard. *The Films of Robert Wise*. Lanham, MD: Scarecrow Press, 2007.

Kirkham, Pat. "Reassessing the Saul Bass and Alfred Hitchcock Collaboration." *West 86th: A Journal of Decorative Arts, Design, History, and Material Culture* 18, 1 (Spring 2011): 50–85.

Kobal, John. *Gotta Sing, Gotta Dance*. London: Hamlyn, 1972.

Laurents, Arthur. *Mainly on Directing: Gypsy, West Side Story, and Other Musicals*. New York: Alfred A. Knopf, 2009.

———. *Original Story By: A Memoir of Broadway and Hollywood*. New York: Applause Theatre Books, 2000.

———. *West Side Story*. 1965. Reprint, New York: Bantam Doubleday, 1996.

Lawson-Peebles, Robert. *Approaches to the American Film Musical*. Exeter: University of Exeter Press, 1996.

Ledbetter, Steven, ed. *A Bernstein Celebration*. Boston: Boston Symphony Orchestra, 1988.

Leemann, Sergio. *Robert Wise on His Films: From Editing Room to Director's Chair*. Los Angeles: Silman-James Press, 1995.

Lehman, Ernest. *West Side Story Screenplay*. MGM Home Entertainment DVD, 2003.

Levitin, Daniel J. *This Is Your Brain on Music: The Science of a Human Obsession*. New York: Plume, 2007.

Mast, Gerald, and Bruce F. Kawin. *A Short History of the Movies*, 11th ed. Boston: Longman, 2011.

Mathew-Walker, Robert. *From Broadway to Hollywood: The Musical and the Cinema*. London: Sanctuary, 1996.

Mirisch, Walter. *I Thought We Were Making Movies, Not History*. Madison: University of Wisconsin Press, 2008.

Monush, Barry. *West Side Story: Music on Film*. Milwaukee: Limelight Editions, 2010.

Morden, Ethan. *The Hollywood Musical*. New York: St. Martin's, 1981.

Negrón-Muntaner, Frances. *Boricua Pop: Puerto Ricans and the Latinization of American Culture*. New York: New York University Press, 2004.

———. "Feeling Pretty: *West Side Story* and Puerto Rican Identity Discourses." *Social Text* 18, 2 (Summer 2000): 83–106.

Nixon, Marni, and Stephen Cole. *I Could Have Sung All Night: My Story*. New York: Billboard Books, 2006.

Peyser, Joan. *Bernstein: A Biography*. New York: Beech Tree Books, 1987.

Picó, Fernando. *Historia General de Puerto Rico*. San Juan, PR: Ediciones Huracán, 1986.

Reyes, Luis, and Peter Rubie. *Hispanics in Hollywood*. New York: Garland, 1994.

Sandoval-Sánchez, Alberto. *José, Can You See? Latinos On and Off Broadway*. Madison: University of Wisconsin Press, 1999.

Schatz, Thomas. *Hollywood Genres*. New York: McGraw-Hill, 1981.

Secrest, Meryle. *Leonard Bernstein: A Life*. New York: Alfred A. Knopf, 1994.

———. *Stephen Sondheim: A Life*. New York: Dell, 1999.

Smith, Susan. *The Musical: Race, Gender, and Performance*. London: Wallflower, 2005.

Tinkcom, Matthew. "Working Like a Homosexual: Camp Visual Codes and the Labor of Gay Subjects in the MGM Freed Unit." In *Hollywood Musicals: The Film Reader*, ed. Steven Cohan, 115–128. London: Routledge, 2002.

Vaill, Amanda. *Somewhere: The Life of Jerome Robbins*. New York: Broadway, 2006.

Wells, Elizabeth A. West Side Story: *Cultural Perspectives on an American Musical*. Lanham, MD: Scarecrow Press, 2011.

Wollen, Peter. *Singin' in the Rain*. London: British Film Institute, 1992.

Zadan, Craig. *Sondheim & Co*. New York: Harper & Row, 1989.

ABOUT THE AUTHOR

Ernesto R. Acevedo-Muñoz is director of the Film Studies Program at the University of Colorado at Boulder. He is the author of the books *Pedro Almodóvar* and *Buñuel and Mexico: The Crisis of National Cinema*. His essays have appeared in various journals and edited volumes, including *Quarterly Review of Film & Video*, *Film & History*, *Lit*, *Letras peninsulares*, *After Hitchcock*, *Authorship in Film Adaptation*, *Contemporary Spanish Cinema and Genre*, *A Companion to Luis Buñuel*, and *Genre, Gender, Race, and World Cinemas*.

INDEX